THE ANCIENT GREEK HISTORIANS

BY
J. B. BURY

DOVER PUBLICATIONS, INC.
NEW YORK
NEW YORK

ΓΑΡΔΙΝΕΡ ΜΑΡΤΙΝΩΙ ΛΑΙΝ

ΦΙΛΕΛΛΗΝΙ ΦΙΛΕΛΛΗΝ

This new Dover edition first published in 1958 is an unabridged and unaltered republication of the first edition. It is published by special arrangement with St. Martins Press.

PREFACE

THIS volume consists of the Lane Lectures which I had the honour of delivering at Harvard University in spring 1908, under the auspices of the Classical Department. They are printed very nearly as they were originally written, though some of my kind hearers, if they should glance through, may detect a good many passages which were omitted in the Lecture Hall. The book amounts to a historical survey of Greek historiography, down to the first century B.C., and such as it is, I dedicate it to Mr. Gardiner M. Lane, who founded the lecturership some years ago in the interests of humanistic study.

The lecture on Herodotus would have gained much if Mr. Macan's admirable work on the last three Books had appeared in time for me to use it. It was satisfactory to find that he had established the priority of those Books with a convincing array of arguments. I have inconsistently included his edition of VII.-IX. in the Bibliography; for the purpose of the list is to make a general acknowledgment of obligations which in lectures of this kind could not conveniently be acknowledged in

detail. There are not very many questions connected with the Greek historians which I have not
at one time or another talked over with my friend
Mr. Mahaffy, and I feel sure that I owe him much
which neither of us could now verify.

September 5, 1908.

CONTENTS

ix

LECTURE I

THE RISE OF GREEK HISTORY IN IONIA

In these lectures I propose to trace the genesis and the development of the historical literature of the Greeks. I will attempt to bring into a connected view the principles, the governing ideas, and the methods of the Greek historians, and to relate them to the general movements of Greek thought and Greek history. I need hardly apologize for devoting much of our time to Herodotus and Thucydides, who, however familiar to us from childhood, have the secret of engaging an interest that is never exhausted and never grows stale. As a Hellenist, I shall be happy if I succeed in illustrating the fact that, as in poetry and letters generally, as in art, as in philosophy, and in mathematics, so too in history, our debt to the Greeks transcends calculation. They were not the first to chronicle human events, but they were the first to apply criticism. And that means, they originated history.

§ 1. *The historical aspect of the Epics*

Long before history, in the proper sense of the word, came to be written, the early Greeks possessed a literature which was equivalent to history for them and was accepted with unreserved credence—their epic poems. The Homeric lays not only entertained the imagination, but also satisfied what we may call the historical interest, of the audiences who heard them recited. This interest in history was practical, not antiquarian; the story of the past made a direct appeal to their pride, while it was associated with their religious piety towards their ancestors. Every self-respecting city sought to connect itself, through its ancient clans, with the Homeric heroes, and this constituted the highest title to prestige in the Greek world. The poems which could confer such a title were looked up to as authoritative historical documents. In disputes about territory the *Iliad* was appealed to as a valid witness. The enormous authority of Homer, the deep hold which the Trojan epics had won on the minds and hearts of the Greeks, may partly explain the puzzle, why it was so long before it occurred to them to record recent or contemporary events. For when we consider the early growth of their political intelligence, the paucity of their historical records must strike us with surprise. In the seventh century they were far advanced in political

experience. Sparta, for instance, had a complicated constitution; yearly magistrates had been
introduced at Athens. The number of the small
independent states which had to live together,
some of which had special relations to one another,
tended to develop the political sense. Intensity
of political life had been the outcome of the
institution of the *polis*, and the Hellenic world
was the scene of numerous and various experiments in government. In these conditions,
political literature originated. Archilochus, Tyr-
taeus, Solon, and Theognis were the most eminent
of the ancient publicists who dealt with current
politics in metrical pamphlets. But the Greeks
of this period felt no impulse to record their
experiences in historical records; the only history
they cared for was still furnished by the epics.
Long before this, Egypt and Assyria had
abundant contemporary records, narratives of
conquests and achievements, inscribed for the
glorification of some powerful monarch. But the
early Greeks, even despots, were free from the
kind of self-consciousness which prompted an
Assur-bani-pal to draw up a narrative of his
deeds; Periander and Peisistratus did not think
of securing posthumous fame by such appeals to
posterity. Had Peisistratus been an oriental ruler,
he would have invited his literary friends to
celebrate his own career; being a Greek of his
time, he appointed a committee of men of letters
to edit the Homeric poems. There were indeed

some records kept in the seventh century, and
perhaps sooner, which at a later time were to
prove useful; but they were bare enumerations
of names, such as lists of magistrates or priests.

Now it is important to realise that the historical
interest of the Greeks of those days, concentrated
as it was on the epic traditions, was active and
productive. The epics were still growing in the
seventh century, though the period of growth was
soon to be over. It is almost certain that the
Iliad and *Odyssey* did not reach the fulness of
their present compass much before 600 B.C. I
need only ask you to recall the lectures which
Mr. Gilbert Murray delivered at this University
last year; some things he said happen to
prepare the way for the consideration of the
origins of historiography. He insisted, rightly as
I think, on the fact that the groundwork and
principal motives of the Homeric epics were
historical; and he showed, with admirable insight,
how the development of the poems, in its successive stages, responded to, and reflected, the ideas,
manners, and tastes of successive periods. But
besides this moral and social criticism which Mr.
Murray traced, there was another kind of criticism
which betrayed the spirit of historical inquiry.
The epics relating to the Trojan war, which
existed, let us say, about 800 B.C. in order to fix
our ideas, would raise in an inquiring mind many
questions as to the course of the war, its final
conclusion, the fortunes of many heroes who took

part in it,—questions to which Homer gave no answer. To quench the thirst for such information was the office of later poets, who related events which the older bards did not know or assumed as known. They had to fill up interstices and to explain inconsistencies, and this process necessarily entailed a definite consideration of chronological sequence, an element which the original creators of myth do not take into serious account. It is impossible to say how far these later poets of the Homeric school drew upon local legends, how far upon their own invention, but in their hands the traditions of the Trojan expedition and its heroes were wrought into a corpus of Trojan epics, chronologically connected, in which the *Iliad* and the *Odyssey* had their places.

The new instinct for systematizing tradition gave rise at the same time to the school of genealogical poets, of which Hesiod was the most distinguished and perhaps the first. Their aim was to work into a consistent system the relationships of the gods and heroes, deriving them from the primeval beings who generated the world, and tracing thereby to the origin of things the pedigrees of the royal families which ruled in the states of Hellas.[1] The interest in genealogies

---

[1] Hesiod's *Theogony* contains a first crude idea of a history of civilisation in the legend of the Five Ages of man, which evidently brings up to date an older version in which the ages were Four. The fanciful notion of marking the degeneration of the race by four ages named after four metals is improved upon by interpolating the age of Homeric heroes before the last or iron age.

linking actual families with legendary heroes [1] was closely allied to the interest in "origins" connecting the foundations of cities with the heroic age. This interest gave rise to a group of what we may call local epics, approximating in style and character to the Hesiodic school, recording the mythical origins (κτίσεις) and the pedigrees of the founders. We know, for instance, of the *Corinthiaca*, ascribed to Eumelus, which may have been the source of certain later sections of the *Iliad*;[2] of the Naupactian poem; of the *Phoronis* which took its name from Phoroneus, reputed the first King of Argos.

In all this intellectual activity, we can recognise in a crude form the instinct of historical inquiry, guided by the ideas of consistency and chronological order. The genealogies inevitably brought chronology into the foreground. We can also see that the poets possessed a certain kind of historical sense. They were conscious up to a certain point of the differences between their own civilisation and that of the heroic age, and this consciousness expressed itself in the archaism which we can observe in the *Iliad* and *Odyssey*. The poets always retained, for instance, the obsolete bronze armour of antiquity.

One epic poem, belonging to the seventh or perhaps the sixth century, claims a special mention

---

[1] In this connexion Mahaffy notes an "anxiety to show hereditary rights in all the usurpers of power throughout early Greek history" (*Prose Writers*, i. 10).

[2] Cp. Murray, *Rise of the Greek Epic*, p. 162.

here, the *Arimaspea* ascribed to Aristeas of Proconnesus.   The subject of this work was Scythia,
which the author seems to have visited, and its
importance for our present purpose is that it
anticipated the interest in geography and ethnography which, as we shall see, accompanied the rise
of history proper.   It seems too to have contained
a reference to an event of what for Aristeas was
modern history, the movement of the Cimmerians
in the seventh century, a movement which he very
properly explained by the pressure of neighbouring
peoples.[1]   The *Arimaspea* however is not altogether
isolated.   A geographical interest is distinctly
present in the *Odyssey*; M. Bérard has illustrated
its significance and the historical background.
But perhaps it is rather in the ancient Argonautic
poems, ranging into the same regions which
Aristeas visited, that we may seek the inspiration
of the *Arimaspea*.

Up to the middle or end of the sixth century,
then, their epic poetry satisfied the historical
interest of the Greeks.   For us it is mythical, for
them it was historical.   And further, during the
later centuries of the epic period, it was becoming
quasi-historical in form.   The body of traditions
was being submitted to crude and rudimentary
processes of what we may call historical inquiry.

------

[1] The main authority for Aristeas is Herodotus iv. 13-16 (cp. Macan's
notes).   The date here (15) assigned, " 240 years ago," is obviously that
of the foundation of Cyzicus (*c.* 680 B.C.) and may be used to fix the composition of Book IV. to *c.* 440 B.C.   For the guess that Aristeas lived in the
sixth century, it may be said that Dionysius, *De Thuc.* 23, brackets him
with Cadmus ; but this is hardly enough to establish even a presumption.

The later poets of the Homeric school, and the poets of the Hesiodic school, worked in obedience to the need of systematic arrangement and chronological order. There was no absolute chronology, no dates; but time-sequence determined the completion of the Trojan cycle, and the relation of the Trojan to other cycles (such as the Theban), and, in the very nature of the subject, it controlled the genealogical poems. Scattered and contradictory traditions were harmonized more or less into a superficially consistent picture of the past by the activity of these poets. Their work must have counted for a great deal in both satisfying and stimulating the self-consciousness of the Greeks.

§ 2. *The foundation of history by Hecataeus*

It might be expected that such an examination of the ancient literature and traditions, though carried out with no under-thought of questioning their truth as a whole, would have sown the germs of criticism and prepared the way for incredulity. This is a difficult question, as our knowledge of this literature is so fragmentary. We can point at least to the notorious scepticism of Stesichorus about the story of Helen. But we can do more. The truth seems to be that towards the end of the epic period there arose in Ionia a spirit which it would be going too far to describe as incredulous, but which was certainly flippant and sceptical and might at any moment break out into positive incredulity. This spirit is revealed, as Mr. Murray has well shown, in some late parts of the *Iliad*, especially in the episode of the Beguiling of Zeus; it appears in the *Odyssey* in the lay of Demodocus, which tells of the punishment of Ares and Aphrodite by the injured husband Hephaestus.

Such tendencies to scepticism, evolved by the Ionian temper, were reinforced by the rise of Ionian science and philosophy. Science and philosophy meant criticism, and it would not be long before criticism which the early thinkers applied to the material world would be systematically applied to human tradition also, and the result would be, in some form or other, the distinction of history from myth.

At the same time the mythopoeic instinct of the Greeks was still potent and still felicitous in its operation. But myth assumed a new shape. Supernatural beings no longer appeared upon the stage; and, with the exception of oracles, omens, and visions, the supernatural *mise en scène* was discarded. Fictions gathered round historical persons, contemporary or recent, but all these stories, such as the saving of Cypselus, the wooers of Agarista, the ring of Polycrates, kept well within the fence of the possibilities of human experience. They are not in the crude sense incredible, ἄπιστα τῷ καθ᾽ ἡμᾶς βίῳ. This new order of myths corresponds to a new interest, which we might call the philosophy of life; it is reflected in the gnomic poetry of the period. Sages have

taken the place of heroes; the Septemvirate of
Wise Men was one of the mythical creations.
The authority of Delphi is established beside the
authority of Homer, and Delphi seems to have
been a centre for fiction of this order.

Now let us suppose that before the end of the
sixth century a thoughtful man began to reflect
upon the past fortunes of the Greeks. He would
be struck by the fact that the character of their
history had completely changed. The age of the
heroes, as described in the epics, was marked by
divine interventions, frequent intercourse between
gods and men, startling metamorphoses, and all
kinds of miracles. How was it that the character
of human experience had changed and that such
marvels had ceased to happen? It was inevitable
that the question should be asked: can we believe
the epic poets and take all they tell us for literal
fact? And we find that before 500 B.C. a philosopher of Ionia, Xenophanes, had arraigned the
credibility of Homer and Hesiod.[1] He rejected
the anthropomorphisms of popular theology, and
branded the Greek myths as ancient fictions (πλά-
σματα τῶν προτέρων). His rationalism was in the
interest of cosmic law. He was applying, whether
explicitly or not, the principle formulated by later

---

[1] It is believed that much about the same time a western Greek,
Theagenes of Rhegium, was attempting to interpret Homer allegorically.
According to Tatian, *adv. Graecos* 31, he flourished in the time of
Cambyses; schol. Ven. to *Il.* Υ 67 (533 ed. Bekker) he was the first to
write on Homer, and he introduced allegorical interpretation; the schol.
on Dionysius Thrax (Bekker, *Anecd. Gr.* 729) suggests that he dealt with
grammar.

rationalists that what was possible once is possible still, and what is incredible now is incredible always. And he was also concerned, in the cause of ethics, to denounce the attribution to the gods of conduct condemned by the contemporary moral standards of Greece.[1]

Besides the efforts of Ionian men of science to explain nature by reason,—besides the dawn of philosophy,—there was another fact which contributed, in the second part of the sixth century, to widen the horizon of intelligent minds in Ionia. The power of Persia had been extended to the Aegean, and the Asiatic Greeks had been incorporated in the Persian empire. A natural consequence was the stimulation of interest and curiosity among those Greeks about the other lands of the great realm to which they were now attached; and their new position provided facilities for gratifying this curiosity. Oriental geography and history presented to the Greeks a new field of study, and this exercised, as we shall see, an important influence in bringing history to the birth.

Its birth is associated with the name of Hecataeus of Miletus. He was, first and foremost, a geographer. I do not dispute the title of Anaximander to be called the "father of geography," but Hecataeus may be considered one of the

---

[1] It is remarkable that Xenophanes wrote two epic poems on quasi-historical subjects—the Origin of his native home Colophon, and the colonisation of his adoptive home Elea; but no traces of these works have survived. It would be interesting to know how he handled definite traditions.

founders of geographical science; his chief contributions to knowledge were in that field. Born
perhaps near the middle of the sixth century, he
not only travelled in Greek lands and on the
shores of the Black Sea, but explored the interior
parts of the Persian empire, and Egypt, which had
been annexed by Cambyses. Perhaps his travels
extended to southern Spain. Everywhere he
collected facts for a geographical work which was
published under the title of a *Map of the World*.
But this work ranged beyond the sphere of pure
geography. There is no doubt that it contained,
besides descriptions of countries and places, a great
deal of ethnography and history, and especially it
introduced the Greeks to oriental history and
sketched for the first time the successive monarchies
of Assyria, Media, and Persia. The writer almost
certainly touched upon the Ionian history of his
own day, in which he himself played a part.
Herodotus, you may remember, mentions advice
tendered by Hecataeus to the Ionians on more
than one occasion, advice which they did not
follow. The most likely person to record advice
which has not been followed is the adviser; and
we may pretty confidently assume that the source
of Herodotus was Hecataeus himself.

Hecataeus thus initiated the composition of
"modern" history, though only in a work which was
geographical in its title and main argument. He
also wrote a work on the ancient history of Greece.
It was a prose compilation from the genealogical

epics. But, though its title, *Genealogies*, shows
how potent the influence of the epics was, it was
a critical investigation. The opening words are
striking and might have stirred a reader to ex-
pectancy of a thoroughgoing and drastic revision
of what currently passed for the ancient history of
Hellas. "What I write here," says Hecataeus,
"is the account which I considered to be true.
For the stories of the Greeks are numerous, and in
my opinion ridiculous." The actual fragments of
the work would not enable us to judge to what
lengths his scepticism ventured. The few instances
of rationalistic interpretation which we can note are
of a sufficiently innocent kind, but show us that,
while he did not adopt the doctrine of Xenophanes
that the myths are fictions, he applied a canon of
inner probability. For instance, he explained the
hound of Hades which Heracles was related to
have dragged up from the under-world, as the
name of a terrible serpent which haunted Taenarum.
Again, he transported the home of Geryones and
his cattle from distant Spain to the more accessible
pastures of Epirus.[1]

But a clearer view of the attitude of Hecataeus
may be derived from certain passages in Herodotus
to which I shall have to draw attention in the next
lecture. We shall then see that his scepticism in
regard to the ancient history of the Greeks had

---

[1] It seems probable it was from his geographical work that Herodotus
derived the explanation of the legend of the nursing of Cyrus by a female
dog, as meaning that he was suckled by a woman named Spako, which
signified dog in the Medic language (Präšek).

been stimulated by the acquaintance he made in Egypt with the historical traditions of the Egyptians. There he made the discovery that in days when gods were supposed to be walking abroad on the hills and in the vales of Hellas, Egypt at the distance of a few days' voyage was managed exclusively by mere human beings. It was an obvious inference that the age of the gods in Greece must be relegated to as remote a date as the age of the gods in Egypt, and that the heroic age of the not very distant ancestors of the existing Greeks must be divested of the supernatural atmosphere with which poetical fable had encompassed it. We may conclude that the prefatory announcement of Hecataeus was not excessive, and that his rationalism was more complete than the few meagre fragments of the work might lead us to suppose.

Hecataeus, as I have said, wrote in prose. His choice of prose was a proof of his competence and a condition of his achievement. But prose had, in all probability, been used already at Miletus for the treatment of a historical subject. The very existence of Cadmus the Milesian has been called in question by some modern critics, and he is certainly a misty figure. The evidence seems to me—though I speak with diffidence—to point to the conclusion that he existed, and was one of the earliest prose writers of Ionia.[1] My idea of Cadmus is that he

---

[1] Chief sources for Cadmus: Dionys. Hal. *De Thuc.* 23 ; Strabo i. 2. 6 ; Pliny, *N.H.* v. 31, vii. 56 ; Josephus, *c. Ap.* i. 2 ; Suidas, *sub*

lived in the early part of the sixth century, contemporary with Anaximander and Pherecydes of Syros, and wrote a book on the Origins of Miletus and other Ionian cities, a work which was notable only because it was written in prose, and not differing in treatment or character from epics like the *Corinthiaca* and *Phoronis*. This is perhaps the best we can do for the reputation of Cadmus; he was a very early prose writer or *logographer*, but there is no reason to suppose that he was more of a historian than Eumelus or Eugammon. The claim of Hecataeus to be the founder of history cannot be disputed in his favour.

A logographer, as you know, means a writer of prose, not specially a historian.

The early historical literature of the Greeks had no distinctive name. It formed part of the general prose literature which was then springing up in Ionia and which included philosophical and scientific works, and, for instance, the fables of Aesop. In their nomenclature, the Greeks regarded only the

nomine. The passages of Strabo and Pliny show that the creation of prose was variously ascribed to Cadmus and Pherecydes (of Syros). This was, of course, the result of Alexandrine investigation. From Dionysius we learn that an extant work which bore the name of Cadmus was strongly suspected of being a fabrication. We may take it for granted that it was spurious, but it seems highly probable that its subject was that of the genuine work which had long since perished. Hence, I think, we may pretty securely accept the information of Suidas (whether derived from the pseudo-Cadmus or from Alexandrine sources) that Cadmus composed κτίσιν Μιλήτου καὶ τῆς ὅλης Ἰωνίας. From Dionysius we also infer that Cadmus belonged to a distinctly older generation than Hecataeus. The posthumous rivalry between him and Pherecydes for the origination of literary prose points to the first half of the sixth century; for Anaximander's prose treatise on Nature cannot have been much later than 550 b.c. Cp. Gomperz, *Griechische Denker*, i. p. 41.

difference of form.   The *epopoioi* had now to be
distinguished from the *logopoioi*, the epic poets
who composed verse from the logo-poets who
composed prose.   The *logopoioi* were also called
logographoi, which means exactly the same thing,
only emphasizing the fact that they used the pen.
Heracleitus and Sophron were as much logographers
as Hecataeus.

History had at first no distinctive name.   The
term ἱστορίη did not then mean what it came to
mean later.   Yet, as it was used by the Ionians,
we may say that it suggested the new element
which discriminated the *logoi* of Hecataeus from
the epics (and, as I suggest, from Cadmus).   You
remember how in Homer a legal dispute is brought
before a ἵστωρ, a man of skill who inquires into the
alleged facts and decides what the true facts are.
ἱστορίη meant an inquisition of this kind.   We saw
that the later epic poets did a certain amount of
inquiring and comparing, and, in so far as they did
this, they were leading up to history.   But in the
preface to the *Genealogies* of Hecataeus the conception of a historical inquiry stands revealed.
He endeavoured to deal with his data more or less
like a ἵστωρ, and to elicit the truth, applying
canons of common sense.   Of course his methods
were unsound ; but in his aim and effort he was a
pioneer, and prose, as he saw, was the right vehicle
for moving along the new paths which he opened up.

The rise of prose was probably a condition of
the rise of history ; it is almost inconceivable that

history could have emerged from its shell if the new vehicle of critical thought had not been there to carry it. It was not indeed a foregone conclusion that Hecataeus should choose prose. Verse and prose were still rivals, they had not yet clearly differentiated their spheres. If Cadmus had recorded the foundation of Miletus in prose, Xenophanes related the foundation of Colophon in metre. Parmenides was writing verse, while Heracleitus was expressing his deeper thoughts in prose ; it is not insignificant that Heracleitus was incomparably the greater thinker. In the choice of prose the founder of history displayed his insight.[1]

Both sides of the activity of Hecataeus, the genealogical in which he is a mythographer, the geographical in which he is also a historian, had a far-reaching influence on the development of Greek historiography ; and announce on the very threshold its weakness and its strength. In treating their " ancient " history the Greeks were always to remain under the influence of the epics : the sceptre was never to fall from the hands of Homer and Hesiod ; and the historical investigation of early Greece was never to be anything but at best a more or less clarified and arbitrarily rationalised mythography. On the other hand, it was the treatment of Persia and the East in the Geography of Hecataeus that inaugurated " modern " and

---

[1] The fragments do not enable us to appreciate his style. According to Hermogenes (*De gen. dic.* ii. 12) his prose had a charm, but he was less careful in composition than Herodotus.

"contemporary" history in which the Greeks achieved such high excellence.

§ 3. *Early Mythographers*

I may take "ancient" history first. The *Genealogies* of Hecataeus soon led to new works on the same subject. In the next generation Pherecydes of Leros, who settled at Athens, and Acusilaus of Argos—they seem to have flourished before the middle of the fifth century —again served up the epic legends in prose. These writers have no claim to the title of historians ; they were simply mythographers and it would be well always to describe them as such.

The work of Pherecydes was distinguished by its comprehensiveness. He modified the traditions for various reasons, but not on any systematic principle. For instance, on chronological grounds he makes Philammon, instead of Orpheus, accompany the Argonauts. In order to connect the poet Homer with the poet Orpheus, he invents genealogical intermediaries. The interpolation of links in pedigrees is a feature of his method ; and here he is working simply on the lines, and in the spirit, of the later epic poets themselves. If he modifies a legend, it is not to rationalise, but rather in the interests of popular superstition. The old legend made Apollo slay the Cyclôpes because they furnished Zeus with the thunderbolts which destroyed Asclepius. Pherecydes makes

him slay not the Cyclôpes but the sons of the
Cyclôpes, evidently to indulge the popular belief
that the Cyclôpes are still busy with the manufacture of thunder.[1] We may say then that
Pherecydes was a systematizer of the epic traditions on conservative lines, contrasting not only
with the revolutionary method of Hecataeus, but
with the freer treatment of the legends by the
Attic tragedians.

In Acusilaus we can detect the influence of
Hecataeus. He cannot resist the temptation to
rationalise up to a certain point. He will not
admit, for instance, that Zeus could change himself into a bull, and so he holds the animal which
carried off Europa to have been a mere common
bull sent by Zeus, not the metamorphosed god.
He describes the fleece of Colchis as not golden
but purple, and explains that it was empurpled by
sea-water. More interesting than these halting
concessions to improbable probability is his reconstruction of the causes of the Trojan war. He
asked himself why the goddess Aphrodite should
have united herself to the Trojan Anchises. Such
an occurrence as the union of a goddess with a
mortal required a motive. He found it in an
oracle that the descendants of Anchises should
reign when the kingdom of Priam had fallen.
When her son Aeneas grew to manhood, the
object of Aphrodite was to bring about the fall

---

[1] Wilamowitz-Möllendorff, *Isyllos*, 65. For the story of Cephalus and
Procris as told in the epics, Pherecydes substituted what seems to have
been the family tradition of the Cephalidae. Bertsch, *Pherek. Studien*, p. 2.

of Priam's dynasty, and for this purpose she caused
Paris to fall in love with Helen.   Then when
Helen had been carried off, she helped the Trojans
in order that they might not, in despair at defeat,
surrender Helen and save the throne of Priam.
The story of the judgment of Paris, which, according to the *Cypria*, was the original cause of the
war, is thus rejected, and the war is attributed to
the ambitious schemes and Machiavellian policy
of Aphrodite.   This is rationalism of a sort.   The
accepted view ascribed the cause of a great movement to the vanity of a goddess; Acusilaus,
retaining the action of the goddess, explained her
motive as political ambition, and so, raising the
transaction to a higher level, fancied that he made
it more credible.

A later writer, Herodorus of Heraclea, carried
the method of Hecataeus much further than
Acusilaus.   It will be enough to illustrate the
character of his mythography by one instance.
The legend told that Apollo and Poseidon built
the walls of Troy for King Laomedon.   According
to Herodorus, what really happened was this.
Laomedon built the walls in the ordinary way, but
he defrayed the expenses by the sacred treasures
which had been accumulated in the shrines of
Poseidon and Apollo.   This is an example of the
method of interpretation by which Herodorus
sought to explain away the miraculous.[1]

---

[1] Murray has an interesting section on Herodorus in his *History of
Greek Literature*, pp. 127 sq.

The work of Pherecydes then represents a conservative reaction against the rationalism of Hecataeus. The compilations of Acusilaus represent a compromise between rationalism and conservatism, but leaning heavily to the conservative side. Herodorus took up the rationalistic method of Hecataeus, and developed it further. Reason was a gainer by the work of Hecataeus; it is a landmark in the progress of criticism; but the Hecataean method could not advance positive knowledge. It led, beyond Herodorus, to Palaephatus and Euemerus; it led ultimately nowhere, and I will not follow it. It was not the mythographers, but the Attic tragedians, whose criticism of mythology was interesting and illuminating, Aeschylus by moralising and Euripides by discrediting it.

§ 4. *Early Historians*

Hecataeus, the historian, as distinguished from the mythographer, had two immediate successors who took up the subject of oriental history in which he had shown the way. Charon of Lampsacus[1] composed a history of Persia coming down at least as far as the destruction of the fleet of Mardonius by a storm off Mount Athos in 492 B.C., but probably including the invasion of Xerxes, of which he was in the fullest sense a contem-

---

[1] His *Hôroi* (see below, p. 29) seems to have been published after 465-4 B.C. Compare Schwartz's article in Pauly-Wissowa. I cannot see any proof that the *Persica* was merely an excerpt from the *Hôroi*.

porary.[1] His narrative was probably brief, but as
one of the first historical works which descended
to the writer's own age it possessed considerable
importance for the growth of historical composition. There was another writer of the same period
who was perhaps equally important and treated
the same subject as Charon. Dionysius of Miletus
likewise wrote a history of Persia which came
down to the death of Darius and included the
defeat at Marathon. But he followed this up by a
continuation which had still greater interest, entitled *The Sequel to the Reign of Darius*; which
narrated the events of the Persian war.[2]

Now while these works of Charon and Dionysius included very important episodes in the
history of Greece, they were properly and formally
histories of Persia. The first Greek writers who
wrote modern history wrote of Greece only incidentally. Their theme was the great empire which
had subjugated a part of Greece and attempted
to subjugate it all. The circumstance that the
writers, who undertook to record the relations of
Greece with Persia, conceived those relations as
part of the history of the Persian state, had an
advantage for the unity of the subject. To write

[1] This is the most natural inference from Dionysius, *Letter to Pompey*,
3. 7 Ἑλλανίκου τε καὶ Χάρωνος τὴν αὐτὴν ὑπόθεσιν (as Herodotus) προεκ-
δεδωκότων. (The *Persica* of Hellanicus cannot have been prior to the
composition of Herodotus vii.-ix.)

[2] One fragment of Dionysius (*Persica*) has been preserved, in the
scholia on Herodotus (cod. B) iii. 61 (ὁ μάγος Πατιζείθης): Διονύσιος ὁ
Μιλήσιος Πανξούθην ὀνομάζεσθαι τοῦτον λέγει. See Stein's *Herodotus* (ed.
1869-71), vol. ii. p. 438. I mention this solitary fragment, because it does
not appear in Müller's *F.II.G.*

the history of Greece at almost any period without
dissipating the interest is a task of immense difficulty, as any one knows who has tried, because
there is no constant unity or fixed centre to which
the actions and aims of the numerous states can be
subordinated or related. Even in the case of the
Persian invasion, one of the few occasions on
which most of the Greek cities were affected by
a common interest, though acting in various ways
and from various motives, it facilitated the task of
the narrator to polarise the events of the campaigns by following the camp of the invader and
describing them as part of Persian history, though
with Hellenic sympathy. But this method of
treatment was a heritage from Hecataeus. The
impulse which led to the "Persian" books of
Charon and Dionysius came from the geographical
work of Hecataeus, and in all probability he was
one of their chief guides for oriental history up to
the Ionic revolt.

There is one other observation I would make
about the lost history of Dionysius. He was an
Ionian, writing after Ionia had been delivered from
the Persian yoke and had entered the confederacy
of Delos, with the prospect of becoming dependent
on Athens. The history of Ionia had not been
brilliant, politically, during the past hundred years.
It had been subdued first by Lydia and then by
Persia; it had revolted from Persia and ignomin-
iously failed; it had been compelled to aid its
master in attempting to enslave the free Hellenes.

It held a somewhat undignified position between
Persia and free Greece. The Ionian point of
view was therefore different, necessarily, from the
Spartan or the Athenian; and the Ionians had
some reason to feel that their actions were open to
misconstruction, and that a rôle, not too heroic,
would gain in their own telling. In any case the
story of the Great Invasion told at Miletus would
have a considerably different colouring from the
same story related at Susa or at Athens. We may
reasonably suspect that the history of the war by
Dionysius had a value for Ionian self-love; that it
may have done less than justice to the victorious
Greeks; but that it probably did more justice to
Persia than the enemy would have received from
an Athenian writer. This Ionian logos of the
Persian war was, we may conjecture, a challenge
to unreserved admirers of Athens; we shall see
in the next lecture how such a challenge was
taken up.

There is another writer of this early school of
historians whose name I cannot pass over, the
Carian Greek, Scylax of Caryanda. He was
employed by Darius to survey the course of the
river Indus, and he published an account of his
exploration. But he also wrote a work of contemporary history which centred round the figure
of his fellow-countryman, Heracleides, Prince of
Mylasae, who deserted the Persian cause and
helped the Greeks in the invasion of Xerxes. A
chance ray of light has recently been shed on

Heracleides by an Egyptian papyrus, which contains a fragment of the work of the historian
Sosylus on the Second Punic war.[1] This fragment relates to a naval action, probably the battle
fought at the mouth of the Ebro in 217 B.C. The
author illustrates a point in the naval tactics by
comparing a certain action of Heracleides which
thwarted a Phoenician manœuvre at the battle of
Artemisium. The episode is not mentioned by
Herodotus (though he refers to Heracleides elsewhere) and it probably comes from the work of
Scylax.[2] How far that work was what could be
called biographical we cannot tell, but it is at least
noteworthy as the earliest Greek book we know of
that made an individual the centre of a historical
narrative.

We shall not wrong these early historians if we
describe them as credulous and uncritical. The
able literary critic, Dionysius of Halicarnassus, in
whose days many of their works were still in existence, says that their aim was simply to compile
and publish traditions and records, " without
adding or subtracting anything"; and he appre-
ciates their style as clear, concise, appropriate to
the subject, bare of any artificial technique, though
not careless or ungraceful.[3]

---

[1] Edited, interpreted, and discussed by Wilcken, *Hermes*, xli. pp. 103
sqq., 1906.

[2] On this work see Gutschmid, *Kleine Schriften*, iv. p. 144, who
thought it must be part of a large work, and Wilcken, *op. cit.* pp. 125-6.

[3] *De Thucydide* 5. Dionysius distinguishes three chronological
groups of historians : (1) Cadmus, whom he associates with Aristeas ;
(2) Eugeon, Deiochus, Eudemus, Democles, Hecataeus, Acusilaus,

The historical impulse initiated by Hecataeus extended after a time beyond Ionia into the neighbouring land of Lydia, which had been permeated by Greek culture under the last Lydian kings. The Lydian Xanthus composed in Greek a history of his country for which he used local traditions and perhaps consulted inscriptions in the palace of Sardis.[1] But in the development of historiography he is less important than two other writers who, like him, wrote during the latter half of the fifth century, Antiochus of Syracuse and Hellanicus of Lesbos. Antiochus composed a work on the history of the western Greeks. He investigated the early history of Sicily and Italy and the plantation of the Greek colonies in those lands. So far he was dealing with the subject of origins, in which the early historians inherited an interest from their epic predecessors, whose legends they supplemented and modified by local traditions. (The epic itself had here a late offshoot in the poem which Panyassis of Halicarnassus produced towards the middle of the fifth century on the colonisation of the Ionian towns.) But the great

---

Charon, Melesagoras (perhaps Διονύσιος ὁ Μιλήσιος has fallen out after Ἑκαταῖος ὁ M.); (3) Hellanicus, Damastes, Xenomedes, Xanthus, καὶ ἄλλοι σύχνοι. 450 b.c. would roughly mark the division between 2 and 3. The work of Eugeon (Euagon) of Samos was appealed to c. 200 b.c. in a dispute between Samos and Priene which was decided by Rhodes (see Greek Inscriptions in the British Museum, cccciii. 109, 120). Deiochus wrote a chronicle of Cyzicus. For Democles see Strabo i. 58 and xii. 551; for Damastes, F.H.G. ii. 64-7. The work which passed under the name of (A)melesagoras (F.H.G. ii. 21) was a fraud : see Wilamowitz-Möllendorff, Antigonos von Karystos, p. 24.

[1] Gutschmid, Kleine Schriften, iv. pp. 307 sqq.

significance of Antiochus is that he wrote the
modern and contemporary history of an important
section of the Greek world.   A comprehensive
history of western Hellas was a step towards a
comprehensive history of Hellas as a whole.

His contemporary, Hellanicus of Lesbos, indicated, and prepared the way for, a further advance ;
and it is important to grasp his significance in our
development.   It has been usual to classify him
with the elder successors of Hecataeus, because he
wrote in Ionic Greek and covered practically all
the fields which they had covered.   But he broke
new ground and became, as has been said, "the
corner-stone" of the historical tradition of the
Greeks.   The range of his literary activity was
wide.   He wrote on the history of Persia ; on the
customs of the barbarians ; on the mythical period
of Greece ; on the origins of the Greek cities in
Asia ; on the later history of Greece and especially
the history of Athens.   His principal achievement
was the construction of a systematic chronology
which laid the foundations for subsequent research.

The subject of chronology must have been
pressed on the attention of Hecataeus, not only
by his research into Greek genealogies, but by
his study of Egyptian and oriental history.   The
Greeks had not yet invented any method of
chronicling events.   They had, as we saw, no
chronological records, except lists of names, like
those of the priestesses of Hera at Argos, of the
archons at Athens, of the priests of Poseidon at

Halicarnassus.   It was only rarely that a name in
these lists would yield the precise date of an event,
such as the archonship of Solon which supplied at
once the date of his reforms.   Beyond these very
barren records the only data were the genealogies.
These furnished a very rough method of reckoning
periods of time by generations.   But there must
have been considerable perplexity how the genera-
tion-unit should be calculated in terms of years.
Ultimately it became usual to reckon three
generations as equivalent to a hundred years, so
that the unit was roughly 33 years.   But there
are early traces of another system which equated
the generation with 23 years,[1] a principle which
would yield widely different results.   There was
another system based on 40 years.   It is probable
that Hecataeus reckoned generally with generations, and not years, as his units, for the more
distant past.   But for "modern" history he had
valuable auxiliary data of a precise kind.   The
oriental monarchies had an exact method of reckoning by means of the regnal years of the kings, and
records of events dated in this way were preserved.
These dates at once supplied synchronisms with
events in Greek history and fixed a number of
chronological landmarks, such as the capture of
Sardis.   But it is not likely that chronology was
treated by Hecataeus more carefully or methodi-
cally than by Herodotus; its fundamental importance was not realised till later.

[1] See Herodotus i. 7 : 22 generations = 505 years.

The problem which Hellanicus undertook was to reconstruct a complete chronicle of Greek history, with the help of the genealogies, lists such as that of the Athenian archons, and the oriental dates. It is possible that attempts had been made to work out this highly speculative problem already. Charon had compiled a book called the *Hôroi* of Lampsacus. It is generally assumed to have been a local history or chronicle of his native city. But the fragments suggest that it had a wider range than the affairs of Lampsacus. Perhaps the work consisted of annals, dated by yearly magistrates of Lampsacus, but recording, as well as local events, other events also of general historical interest. We have a parallel in a vast number of medieval chronicles which possess at once a local and a general side. Annals of Paderborn, for instance, take special account of Paderborn affairs, but also record the general history of the Western Empire. This is only a conjecture,[1] and in any case it was reserved for Hellanicus, even if he had the help of previous attempts, to achieve the construction of a chronicle which in its main lines found general acceptance, and influenced the course of subsequent chronological study. He made the list of the Argive priestesses of Hera the framework of his general chronicle of Greece.[2] He also compiled a special chronicle of Attic history, in which events were naturally arranged under the archon years

---

[1] Of Seeck ; see *Klio* iv. pp. 289-90. We have no data to conjecture the scope of Eugeon's *Hôroi* of Samos.

[2] Kullmer refers p. 52 to the Ambracian-Acarnanian war of 429 B.C.

from the year 683-2 onward. In its first form,
this work came down to the year 411. After the
termination of the Peloponnesian war the author
continued it to 404 B.C.[1] The notices of events
were brief, but it was not without a certain political colouring, evincing sympathy with Athenian
democratic patriotism.

Without entering upon a minute criticism of
the method of Hellanicus, it is enough to say that,
mistaking the character of mythical traditions, he
erected an ingenious edifice on foundations which
had no solidity. The most perfect genealogies
could not even approximately determine absolute
dates ; and the genealogies were full of inconsistencies which had to be overcome by arbitrary
interpolations and manipulations. Moreover, quite
recent events, which had not been recorded at the
time, might present almost insuperable difficulties
to a chronographer. One case, which we can
control, will illustrate how dangerous the procedure
of Hellanicus was. If he had consulted a certain
inscription, which we are fortunate enough to have
recovered, he could have found that several military
events which he chronicled occurred in the same
archonship, corresponding to the latter half of
459 B.C. and the former half of 458 B.C. Ignorant
of this authentic evidence, he distributed these
events over three archonships.[2] Yet these events

---

[1] See Lehmann-Haupt in *Klio* vi. pp. 127 sqq. Apollodorus used the
earlier edition.

[2] We can be virtually certain that the chronology of Ephorus and
Diodorus for the period of the Fifty Years depended on Hellanicus, so far

must have happened within his own lifetime.
His whole chronology of the thirty-five years
after the Persian war was arbitrary; and it
illustrates how in the absence of records precise chronology is hopeless. The instance of
error which I have given suggests another
observation. There were numerous stones at
Athens, officially inscribed and precisely dated,
from which, if they were all preserved, a modern
student would probably construct without difficulty
and with absolute certainty an exact chronicle of
Athenian history in the fifth century. But it
never occurred to Hellanicus to look for them,
and in this he was only like most other Greek
historians. The Greeks used such records when
they came across them, but as a rule they did not
seek them out systematically. Was the labour of
deciphering them too laborious? It is remarkable
that Thucydides describes a sixth-century inscription, which he quotes, as written "in faint characters"; yet a portion of that same inscription
which has survived seems to a modern epigrapher
quite clear, after more than two thousand years.

When we realise the nature of the data and the
methods of the first chronologists whose ingenious
constructions determined the received tradition,
we shall hardly be prepared to dispute the con-

as Ephorus may not have modified it by the indications of Thucydides.
For Thucydides and Hellanicus seem to have been the only fifth-century
historians who recorded that period. Diodorus distributes over the years
460-59, 459-8, 458-7 events in Egypt, at Halieis, and Aegina, and
Megara, which, the well-known Erechtheid stone (*C.I.A.* i. 433) instructs
us, occurred in the same civil year (459-8).

clusion at which Mahaffy arrived more than
twenty-five years ago, that there are no well-
established exact dates in Greek history before the
seventh century.[1] For the seventh and even for
the sixth there are only a few. Nay, we can hardly
say that a clear and definite chronicle begins before
445 B.C., the year of the Thirty Years' Peace.

It is to be deplored that the early historians
failed to realise how desirable it was to reckon
time by a fixed chronological era. The practical
Romans dated historical events from the Foundation of the City. The Greeks might have adopted,
for instance, the year of the invasion of Xerxes.
They could have dated Before and After, $\pi\rho\grave{o}$ $\tau\hat{\omega}\nu$
$M\eta\delta\iota\kappa\hat{\omega}\nu$ and $\mu\epsilon\tau\grave{a}$ $\tau\grave{a}$ $M\eta\delta\iota\kappa\acute{a}$, as we do with our
era. But the most natural, and perhaps the best,
chronological starting-point would have been the
Trojan war. It did not matter in the least that
the actual date of that event could not be known
with certainty, so long as a definite year was fixed
upon. Our era is not the true date of the Nativity;
the true date cannot be ascertained; but this does
not affect the utility of the conventional era. Now
as a matter of fact the Trojan war was occasionally used, as a sort of reference date, by fifth-
century historians,[2] and it is much to be regretted
that Hellanicus did not systematically adopt this

---

[1] The subject of the early list of Olympian victors, constructed by
Hippias of Elis without trustworthy data, has recently been discussed by
A. Körte (*Hermes* xxxix. pp. 224 sqq., 1904), who confirms in essential
points the conclusions of Mahaffy.

[2] Herodotus ii. 145 *ad fin.*

method of reckoning. The years of magistrates
or priests are not only clumsy, but convey
no chronological idea. For it is to be observed
that when dates are expressed by cardinal numbers
proceeding from a fixed year, not only is calculation
simplified, but the numbers present to the mental
vision a clear historical perspective.

But recognising the defects both in the mechanism and in the methods of Hellanicus, who
attempted the impossible, we must give him credit
for having framed the ideal of a chronological
system which should embrace all the known facts
of history; and if he established many erroneous
dates, it is probable that he also rescued some
that were correct.

§ 5. *Summary*

To sum up. (1) The historical study of their
past by the Greeks arose out of the epic tradition
and was a continuation of the work of the later
epic poets. The tradition of the Homeric and
Hesiodic poets maintained its control to the end.
What we would designate as the post-mythical
or historical period overlapped by means of genealogies with the mythical period; the existing
families of Greece were connected in line of
blood with the heroes and thereby with the gods.
The genealogical principle, lying at the base of
their historical reconstruction, hindered the Greeks
from drawing a hard and fast line between the
mythical and the historical age. The historians

who approached the subject never got beyond
criticism of details and rationalistic interpretation
of miracles. But (2) at the very time when the
study of mythological tradition began to assume a
more critical character, the interest of the Greeks
expanded to the "modern" history and institutions of non-Greek states, and here they were in
a region not mythical, but historical. This intellectual movement originated in Ionia; its main
cause was the Persian conquest, and the resulting
contact of Ionian thinkers with oriental history.
The rise of Ionian science not only promoted the
spirit of criticism, but also created an interest in
geography, for the study of which the new political
status of Ionia furnished opportunities; but it was
principally the new vision of oriental history that
brought to birth Greek historiography. It was
from the "modern" history of the East that the
Greeks went on to study the "modern" history of
Hellas. And the struggle with Persia in the first
twenty years of the fifth century impelled them
to begin to write histories of their own time.
Further, as I will attempt to show more fully in
the next lecture, their contact with the traditions
of non-Greek lands within the Persian empire
suggested to the Greeks a new kind of criticism of
their own mythical traditions. In all three fields
of ancient, modern, and contemporary history, as
well as in the allied sphere of geography, Hecataeus
was a pioneer; his originality lay in responding to
the stimulus from the non-Greek world.

The work of Hellanicus, who conceived the idea of a general history of Greece and laid the slippery foundations of its chronology, has brought us to a date from which we shall have to retrace our steps to examine the work of a greater writer than any of those who have claimed our attention to-day. We have only considered those points of light, obscured by time, which form the Ionian constellation; we have yet to examine a star of the first magnitude which is still as luminous as ever. Herodotus (we must not call him an Ionian) will be the subject of the next lecture.

LECTURE II

HERODOTUS

In the last lecture the necessities of our subject obliged us to consider works of which only scraps have survived, and of which we can form only dim ideas by groping methods, although we may feel tolerably confident as to the general character and value of the literature to which they belong. The names of their authors are forgotten by the world, and their chief function now is to tantalise the special student of literature or history. To-day we come to a work which time has not been allowed to destroy or diminish.

Of the life of Herodotus, son of Lyxes, of Halicarnassus, we know hardly anything except what may be gleaned from his own statements. Born early in the fifth century, he left his birthplace before 454 B.C., banished by Lygdamis the tyrant, who put his cousin Panyassis, the epic poet, to death. He stayed apparently for some time in Samos, and then went to Athens, whence he proceeded to Italy as one of the first citizens of the new colony of Thurii (443 B.C.). He survived the first years of the Peloponnesian war

(431-0 B.C.[1]). Into this framework we have to
fit his travels, which included the coasts of the
Euxine, Babylon, Phoenicia, Egypt, and probably
Cyrene. It is not necessary to discuss the disputed subject of the chronology of his journeys.
I need only say that his most important journeys,
those to Babylonia and Egypt, were probably
undertaken in the later period of his life, while
he was a citizen of Thurii. The years which
elapsed between his banishment from his native
city and his departure for his new home seem to
have been spent in Greece, perhaps chiefly at
Athens, and to have been devoted, as we shall
see, to investigating and composing the story of
the invasion of Xerxes. Though he may naturally
have visited Athens again, on his way to or from
the East, there is no evidence to entitle us to
presume, as some have thought, that he deserted
Thurii permanently and dwelled at Athens during
the last years of his life.[2]

The argument of his history is a narrative of
the relations between the Greeks and the oriental
powers from the accession of Croesus to the
capture of Sestos in 478 B.C.—a "modern" history
in the fullest sense of the term. The division into
nine Books is not due to the author himself, for

---

[1] There are passages which cannot have been written before 431-0
B.C. vii. 233 (cp. Thucydides ii. 2) and ix. 73 (cp. Thuc. ii. 23) imply 431
B.C.; vii. 137 (cp. Thuc. ii. 67) implies 430 B.C. Cp. also iii. 160; and v. 77.
The reference to Artaxerxes in vi. 98 does not imply that the words were
written after his death (425 B.C.); cp. Macan's note *ad loc.*

[2] Compare the pertinent remarks of Wachsmuth, *Rheinisches Museum*,
lvi. 215-8 (1901).

in his day such divisions had not yet come into
fashion. But the Alexandrine editor who was
responsible for it was a man of extraordinary
insight. His distribution perfectly exhibits the
construction of the book and could not be improved by any change. But it can be rendered
more perspicuous by observing that each of the
nine Books is truly a sub-division and that the
primary partition is a threefold one.[1] The work
falls naturally into three sections, each consisting
of three parts. The first section, or triad of
Books, comprises the reigns of Cyrus and Cambyses,
and the accession of Darius; the second deals with
the reign of Darius; the third with that of
Xerxes. The first is mainly concerned with
Asia including Egypt; the second with Europe;
the third with Hellas. The first displays the rise
and the triumphs of the power of Persia; the
last relates the defeat of Persia by Greece; while
the middle triad represents a chequered picture,
Persian failure in Scythia and at Marathon, Greek
failure in Ionia. And each of the nine sub-
divisions has a leading theme which constitutes
a minor unity. Cyrus is the theme of the first
Book, Egypt of the second, Scythia of the fourth,
the Ionian rebellion of the fifth, Marathon of the
sixth. The seventh describes the invasion of
Xerxes up to his success at Thermopylae; the
eighth relates the reversal of fortune at Salamis;
the final triumphs of Greece at Plataea and Mycale

---

[1] This has been well brought out by Macan.

occupy the ninth. In the third alone the unity is less marked ; yet there is a central interest in the dynastic revolution which set Darius on the throne. Thus the unity of the whole composition sharply displays itself in three parts, of which each again is threefold.[1] The simplicity with which this architectural symmetry has been managed, without any apparent violence, constraint, or formality, was an achievement of consummate craft. The writer's management of the digressions, for which he is notorious, is hardly less striking, exhibiting a rare skill in the choice of the best and perhaps the only fitting places to stow away loose material he wished to make use of.

But, perfect as is the architectural unity of the work of Herodotus, it would seem that the plan as it was finally carried out was not conceived when he commenced to write, and that the unity was achieved not in conformity to a design thought out from the beginning, but by a process of expansion due to an after-thought. There is a variety of internal evidence which points convincingly to the conclusion that the last three Books were composed before the first six, and there are indications that he wrote this portion between 456 and 445 B.C., before he began his travels.[2] The natural inference is that he originally contemplated no more than a history of the

---

[1] In the last part the unity is much more marked than the triplicity ; in fact, the division of Book VII. from Book VIII. is somewhat arbitrary.

[2] The most complete appreciation of the evidence will be found in the Introduction to Macan's ed. of *Herodotus*, vii.-ix. (§ 7 and § 8).

invasion of Xerxes; and that it was in the course of his travels that he conceived the idea of a larger work, of which the "Invasion of Xerxes" should form the finale. The idea doubtless shaped itself gradually; and the first six Books were not composed in the order in which they stand. But the author has worked with such skill that only a searching analysis has detected the series of facts which demonstrate the priority of the last three Books[1] and make it clear that the Persian war was his original inspiration.

At whatever moment the idea of expanding his original history to its fuller compass presented itself, whether it was suggested by his journeys or prompted him to become a traveller, it was certainly connected closely with his travels, and the occurrence of long geographical excursus is one of the most striking features of the expansion.

So strongly marked indeed is the geographical element, so long are the geographical sections, in the work of Herodotus, that some critics have been led to think that considerable parts of it were originally intended to form part of a

---

[1] Some few additions were made subsequently : thus in vii. 93 and 108 there are references to passages in the books which are earlier in order but were later in composition. It is probable that the whole work never received a final revision, and this would be sufficient to explain the unfulfilled promise of vii. 213, which is the insufficient but only real argument for the hypothesis that the ninth Book is not complete. [How gratuitous this hypothesis is, Macan shows at length, *ib.* § 6.] On the other hand it seems not improbable that Herodotus intended to include in the early portion of his work a summary of Babylonian history ('Ασσύριοι λόγοι) : this seems to me more likely than that in i. 106 and 184 he is referring to another work.

geography, and were afterwards incorporated in
his history.   There is nothing that compels us to
adopt a hypothesis of this kind.   Association with
geography was a characteristic of the early
historical literature of the Greeks, and these
excursus in Herodotus attest the influence of the
Hecataean school, and were natural in the work
of a historian who was himself a traveller.   And
it is worth observing that when he was writing,
both Egypt and Scythia, the subjects of his
longest historico-geographical digressions, had a
particular practical interest for the Athenians;
and of the Greek public it was unquestionably
the Athenians to whom the historian designed
his work pre-eminently to appeal.   I need only
remind you of the Athenian adventure in Egypt
in the middle of the fifth century and of the
voyage of Pericles in the Euxine Sea.   It has
even been conjectured that this Periclean expedition (444 B.C.) was the occasion of the historian's
visit to the Pontic regions.   However this may
be, it is not insignificant, in judging these digressions, that Egypt and Scythia possessed, at the
time Herodotus wrote, an interest of a political
kind, subordinate indeed to that of Persia, but
distinctly actual.

It is also to be noted that the digressions in
general had an artistic justification.   They are an
epic feature, deliberately designed;[1] one of the
epic notes of the work.   Homer was the literary

---

[1] He says expressly that προσθῆκαι are a feature of his work, iv. 30.

master of Herodotus; without imitating him in any obvious way, the first great master of prose studied and caught the secrets of his effects. By means of digressions he achieved epic variety. We cannot do better than read the observations of the accomplished literary critic Dionysius.[1] "Herodotus knew that every narrative of great length wearies the ears of the hearer, if it dwell without a break on the same subject; but, if pauses are introduced at intervals, it affects the mind agreeably. And so he desired to lend variety to his work and imitated Homer. If we take up his book, we admire it to the last syllable, and always want more."

Besides diversifying his work with digressions and episodes, Herodotus adopted another epic feature, not less characteristic. Like Homer, the historian makes his characters speak. He introduces not only short and pointed conversations, but dialogues and orations of considerable length. For instance, Xerxes, Mardonius, and Artabanus make each a speech in Council before it is decided to invade Greece. I may recall the conversations of Solon with Croesus, of Xerxes with Artabanus and with Demaratus; and the speech made by the Corinthian envoy when the Spartans were considering the policy of forcing Athens to restore the Peisistratids.[2] If the historian were charged

---

[1] *Letter to Pompeius*, 3. Longinus calls Herodotus ὁμηρικώτατος, *De subl.* 13. 4.

[2] v. 92. Compare Stahl's article mentioned in the Bibliography.

with abusing this artifice by introducing in the
Corinthian envoy's speech a long episode from
Corinthian history, which is really quite irrelevant,
he could appeal to the discourses of Phoenix and
Nestor in Homer; and this case illustrates the
fact that in introducing speeches he was influenced
by the Ionian epic and not by the Athenian drama.
It is impossible to say whether any of the older
prose writers had adopted this practice, which
makes the scenes vivid and the work alive. The
bits of Hecataeus we possess are too brief to
judge; but I may note that in one case at least
he put words into the mouth of an actor.[1]

The Homeric qualities of Herodotus, which
communicate to his history an epic flavour, accord
with the object to produce a work which like
Homer should fascinate the minds of men. It
was his aim to hold his audience or readers
entertained; to do for his own world in prose
what Homer had done for the ancient world in
numbers. We cannot tell how far any of his
prose predecessors had sought to make their
works attractive or entertaining,[2] or whether the
influence of epic poetry affected their method
of presentation. But we may confidently say
that Herodotus was the first who discerned in
"modern" history the possibilities of a treatment

---

[1] Fr. 353 (Longinus, *De subl.* 27).   Cp. Mahaffy, *Prose Writers*,
i. p. 33. The statement in Marcellinus, *Vita Thuc.* 38, has not much
weight.

[2] Thucydides i. 23 (λογογράφοι) is not conclusive; he was thinking
chiefly, perhaps only, of Herodotus.

which was epic, and not Hesiodic but Homeric, in spirit and style.

His theme, the struggle of Greece with the Orient, possessed for him a deeper meaning than the political result of the Persian war. It was the contact and collision of two different types of civilisation, of peoples of two different characters and different political institutions. In the last division of his work, where the final struggle of Persia and Greece is related, this contrast between the slavery of the barbarian and the liberty of the Greek, between oriental autocracy and Hellenic constitutionalism, is ever present and is forcibly brought out. But the contrast of Hellenic with oriental culture pervades the whole work; it informs the unity of the external theme with the deeper unity of an inner meaning. It is the key-note of the history of Herodotus. The digressions and stories which delay the action, besides their intrinsic interest, and besides their epic use as pleasant pauses, have also the value of sounding that note, and of contributing distinctly, but without emphasis or iteration, towards impressing that contrast on the reader's mind. The interview, for example, of Croesus with Solon, the self-confident Eastern potentate with the thoughtful, self-controlled Greek, strikes this chord loudly; and most of the oriental and Hellenic stories are calculated to suggest the antithesis which finds its supreme expression, and is more elaborately wrought out, in the final collision of the Persian wars.

In the execution of this conception the Herodotean work has assumed the character of a study in the history of civilisation. Just as the Homeric poems present a large and living picture of the culture of ancient Greece, so the history of Herodotus gives us panoramic views of the Hellenic civilisation of the sixth century, and describes the cultures of all the Eastern peoples who directly or indirectly come within range.

And if it is a study in the history of civilisation, we may also say that it has certain features of a universal history. It is not universal either in space or in time. Not in time; it does not attempt to go back far in Greek history, and only touches upon the ancient period incidentally. Not in space, for it hardly touches upon the Western Greeks at all, and does not include what Hecataeus would have supplied about the peoples of the Western Mediterranean. But it has the higher quality of what we mean by universal history or *Weltgeschichte*, in focussing under one point of view, and fitting into a connected narrative, the histories of the various peoples who came into relations with one another, within a given range; so that they are drawn out of their isolation and recognised to have a meaning, greater or less, in the common history of man. Within that range, which is determined by his theme, Herodotus is irreproachably comprehensive; and his book, though he never formulates the idea, is a lesson in the unity of history.

Although Herodotus does not enter upon the
history of the heroic period, he has frequently
occasion to refer to mythical tradition, and here
he shows himself distinctly a sceptic. Not that
he was a rationalist in regard to theology generally,
or had any clear and consistent philosophical view.
He looked upon human life as under the control
of superhuman powers, who in exercising their
incalculable government were prompted by motives
of envy and nemesis or righteous anger, who acted
to some extent on principles of justice and retribution, and who might communicate knowledge to
men by means of oracles, portents, or dreams.
But any further converse of gods with men, any
divine appearances alleged to have happened in
recent times, Herodotus is not prepared to accept,
though he is never dogmatic. His philosophy was
not strong enough to deny that the gods had ever
carried on the sort of intercourse with men that is
described in the epics, or generated human progeny;
for his ultimate line between the divine and the
human was not fast. But it was a great comfort
for common sense and everyday experience, to push
the age in which such things could happen as far
back as possible. Herodotus reveals unmistakably his incredulity about all the mythical wonders
in which, according to tradition, ancestors of
living people, some fifteen or twenty generations
back, played bright or shady parts. He accepted
the genealogies, but when he got to Perseus or
Heracles, he did not regard them as sons of a god.

Heracles is the son of Amphitryon, Helen is the daughter of Tyndareus. Sometimes he relates legends or tells tales involving superhuman agency, but he never takes any responsibility for them, and occasionally treats them with delicate irony. He mentions a legend of the Thessalians that the ravine through which the Peneius makes its way to the sea was wrought by Poseidon. "Their tale is plausible; and any one who thinks that Poseidon shakes the earth and that clefts produced by earthquakes are the works of that god, would on seeing this mountain-ravine ascribe it to Poseidon. For it appeared to me to be the result of an earthquake." Gibbon might have taken lessons in the art of irony from Herodotus as well as from Pascal. Consider again the admirable caution with which he speaks of the divine snake said to live on the Athenian Acropolis. "The Athenians say that a great snake lives in the Sanctuary as guardian of the citadel; and they present a honey-cake every month as to a creature existing" (ὡς ἐόντι). This commits him to nothing.

But though disposed to accept only what experience led him to regard as possible, in any given case, Herodotus, as I have said, did not draw theoretically a hard and fast line between the human and the divine; and he did not reject as ridiculous the notion that at one time gods moved visibly on the earth and consorted with men. Why then did he reject the divine parentage of heroes like Heracles and Perseus? It is important

to comprehend the reason for this scepticism which
he derived from Hecataeus. I touched on this
point in the first lecture. It was not due to the
canons of Ionian science or to the influence of
Ionian philosophy. It was due to the study of
comparative mythology which had opened for
Hecataeus a new perspective of the world's history.
The Egyptian studies which Herodotus pursued in
the footsteps of the Milesian traveller taught him
that human history in that country went back for
thousands of years before the age of the gods was
reached. The Egyptians, for instance, had a god
corresponding to Heracles, and they reckoned that
17,000 years had elapsed since he had appeared in
Egypt. Hence the conclusion which Herodotus
accepts that there was an ancient god Heracles,
but that he must be sharply distinguished from
the human son of Amphitryon, ancestor of the
Heracleidae.[1] The Greek tradition that the age in
which gods walked the earth was still current some
eight or nine hundred years ago could not be true.
For even apart from the suggestions of comparative mythology, it was inadmissible to suppose that
while Egypt was in a prosaic age of mere men,
Greece was trodden by deities and the scene of
miracles; and the Egyptian tradition was vouched
for by records. The argument demolished the
received mythology of the heroic age so far as it
was superhuman.

---

[1] Similarly Pan son of Penelope, Dionysus son of Semele, are to be
distinguished from the synonymous gods.

Herodotus deserves credit for having accepted the argument, to which contemporary writers like Pherecydes were deaf; and if he asks pardon from the gods and heroes for his boldness, this does not mean that he felt hesitation or reluctance; it was merely an insincere and graceful genuflexion. He was doing what a Christian preacher sometimes does, when having delivered an extremely heterodox sermon he winds up with a formal homage to orthodox dogma. Herodotus is extremely courteous, perhaps ironically courteous, to both parties. He says, as it were, to the gods and heroes, "Please, do not be angry with me,—supposing you to exist. But at this time of day, you know, one must really draw the line somewhere." On the other hand he says to the infidels who disbelieve in oracular prophecy, "I know you will think me credulous. But still in this case the evidence is so remarkably clear that I do not see my way to resisting it."[1] The mythological argument, however, of which I am speaking was not due to Herodotus himself. He may have put it in his own way, and added some points, but he owed it, as I have said, to Hecataeus. It has long been recognised that his description of Egypt is not an original work, put together exclusively from his own observations and inquiries, but largely reproduces the account which Hecataeus had given in his *Map of the World*. When Herodotus visited Egypt, he doubtless had the book of

---

[1] Cp. viii. 77.

Hecataeus with him, and used it like a barrister's brief for cross-examining the temple-servants and guiding him in his investigations. He added corrections and new information, but the great Ionian supplied the groundwork. He does not say so; he does not acknowledge his debt to Hecataeus; for, as you know, the ancients had very different views from the moderns about literary obligations. It was not the fashion or etiquette to name your authorities except for some special reason,—for instance, to criticize them, or to display your own learning; and you were not considered a plagiarist if you plundered somebody else's work without mentioning his name. Hecataeus brought out the importance of the Nile by the striking phrase that Egypt was the gift of the river; Herodotus adopts the phrase as if it were his own. One of the most convincing tests by which suspected plagiarism can be established is the occurrence of the same mistakes. Now Herodotus reproduces the errors which Hecataeus had committed about the hippopotamus. But there are a whole series of points in which we can trace the contact between the two writers in regard to Egypt. As for the mythology, we are left in no doubt because Herodotus names Hecataeus in this connexion. "When Hecataeus was in Thebes he told his pedigree to the priests and connected himself with a god in the sixteenth generation. And the priests did to him what they did to me, though *I* did not relate *my* pedigree. They took him into

the hall of the temple and showed him wooden
statues of the high priests. The high priesthood
descends from father to son, and each high priest
sets up his own statue in his lifetime. They
counted 345 statues, and they set this genealogy
against that of Hecataeus, but *they* did not derive
their pedigree from a god or a hero."[1]

The author's motive in naming his predecessor
here is, obviously, to rally him for having "given
himself away" by stating his own genealogy and
divine ancestry to the priests. "*I* was not so
incautious" is the implication. But we have no
right to infer that Hecataeus had not already
drawn the sceptical conclusions which Herodotus
explains. The sceptical words with which Hecataeus introduced his *Genealogies* show that he was
not deaf to the lessons in history which he learned
in Egyptian temples. His very expression, when
he says that "the *logoi* of the Hellenes are absurd,"
not "the stories of the poets," suggests the contrast of non-Hellenes whose *logoi* he had compared.
The distinction of what the Greeks say from what
the Persians, Phoenicians, or Egyptians say often
recurs in Herodotus, and is an echo, I believe,
from Hecataeus.[2] But we have another proof.
Herodotus cites the Egyptian priests as dating
the age of the gods in relation to the reign of

---

[1] ii. 143.

[2] When Herodotus cites what οἱ Ἕλληνες say, it is sometimes assumed
that he means Hecataeus (or some other Ionian writer). In that case he
would have said οἱ Ἴωνες. He is really quoting criticisms of Hecataeus
on οἱ Ἕλληνες, that is, on the current mythology of epic tradition.

Amasis. As the visit of Hecataeus to Egypt would have fallen not long after the death of Amasis, the dating indicates that Herodotus was copying the statement of Hecataeus.

The note of scepticism, perhaps we may say the characteristic note of Ionian scepticism, is struck in the first paragraphs of the Herodotean work. It opens with the statement of a theory that the wars of the Greeks and Persians were the manifestation of a secular antagonism between Asia and Europe—what our English historian, Freeman, was fond of calling the Eternal Question. This at least is the abstract way we should formulate the tenor of the statement which I may abbreviate as follows:—"The quarrel began thus : Phoenician traders carried off from Argos Io the king's daughter. Subsequently Greek adventurers from Crete carried off the princess Europa from Tyre. The next aggression came from the Greek side, when the Argonauts ravished Medea from Colchis. The Asiatic reply to this outrage was the rape of Helen by Paris. The Trojan war which followed generated in Asia a feeling of hostility to the Greeks, and the Persian war was the ultimate issue of this feeling." But the theory was not originated by Herodotus. He disavows all responsibility. It was a theory of the Persians, he tells us, and he states it only to set it aside in his ironical way.

The whole passage reads as if it might be the condensation of a friendly discussion between a

Greek and a Persian as to the responsibility for the Persian war. It was undeniable that the Persians and not the Greeks had been the aggressors; the conquest of Ionia by Cyrus had been the beginning. The Persian advocate could only remove the blame from Asia by going farther back. The summary I gave of the argument does not reproduce its flavour, and I will take the liberty of throwing it into the form of a dialogue.

Persian. The Greeks had no business in Asia. They belong to Europe, and they should have stayed there. Their expedition against Troy was the first trespass; it began their encroachments on a continent which belongs to Asiatic peoples of whom the Persians are the heirs.

Greek. Oh, but you are forgetting that on that occasion the Trojans were the offenders; Paris carried off Helen.

Persian. That was no sufficient reason; but even if it were, the act of Paris was only a reprisal for the Greek crimes of carrying off Medea and Europa. And the Asiatics were far too sensible to make a *causa belli* of such foolish elopements.

Greek. Well, if you go back so far, you must go back farther still. What about the rape of Io from Argos?

Persian. Well, yes, I admit it. That was a Phoenician business, and we Persians must allow that the Phoenicians began the mischief, though we hold you really responsible, through your folly

in taking such an affair seriously. Only fools
would make war on account of such escapades.
Men of the world know that, if these women were
carried off, they were not more reluctant than
they should be.[1]

Evidently we have here an invention of Ionian
esprit. The nature of the argument, dealing as it
does entirely with Greek legend, shows that the
Persian was a fictitious disputant ; and the attribution of the theory to a Persian is an effect of
literary subtlety quite in the manner of Voltaire.
Though Herodotus thought little of this speculation about ancient wrongs, he seems to have taken
it as seriously meant. " Whatever we think about
all this," he says, " I will begin with the first Eastern
monarch who undoubtedly committed injustice
against Greece, Croesus, who subdued Ionia without
provocation." But it is highly significant that he
should place in the portals of his work a speculation
which set mythical tradition in a ridiculous light.

The passage I have discussed is one of several
that evince those acute tendencies in the Hellenic
mind which culminated in the movement of the
Sophists. For instance, the story of the wife of
Intaphernes. She chose to save her brother rather
than her husband or children, on the ground that
husband and children might be replaced but she
could never have another brother. That is a clever
Ionian subtlety ; there is no reason to suppose that
it was invented in the period of the Sophists. Or

---

[1] Plutarch, Περὶ τῆς Ἡροδότου κακοηθείας, 2, takes this quite seriously.

take the demonstration of the power of custom by
Darius. He dismayed some Greeks by the question what they would take to eat their dead
fathers, and then equally horrified some Indians
of a tribe who ate dead parents, by asking them
how much they would take to cremate theirs.
The immense power of custom was an observation
redolent of the age of the Wise Men; Pindar,
whom Herodotus quotes, designated Custom as
king of the world; and the idea afterwards became
the basis of sophistic theories. The story quoted
by Herodotus is a drastic Ionian illustration.

Again, the famous discussion of the comparative
merits of democracy, aristocracy, and monarchy by
the seven Persian conspirators who overthrew the
false Smerdis, belongs also to pre-sophistic speculation. It is obviously a fiction; for the discussion
was appropriate in the Greek world, but was quite
out of place in Persia. But it was not a fiction of
Herodotus, for he states expressly (careful though
he generally is not to commit himself) that these
opinions were really uttered by the Persian noble-
men, although some of the Greeks consider this
incredible. The historian was taken in, just as he
was taken in by the persiflage about the rapes of
the fair women of legend. There can hardly be
much doubt that some publicist threw his reflexions on the comparative merits of constitutions
into the shape of this historical deliberation. The
distinction of three fundamental types of constitution is older than the period of the Sophists; it is

recognised in an ode of Pindar not later than 473
B.C., and it was then probably a commonplace.[1]
We may suspect that we have to do with some
publication of the first half of the fifth century.

Now there is one feature common to these
passages. Greek ideas and reflexions are transferred to an Eastern setting or connected with
Persian history. Their origin was assuredly
Ionian.[2] They betray the naïve interest of the
Ionians in their masters, and show the Greek mind
projecting its own reflexions into a world of which
it had only a half-knowledge, with the instinct
of making that world more interesting and sympathetic.[3]

But I must return to the scepticism of Herodotus. I have already observed that in the historical
post - Homeric period the mythopoeic faculty of
the Greeks did not slumber, but myth now took
the form of the historical anecdote, or, as the
Germans call it, "historische Novelle." Here

---

[1] *Pyth.* ii. 87-8.

[2] The clear allusion of Otanes, in his defence of democracy, to the
Athenian constitution under the lot-system does not necessitate by any
means an Athenian origin.—It may be conjectured that the peculiar
privileged position which Otanes and his descendants were said to have
held in the Persian realm suggested the idea of transferring this singularly
Hellenic discussion to Susa. Otanes, it is said, was exempted from subjection to the kings because, though he was the leading organizer of the
conspiracy, he resigned all claims to the throne which Darius secured.
He was thus neither ruler nor subject, an anomalous position which in
Greece had a sort of parallel in the membership of a democracy. Hence
the suggestion that Otanes believed in democracy, and, when he did not
convince his fellow-conspirators, obtained for himself personally and his
family the freedom which a democracy bestows.

[3] I have been here expressing dissent from the view of some critics that
the passages enumerated indicate sophistic influence.

they showed consummate felicity in constructing
stories with historical background, historical actors,
historical motives, and possessing, many of them,
a perpetual value because they are seasoned with
worldly wisdom and enshrine some criticism of life.
These tales differ from the old myths not only in
the tendency to point a moral, but also in the
circumstance that for the most part they do not
involve physical impossibilities, though they may
imply highly improbable coincidences, or what we
may call psychical or political impossibilities. The
work of Herodotus is richly furnished with these
tales; he had a wonderful *flair* for a good story;
and the gracious garrulity with which he tells historical anecdotes is one of the charms which will
secure him readers till the world's end. Gibbon
happily observed that Herodotus "sometimes
writes for children and sometimes for philosophers"; the anecdotes he relates often appeal
to both. He accepts them generally at their face
value, and most of them have been taken as more
or less literally true till very recent times. The
story of the intercourse between Croesus and
Solon was rejected as fiction only because it seemed
impossible to reconcile it with chronology.[1] But
we are now more sceptical about good stories of
this type, and we have come to see how often they

---

[1] It may be held, however, that this is still an open question. A
fragment of an anonymous Dialogue, discovered by Grenfell and Hunt
(*Oxyrhynchus Papyri*, iv. No. 664), represents Solon as in Ionia when
Peisistratus became tyrant (560 B.C.). If this were so, the meeting with
Croesus would become chronologically possible.

are wrought upon, or woven into, some ancient *motif*, which is adapted to a historical setting. The tale of the funeral pyre of Croesus sprang from the burning of the Assyrian god Sandan; it was an up-to-date version of the legend of Sardanapalus. The story of the ring of Polycrates turns on an old motive, the finding of something lost in a fish's belly, but its point in connexion with Polycrates has been explained only the other day. The casting of the ring into the sea was symbolic of thalassocracy; it was the same mythical ring as that of Minos, which in the poem of Bacchylides Theseus sought in the halls of Amphitrite; its recovery was fatal to the ruler of the seas.[1]

Herodotus is the Homer of this later form of historical myths, in which the supernatural machinery consisted of oracles or significant dreams or marvellous coincidences. They corresponded to his wavering standard of the credible and probable, which generally excluded what seemed physically impossible. For instance, he positively refuses to believe that statues assumed a sitting posture.[2] He duly records the story that a certain man dived under water a distance of several miles. It was the private opinion of Herodotus that that man arrived in a boat.[3]

---

[1] S. Reinach, "Xerxès et l'Hellespont," in the *Revue archéologique*, sér. 4, vol. vi. pp. 1 sqq., 1905. The symbolic marriage of the Doges of Venice with the Hadriatic is the same story, and Reinach also finds the same *motif* underlying the story of Xerxes and the Hellespont (Herod. vii. 35) and the rite practised by the Phocaeans, *ib.* i. 165, and by the Ionians, Aristotle, 'Αθ. π. 23.

[2] v. 86.

[3] viii. 8.

Perhaps the story of the miraculous deliverance of Delphi from the Persians [1] may be taken to illustrate the ill-defined limits of his faith. Their oracle declared to the Delphian priests that the god would himself provide for the safety of his sanctuary, and when the Persians came they were repelled, with great havoc, by lightning and by the fall of huge boulders from Parnassus. Herodotus relates this without any hint of scepticism, though he emphasizes the miraculous nature of the events. Now you observe that there is nothing impossible in the alleged physical occurrences; the marvel lies in the opportunity of the coincidence and the fulfilment of the oracular announcement. Against a marvel of this order Herodotus had no prejudice. But another miracle was said to have happened on the same occasion. Certain sacred arms, which were preserved within the shrine and were too sacred to be profaned by human touch, were suddenly discovered lying in a heap in front of the temple. A rationalist—Euripides, for instance—would find no difficulty in such an occurrence, assuming the fact to be certain. Herodotus accepts it as a genuine marvel, without any suggestion that human agency, notwithstanding Delphic asseverations to the contrary, might have been concerned in the matter; and the notable thing is that he considers it less wonderful than the intervention of the physical forces which overwhelmed the Persians. If such a phenomenon as

---

[1] viii. 36-39.

the removal of the arms presented itself to us
for criticism—supposing the fact were assured
beyond a doubt, and supposing human agency
were absolutely excluded by the circumstances—
we should regard it as something incomparably
more extraordinary than the unquestionably wonderful coincidence of the storm of lightning.[1] Here,
in fact, Herodotus has failed to draw the line at
what is physically impossible. The truth is that
his faith and doubt are alike instinctive ; he had
never thought the problem out for himself ; he
had never clearly defined the border between the
domains of the credible and the incredible. And
so in this episode he has no sooner given us a
lesson in faith than he relapses into reserve. For
there was yet another marvel to be told. It was
said that two armed warriors of superhuman
stature pursued the flying Persians and dealt death
among their broken ranks. But Herodotus carefully avoids the responsibility of accepting this
story. He gives it on the authority of the
Persians ; he qualifies it by the phrase "as I
am informed" ; and he adds that the Delphians
identified the two warriors with local heroes.

The contrast of the *naïveté* of Herodotus with
his scepticism imparts to his epic a very piquant
quality. Credulity alternates with a cautious reserve, which is especially noticeable when he is

---

[1] I do not add the fall of the rocks ; for this might have been engineered.
The rocks were shown to Herodotus in the temple of Athena Pronaïa
(ch. 39) ; this was just the sort of evidence which would impress him.

aware of more than one version of an occurrence. He is an expert in the art of not committing himself. He says in one passage, " I am bound to state what is said, but I am not bound to believe." [1] Of the tale that Zalmoxis lived for three years in a subterranean chamber, he professes agnosticism ; " I do not disbelieve nor do I absolutely believe it." [2] Occasionally he criticizes and rejects a story, for instance the charge against the Alcmaeonids of treachery at Marathon ; but his common practice is to state conflicting accounts and leave the matter there. This method, as it happens, is much more satisfactory to a modern critic than if Herodotus had selected one version, or had attempted to blend different versions together. But it shows him in the light of a collector of historical material, and an accomplished artist in arranging and presenting it, rather than as what we mean by a historian, who considers it his business to sift the evidence, and decide, if possible, between conflicting accounts.

We are often tempted to think of Herodotus as an Ionian, although he was not a native of Ionia. He wrote in Ionic ; and he cannot be severed from the school of the Ionian historians, to whom his work owed a great deal more than appears on the surface. But if he had heard himself described as an Ionian writer, he would have been vastly indignant. He is at great pains to dissociate himself from Ionia and Ionian interests. In his

[1] vii. 152.   [2] iv. 96.

account of the Ionian revolt and of the part which
the Ionians played in the war with Xerxes, he
shows a hardly veiled contempt for a people which,
as he says, had been thrice enslaved.   He tells us
that the name " Ionian was one of no great repute."
He is careful to record, without any comment, the
Scythian opinion that the Ionians were the most
cowardly and unmanly people in the world.[1]   He
takes frequent opportunities of criticizing adversely
the views of Ionian writers.   Now I think we may
say that this antagonistic attitude was not due
entirely or principally to the fact that he belonged
by birth to Dorian Halicarnassus.   He does indeed
insist on the difference of Dorian and Ionian, but the
contrast on which his anti-Ionian feeling depended
was one within the Ionian race itself—the distinction
of the Athenians from the Ionians of Asia.   We saw
that Herodotus was at Athens before he went to
Italy, and his connexion with Athens impressed its
mark on his political views.   He was a warm
admirer of the Athenians, and looked with favour
and enthusiasm on their empire.   He participated
in their experiment of colonising Thurii, became a
citizen of their daughter-city.   But even if we had
not this external proof of his political sympathy,
his work testifies to it abundantly.   The whole
account not only of the Marathonian campaign but
of the war with Xerxes is one that redounds to the
glory of Athens and flatters Athenian pride.   It is,
in fact, written mainly from the Athenian point of

[1] iv. 142.

view, and represents largely, though not exclusively,
the Athenian version. The Spartans and the part
they took in the war are often handled with irony
—for example, they were always arriving too
late because they were celebrating a feast. The
Corinthians are treated almost with malice. The
story would have had a very different complexion
if it had been written in the Spartan interest; and
even though we have no philo-Spartan historian of
the time, a very good case has been made out for
the view that Sparta showed as true heroism as
Athens.[1] Further, Herodotus takes opportunities
to set forth the mythistorical claims of Athens to
a hegemony of the Greeks, and represents Athens
as asserting those claims at the time of the Persian
war.[2] This is an anachronism. At that time
Sparta was admittedly the leader and dictator;
Athens was a member of the Peloponnesian confederacy, and the strife for supremacy had not
begun. Thus the situation is construed in the
light of the sequel; history is distorted in the
interest of politics; and the grounds of the claim
to hegemony which Herodotus ascribes to the
Athenians of that time are the stock arguments
which we find used in Athenian funeral orations to
illustrate and justify the Athenian empire. In
the Epitaphios which Pericles pronounced over the
citizens killed in the Samian war (439 B.C.) these
arguments from myth and history were doubtless
marshalled; and that Herodotus was present and

<hr>

[1] By E. Meyer.   [2] vii. 161 ; ix. 27.

listened to it is a conjecture of Eduard Meyer, which has some plausibility, since we find that a famous picturesque phrase used by the orator, likening the dead soldiers to the spring taken out of the year, was adopted by the historian and placed in a new setting.[1]

Admiration for the Athenian empire in the third quarter of the fifth century meant admiration for Pericles, the chief inspirer of Athenian policy, and the sympathy of Herodotus with Pericles is revealed in the single passage in which he mentions him, where he records the anecdote of his mother's dream that a lion would be born to her.[2] It is revealed, too, in sympathy with the Alcmaeonid family.[3]

His strong phil-Athenian feelings cannot be disconnected from his tone of prejudice and disparagement in treating the Ionians. When the immediate danger of Persian subjection was over, and the Ionian cities which had been leagued with Athens as an equal were brought to submit to her as a mistress, there was little love lost. The Ionian record of the war was one which would have failed to satisfy Athenian patriots as certainly

---

[1] vii. 162.   [2] vi. 121.

[3] v. 71 rests on the Alcmaeonid tradition. It has been suggested that this sympathy of Herodotus may explain his curious treatment of Themistocles. To this statesman Athens chiefly owed the decisive rôle she played in the war, and though his good counsels are recognised, he is also treated in an unfriendly spirit of detraction, and represented as an intriguer rather than as a statesman. This looks as if the memory of Themistocles were under a cloud, and this partial obscuration were reflected in Herodotus. Afterwards, Thucydides made a point of doing him justice.

as the Herodotean narrative must have failed to please the Ionians. Herodotus expressly argued that the Athenians were "truly the saviours of Greece";[1] but he did more: he gave currency and authority to a story which embodied Athenian tradition and justified Athenian empire, and with such cunning and tact that it has been permanently effective. His admiration for Athens was bound up with his belief in democratic freedom. Until the Peisistratids were overthrown, he says, Athens was an ordinary undistinguished city; but when the Athenians abolished the tyranny and won their freedom, they became by far the first state in Greece.[2]

Herodotus then was a phil-Athenian democrat. If the story is true that the Athenians bestowed on him ten talents (about 12,000 dollars) in recognition of the merits of his work, it was a small remuneration for the service he rendered to the renown of their city.[3] But that he did this service does not degrade his work into anything that could be described as a partisan publication in the offensive sense. It was pragmatical; it reflected the author's political beliefs, and exhibited a strong bias in the preference given to Athenian sources. But it was the work of a historian who cannot help being partial; it was not the work of a partisan who becomes a historian for the sake of his cause.

---

[1] vii. 139.   [2] μακρῷ πρῶτοι, v. 78.

[3] Plutarch, Περὶ τῆς Ἡροδότου κακοηθείας, 26. There is nothing incredible in the story that he recited part of his work at Athens c. 445 B.C. His work then consisted of the last three Books.

Something more particular must be said about the Herodotean story of the Persian invasion. A self-flattering version of the war had become a tradition at Athens. We have an early sketch of it, in a poetical form, in the *Persae* of Aeschylus (472 B.C.); but Herodotus was probably the first to write it down in a historical form, some twenty years later. Oral traditions (gathered at Athens, Sparta, Delphi, and elsewhere) appear profusely in his work, as every one knows. But he could not have constructed his history of the course of the war from oral traditions alone, or composed such a narrative of events, in which he was too young to take part, thirty years or so afterwards, without the help of some earlier record. We have seen that he depended on Hecataeus for Egypt, though this was just one of the portions of his work where autopsy, and information collected orally, might have sufficed. There is little doubt that Hecataeus was his main guide for early oriental history, and that the same writer was also used for the descriptions of Scythia and Libya, along with other geographical works of the Ionian school. When we come to the invasion of Darius and Xerxes, we find, as we might expect, clear indications that Herodotus here too had a written guide. Throughout the narrative, in the last three Books, of the events after Marathon to the end of the second invasion, the historian has naturally to pass backwards and forwards from the Persians to the Greeks. Now there is a remarkable contrast

between the character of the narrative when the
writer takes us to Susa or to the Persian camp,
and when he transports us to the cities or tents of
the Greeks.   In the accounts of what the Greeks
did, we are constantly confronted with more than
one story, representing various oral traditions which
reflect different local interests.   But when we
follow the movements of the Persians, we have a
continuous chronological narrative, by no means
always credible, but all of a piece and marked by
enumerations and details which point to a more or
less contemporary written source, and a source of
which Persian, not Greek, history was formally the
subject.   This source contributes the main thread
of the narrative, round which Herodotus has
wrought all the additional supplementary and
illustrative material he managed to collect.   The
chronology of Persian events after Marathon is
orderly and distinct, contrasting with the un-
certainties which beset the digressions on Greek
history, such as that on the Spartan kings
Cleomenes and Demaratus.   Now we know of a
history of the Persian war prior to Herodotus,
the book of Dionysius of Miletus.   I spoke of
it in the last lecture, and I also pointed out
that the Persian history of Charon of Lampsacus may, not improbably, have come down
to the invasion of Xerxes.   Either of these
books would satisfy the condition that the
war was treated as an episode in Persian,
not Greek, history, so that it is not unlikely

that one of these may have been the source of
Herodotus.[1]

Into the warp thus furnished by an older writer
is wrought a woof of Athenian tradition, varied
here and there by tissue from other sources.   And
it is noteworthy how in the last three Books, com-
prising the invasion of Xerxes, the imminence of
a divine direction of human affairs is strongly
accentuated.   The sceptical tone is less apparent
here than in other parts of the work.   From the
beginning of the seventh Book the dominant note
is changed, at least this is the impression I receive;
the atmosphere becomes charged with a certain
solemnity; it is, I think we might say, rather
Athenian than Ionian.   Is this difference due
to the influence of those Athenian dramas which
had glorified the subject, the tragedies of Phry-
nichus and Aeschylus?

The catastrophe which befals the Persian expedition is not conceived as the work of jealous
gods annoyed by the conspicuous wealth or success
of mere mortals.   It is rather a divine punishment
of the insolence and rashness that are often born of
prosperity.   This is the Aeschylean doctrine:

$$\text{Ζεύς τοι κολαστὴς τῶν ὑπερκόμπων ἄγαν}$$
$$\text{φρονημάτων ἔπεστιν εὔθυνος βαρύς.}^2$$

[1] So Lehmann-Haupt.   There is little evidence for a source of this
kind in the history of the years 500-490 B.C. = Books v. vi.   Chronology
is conspicuously absent, but the few dates we get suggest a Persian
history as their source (Charon or Dionysius?).   See vi. 18, 42 *ad init.*, 43
ad init., 46 *ad init.*

[2] *Persae* 827.   In *Agam.* 749, Aeschylus rejects the vulgar doctrine
(παλαίφατος ἐν βροτοῖς γέρων λόγος) that wealth, inordinately increased,
necessarily leads to unappeasable woe.

> Zeus is a judge who visits heavily
> All whose self-glorious spirit vaults too high.

This Athenian influence in the last Books of Herodotus accords with my conjecture that Athens was his headquarters during a part of the ten years or so which elapsed between his banishment and his sailing for Italy.

Herodotus then made a considerable use of older writers [1]—of whom he only names Hecataeus, and usually for the purpose of hinting something uncomplimentary. As the works of these writers have perished, it is very difficult to form a fair estimate of the achievements of Herodotus himself as a historical investigator—apart from his transcendent gifts as an artist and man of letters. His great service consisted probably in the collection of unwritten material concerning modern Greek history; this floating matter he wrought with masterly skill into a framework of facts constructed by predecessors. His maxims of historical criticism may be set down as three : (1) Suspect superhuman and miraculous occurrences, which contradict ordinary experience. But this, in his application

---

[1] A complete library of Greek prose works on history would have been very small in 450 B.C., and it would not have been very much larger in 430 B.C. It is difficult to suppose that Herodotus would not have been acquainted with all the historical literature that had been published, or that the works of Dionysius and Charon could have escaped him. Besides Hecataeus the only historian to whom he refers is Scylax (iv. 44), but he mentions him as an explorer and not as an author, though obviously his brief account of the exploration is taken from the report of Scylax. Could he have failed to know the book of this Carian writer on Heracleides of Mylasa? It is remarkable that he ignores the part played by Heracleides of Artemisium (see Sosylus fragment, mentioned above, p. 25). Heracleides is mentioned v. 121. The geographical works of the Ionians are referred to in iv. 36.

of it, leaves a wide room for portents, and it does not cover oracles and dreams. (2) When you are confronted by conflicting evidence or differing versions of the same event, keep an open mind; *audi alteram partem.* But this does not save him from a biassed acceptance of Athenian tradition. (3) Autopsy and first-hand oral information are superior to stories at second hand, whether written or oral.[1] This tends to take the naïve form, " I know, for I was there myself," and it placed the historian at the mercy of the vergers and guides in Egyptian temples.

I may illustrate by a couple of examples how Herodotus was sometimes unfortunate in his information gathered on the spot. When he visited Egypt he saw on the great Pyramid inscriptions which disappeared in the Middle Ages. Probably they were of religious import, appropriate to a royal tomb. But Herodotus tells us that they enumerated the sums of money which were expended on the onions and leeks consumed by the workmen who built the pyramid. This was the interpretation with which the guide satisfied the Greek traveller's curiosity.[2] The other instance

---

[1] Compare, *e.g.*, ii. 99. I have little doubt that Herodotus visited and examined the battlefield of Plataea. Our difficulties in reconstructing the battle (elucidated by Grundy, Woodhouse, and Macan) from his description are not an objection. We may remember that the account of the battle of Trasimene by Polybius, who had visited the place and was a master of military science, lends itself to different interpretations. The features of the Pass of Thermopylae as described by Herodotus can be recognised by any traveller to-day ; but he can hardly have been there, for he orients it N.S. instead of E.W.

[2] See Wiedemann, *ad* Her. ii. 125.

I will quote appertains to Babylonian history.
Herodotus saw at Babylon the great buildings of a
king, with whose name even those of us who have
not studied Babylonian annals are probably familiar
—King Nebuchadnezzar. He is correctly informed
as to the time at which they were built—five generations after the reign of Queen Sammuramat whom
he calls Semiramis. But autopsy did not keep him
from falling into a droll error about the potentate
who built them. Nebuchadnezzar has had rather
bad luck. In the book of Daniel he is metamorphosed into a beast of the field; in Herodotus
he is forced to masquerade as a woman. We have
to discover his identity under the mask of Queen
Nitocris.[1]

We must give full credit to Herodotus for
having recognised the principles of criticism which
I have indicated, though his application of them is
unsatisfactory and sporadic. They are maxims of
permanent validity; properly qualified they lie at
the basis of the modern developments of what
is called historical methodology. But notwithstanding the profession of these axioms of common
sense, he was in certain ways so lacking in
common sense that parts of his work might seem
to have been written by a precocious child. He
undertook to write the history of a great war; but
he did not possess the most elementary knowledge
of the conditions of warfare. His fantastic state-

---

[1] This has been shown by Lehmann-Haupt in his paper on Semiramis
(see Bibliography). Herodotus is similarly unlucky about Mithra. He
makes him a goddess, i. 131.

ment of the impossible numbers of the army of
Xerxes exhibits an incompetence which is almost
incredible and is alone enough to stamp Herodotus
as more of an epic poet than a historian.   It
matters not whether he worked out the arithmetic
for himself or accepted it entirely on authority;
this is a case in which to accept is as heinous as to
invent.   Heinous for a historian ; and if we judge
Herodotus by the lowest standard as a historian of
a war, this case invalidates his claim to competence.
But as an epic story-teller he escapes triumphantly.
His catalogue of the Persian host is a counterpart
to the Catalogue of the *Iliad*:

$$\mu\hat{v}\theta ov \ \delta' \ \dot{\omega}\varsigma \ \ddot{o}\tau' \ \dot{a}o\iota\delta\dot{o}\varsigma \ \dot{\epsilon}\pi\iota\sigma\tau a\mu\dot{\epsilon}\nu\omega\varsigma \ \kappa a\tau\dot{\epsilon}\lambda\epsilon\xi a\varsigma.$$

His incompetence in military matters is shown, in
another way, in his account of the campaign of
Thermopylae and Artemisium.   The key to their
actions lay—and it required no technical training
or experience to discern this—in the close connexion and interdependence of the Persian land
army and the Persian fleet, a fact which governed
the Greek measures for defence.   Herodotus,
though he mentions several things which imply
this and enable us more or less to penetrate the
strategy of the combatants, fails completely to
realise the situation and treats the naval and the
land operations as if they were independent.

In his relation of the Persian war, Herodotus
does not neglect the chronology, and it is perhaps
as satisfactory as we could expect.   But it may

fairly be questioned whether the credit for this is
not to be imputed to an earlier writer—Dionysius
or Charon—whom he had the discretion to follow.
It is significant that he does not give any formal
date which a Greek reader could easily interpret,
until he mentions, almost by the way, that the
Persian invasion of Attica occurred in the archonship of Calliades.[1] But while chronology fares
pretty well in the last three Books, the whole work
shows that, while the author copied the dates which
his sources supplied, he never attempted to grapple
with the chronological difficulties of Greek history,
although so many of the episodes which he related
raised the problem of synchronizing Hellenic tradition with oriental records. We have no reason to
suppose that he avoided the problem because he
judged it insoluble ; his indifference to it is another
manifestation of his epic, quasi-historical mind.

The first phase of Greek historiography culmi-
nates and achieves its glory in Herodotus. He
reflects its features—its eager research into geography and ethnography (the indispensable groundwork of history), and its predominant interest in
the East. He adopts from Hecataeus a critical
attitude towards the ancient myths, aided by a
rudimentary comparative mythology. But these

[1] He signalises the years 490-481 by reference to the year of Marathon,
but he does not mention the eponymous archon of that year. Even if he
had done so a reader would have required a list of Attic archons, in order
to follow his dates intelligently. Herodotus does not assist his readers
by reckoning back from a fixed point which they could realise. Thucydides
saw that without such a point dates were entirely in the air, and he dated
backward from the first year of the Peloponnesian war.

elements are transfigured by the magic of his epic art and the spell of a higher historical idea. He was the Homer of the Persian war, and that war originally inspired him. His work presents a picture of sixth - century civilisation; and it is also a universal history in so far as it gathers the greater part of the known world into a narrative which is concentrated upon a single issue. It is fortunate for literature that he was not too critical; if his criticism had been more penetrating and less naïve, he could not have been a second Homer. He belonged entirely in temper and mentality to the period before the sophistic illumination, which he lived to see but not to understand. Before his death, the first truly critical historian of the world had begun to compose. Our attention will next be claimed by Thucydides.

LECTURE III

§ 1. *His life and the growth of his work*

THUCYDIDES belonged by descent to the princely family of Thrace into which Miltiades, the hero of Marathon, had married. He was thus a cousin of the statesman Cimon, and he inherited a rich estate with gold mines in Thrace. And so, while he was an Athenian citizen and connected with a distinguished family of Athens, he had an independent *pied à terre* in a foreign country. His mind was moulded under the influence of that intellectual revolution which we associate with the comprehensive name of the Sophists, the illumination which was flooding the educated world of Hellas with the radiance of reason. Without accepting the positive doctrines of any particular teacher, he learned the greatest lesson of these thinkers : he learned to consider and criticize facts, unprejudiced by authority and tradition. He came to be at home in the "modern" way of thinking, which analysed politics and ethics, and applied logic to every-

thing in the world. We might illustrate how
intense and deep-reaching the sophistic movement was, in the third quarter of the fifth century,
by pointing to the difference between Herodotus
and Thucydides. If you took up the two works
without knowing the dates of their composition,
you would think there might be a hundred years'
development between them. But then consider
the difference between Sophocles and Euripides.

Thucydides must have been at least twenty-five
years old, some think he was as much as forty,
when the Peloponnesian war broke out in 431
B.C. At the very beginning he formed the
resolution to record it, and in the first years of
the war, at least, the composition of the history
was nearly contemporary with the events. In
424 B.C. he was elected to the high office of a
strategos and appointed to command in Thrace;
and the loss of Amphipolis led to his condemnation and banishment. For twenty years he did
not see Athens, and, while he probably lived for
the most part on his Thracian estate, he also
travelled to collect material for his work. It
seems certain that he visited Sicily, for his
narrative of the Athenian expedition could not
have been written by one who had not seen
Syracuse with his own eyes.[1] After the end of
the war he was allowed to return to Athens in
404 B.C. (by the decree of Oenobius). He did not

[1] That he knew Sparta is a legitimate inference from i. 10. 2, and
134. 4.

die before 399 B.C. ; perhaps he was no longer
alive in 396 B.C. ; and he left his book unfinished.[1]

It is evident how these biographical facts, and
they are almost all we know about the man, bear
upon his historical work. His family connexion
at Athens provided him, perhaps, with exceptional
facilities for obtaining authentic information, while
his military training and experience qualified him
to be the historian of a war. His second home in
Thrace gave him an interest independent of
Athens, and helped him to regard the Athenian
empire with a certain detachment which would
have been less easy for one who was a pure-
blooded citizen and had no home outside Attica.
His banishment operated in the same direction,
and afforded him opportunities for intercourse
with the antagonists of his country. The intellectual movement which invaded Athens when
he was a young man was a condition of his mental
growth ; if he had belonged to an earlier generation, he could not have been Thucydides.

But if all these circumstances helped and conditioned the achievements of a profoundly original
mind, which always thought for itself, we must
seek the stimulus which aroused the historical
faculty of Thucydides in—the Athenian empire.
If it was the wonder of the Greek repulse of the
Persian hosts that inspired the epic spirit of

[1] There were conflicting stories as to the manner and the place of his
death. His tomb, which may have been a cenotaph, was shown at
Athens, in the burying-place of the family of his kinsman Cimon, near
the Melitid gate.

Herodotus, it was the phenomenon of the Empire of Athens, a new thing in the history of Hellas,— an empire governed by a democracy, a new thing in the history of the world—that captured the cooler but intense interest of Thucydides. He did not take up his pen to celebrate; his aim was to understand, — to observe critically how that empire behaved in the struggle which was to test its powers. It has not, I think, been sufficiently realised what an original stroke of genius it was to form the idea of recording the history of the war at the very moment of its outbreak. Contemporary history in the strictest meaning of the term was thus initiated. Thucydides watched the events for the purpose of recording them; he collected the material while it was fresh from the making. Further, he designed a history which should be simply a history of the war and of the relations of the militant states, which should confine itself to its theme, and not deviate into geography or anthropology or other things. Thus he was the founder of "political" history in the special sense in which we are accustomed to use the term.

Widely divergent views are held as to the way in which the work of Thucydides was constructed and the stages by which it reached its final though incomplete state. This question is not one of merely meritorious curiosity which may be left to the commentator as his exclusive concern; it affects our general conception of the historian's

point of view, as well as his art, and no study of
Thucydides can evade it.

The history falls into two parts. The first ends
with the Fifty Years' Peace of 421 B.C., which at
the time seemed to conclude the war and terminate
the author's task. The second part is formally
introduced by a personal explanation, in which
Thucydides announces the continuation of his
subject down to the capture of Athens in 404 B.C.
He explains that though we may divide the whole
period 431-404 B.C. into three parts—the first war
of ten years, then seven years of hollow truce, and
then a second war,—the truer view is that there
was only one war lasting twenty-seven years, for
the hollow truce was truly nothing less than war.
This passage was written after 404 B.C. and naturally suggests that Thucydides had only recently
recognised that the indecisive war which he had
recorded was only a portion of a greater and
decisive war, and had determined to extend the
compass of his work to the whole twenty-seven
years. On the other hand, his statements [1] seem
to make it evident that during his banishment he
had followed the course of events and travelled
with a view to continuing his work. This continuation was prompted by the Athenian expedition to Sicily, and was intended to be the history
of what then seemed to him a second war. I
conclude then that there were three stages in his
plan. After the Fifty Years' Peace of 421 B.C.,

[1] v. 26.

his book was to be simply a history of the war
of ten years. The course of the Sicilian expedition began a new war which he determined also
to record, as a chronologically separate episode.
Then the catastrophe of 404 B.C. set in a new
light the significance of all that had happened
since the original outbreak of hostilities in 431 B.C.,
and imparted to the whole series of events a unity
of meaning which they would hardly have acquired
if the struggle had been terminated in 404 B.C. not
by the fall of Athens but by a second edition of
the Fifty Years' Peace. Hence Thucydides rose
to the larger conception of producing a history of
the whole period of twenty-seven years.

Accordingly he found on his return to Athens
that he had three things to do. He had to
compose the history of the ambiguous interval
between the Fifty Years' Peace and the Sicilian
war. Secondly, he had to work up the rough
copy and material of the last ten years. This was
done [1] fully and triumphantly for the Sicilian
episode, but of the rest we only possess the un-
revised draft of the years 412 and 411, known as
Book VIII., for which, perhaps in respect to its
literary shape, and certainly in respect to its
matter (by means of supplementary information
procurable at Athens), much had to be done.
In the third place, it was desirable and even
necessary to make some additions and alterations
in the original, completed but still unpublished,

---

[1] Perhaps before his return.

history of the first ten years, so as to bring it internally as well as externally into the light of the higher unity. This was a natural thought, and it appears to me the only hypothesis that explains the facts without constraint.[1]

§ 2. *His principles of historiography: accuracy and relevance*

In his Introduction Thucydides announces a new conception of historical writing. He sets up a new standard of truth or accurate reproduction of facts, and a new ideal of historical research; judged by which, he finds Herodotus and the Ionian historians wanting. He condemns them expressly for aiming at providing "good reading," as we should say, rather than facts, and for narrating stories, the truth of which cannot possibly be tested. He does not seek himself to furnish entertainment or to win a popular success, but to construct a record which shall be permanently valuable[2] because it is true. He warns his readers that they will find nothing mythical in his work. He saw, as we see, that the mythical element pervaded Herodotus (of whom, evidently, he was chiefly thinking) no less than Homer. His own experience in ascertaining *contemporary* facts taught him, as nothing else could do, how soon and how easily events are

---

[1] See Appendix.
[2] Instructive. I revert to this important point in Lecture VIII.

wont to pass into the borders of myth; he learned thereby the most effective lesson of scepticism in regard to historical tradition.   It was indeed of inestimable importance for the future of history that Thucydides conceived the new idea of recording the war at its commencement.   It made all the difference to his work that he formed the resolve in 431 B.C. and not after the war was over.

Writing the history of the present is always a very different thing from writing the history of the distant past.   The history of the distant past depends entirely on literary and documentary sources; the history of the present always involves unwritten material as well as documents.   But the difference was much greater in the days of Thucydides than it is now.   To-day a writer sitting down to compose a history of his own time would depend mainly on written material, —on official reports, official documents of various kinds, and on the daily press.   He would supplement this, so far as he could, by information derived personally from men of affairs, or by his own experience if he had witnessed or taken part in public events; but the main body of his work would depend on written sources.   The ancient historian, on the contrary, in consequence of the comparative paucity of official reports and the absence of our modern organization for collecting and circulating news, would have to be his own journalist and do all the labour of obtaining facts orally from the most likely sources; and his success might largely depend on accidental facilities. His work would rest mainly on information obtained orally by his own inquiries, supplemented by such documents as were available, such as the texts of treaties or official instructions or letters; whereas the modern work is based principally on printed or written information, supplemented by such private information as may be accessible. It is clear that the ancient conditions made the historian's task more difficult, and demanded from him greater energy and initiative. Few things would be more interesting than a literary diary of Thucydides, telling of his interviews with his informants and showing his ways of collecting and sifting his material. But it was part of his artistic method to cover up all the traces of his procedure, in his finished narrative. He had to compare and criticize the various accounts he received of each transaction; but his literary art required that he should present the final conclusions of his research without indicating divergences of evidence. It is probable that he suppressed entirely details about which he could not satisfy himself. He was very chary of mentioning reports or allegations concerning which he felt in doubt; in the few cases in which he disclaims certainty we may suppose that he accepted the statement as probable.[1] He does not name his informants; nor does he even tell

---

[1] For instance : of the answer of the oracle to the Spartans (ὡς λέγεται), i. 118. 3 ; of the motives of Archidamus, ii. 18. 5 ; of the end of Nicias, vii. 86.

us on what occasions he was himself an eye-witness
of what he describes.   We may make guesses,
but we can only speak with assurance of the
operations which he conducted as strategos.

We are able, however, to gain a slight glimpse
into the historian's workshop because some parts
of his work have been left incomplete.   The
eighth Book is only a preliminary draft.   In it
we find accounts emanating from different informants, Athenian and Peloponnesian, written out so
as to form a continuous narrative, yet containing
contradictions as to matters of fact as well as differences in tendency.[1]   It is possible, for instance, to
detect that some of the Peloponnesian informants
were favourable to Astyochus the Lacedaemonian
commander, and others were not.   It is evident
that we have material which has only been provisionally sifted.   Again, the texts of the three
successive treaties of alliance between Persia and
Sparta are given *verbatim*,[2] and if we consider the
transitory significance of the first two, it seems
improbable that Thucydides intended to reproduce
them *in extenso* in his final draft.   They were
material—material, according to a plausible conjecture, furnished by Alcibiades.   These facts, and
the unsatisfactory nature of the account of the
oligarchic revolution, as compared with the finished
portions of the work, confirm what the style and
the absence of speeches had long ago suggested,

---

[1] See Holzapfel's article mentioned in the Bibliography.
[2] viii. 18, 37, 58.

that Book VIII. was a first draft which, if the writer had lived, would have appeared in a very different shape.

In the fifth Book it may also be shown that there was still revision to be done, though this section was in a more advanced state than Book VIII. Here we find a whole series of documentary texts. Now it was not in accordance with the artistic method of Thucydides, or of ancient historians in general, to introduce into the narrative matter heterogeneous in style; and it is almost incredible that he would have admitted texts not written in Attic Greek. We must, I think, conclude that we have here material which was to be wrought in during a final revision.

In the finished part of the history we can sometimes penetrate to the source of information. It is easy to see that he consulted Plataeans as to the siege of Plataea, and that he received information from Spartans as well as from Athenians about the episode of Pylos and Sphacteria. We can sometimes divine that he has derived his statements from the official instructions given to military commanders; and it has been acutely shown that his enumeration of the allies of the two opposing powers at the beginning of the war was based on the instrument of the Thirty Years' Peace.[1] Sometimes the formulae of decrees or treaties peer through the Thucydidean summary.[2]

---

[1] By Wilamowitz-Möllendorff.
[2] Cp. ii. 24; iv. 16. Wilamowitz-Möllendorff, *Die Thukydides-legende* (see Bibliography).

We have then to take the finished product,
which Thucydides furnishes, on trust. We have
not any considerable body of independent evidence
for testing his accuracy, but so far as we can test
it by the chance testimonies of original documents,
he comes out triumphantly (in those parts which
he completed), and there can be no question that
the stress which he laid on accuracy was not a
phrase.[1] The serious criticisms which can be
brought against him in regard to facts concern
not what he states but what he omits to state.
For instance, the important measure which Athens
adopted in 424 B.C. of raising the tribute of the
subject states is passed over entirely, though it is
a pertinent fact in the story of the war; we have
learned it in recent years by the discovery of parts
of the stone decree. We cannot discern his reasons
for recounting some passages of military history at
great length and passing over others (such as the

---

[1] Some errors are due not to the author but to very early scribes. For
instance, Andocides in i. 51, Methone for Methana in iv. 45 (cp. Wilamowitz-Möllendorff, op. cit.). It is unquestionable that he makes grave
topographical mistakes in his account of the episode of Pylos-Sphacteria.
He has completely misconceived the size of the entrances to the bay, and
he gives the length of Sphacteria as 15 stades, whereas it is really 24.
These errors have led Grundy to deny that Thucydides had ever visited
the spot; while R. M. Burrows (who has shown that the whole narrative
is otherwise in accordance with the topography) thinks that his measure-
ments were wrong. My view is that he first wrote the story from information supplied by eye-witnesses who gave him a general, though partly
inaccurate, idea of the place, and that he afterwards tested it on the spot
and probably added local touches, but omitted to revise the errors of
distance. We have a somewhat similar case in the description of New Carthage by Polybius (see below, p. 194). It is indeed possible that the blunder
in the length of the island may have been exaggerated by a scribe's pen.
For κ was exposed to confusion with (ις or) ιε.—The topography of the
siege of Plataea has been elucidated by Grundy.

attempt of Pericles on Epidaurus) with a bare
mention. But in other cases his silence is a judgment. He rejects, for instance, by ignoring, the
connexion which the gossip of the Athenian
streets alleged between the private life of Pericles
and the origin of the war. But it must be allowed
in general that, in omitting, Thucydides displays a
boldness and masterfulness on which no modern
historian would venture.[1]

His omissions are closely connected with a
general feature of his work. If the first fundamental principle of his ideal of history was
accuracy, the second was relevance; and both
signify his rebound from Herodotus. Discursive-
ness as we saw was the very life-breath of the
epic history of Herodotus; the comprehensiveness
of the Ionian idea of history enabled him to spread
about through a wide range, to string on tale to
tale, to pile digression on digression, artfully, yet
as loosely as the structure of his Ionic prose.
Thucydides conceived the notion of political
history, and he laid down for himself a strict
principle of exclusion. His subject is the war,
and he will not take advantage of opportunities
to digress into the history of culture. He excludes geography, so far as brief notices are not
immediately necessary for the explanation of the

---

[1] Thus no modern historian, probably, would have omitted to note the
psephisma of Charinus, which followed up the decrees excluding Megara
from the markets of Athens and her empire, by excluding Megarians
on penalty of death from the very soil of Attica. Thucydides would have
said that it did not affect the outbreak of the war.

events recorded.   He disdains personal gossip and
anecdotes; he had no use for the spicy memoirs of
Ion and Stesimbrotus.   He rigidly abstains from
dropping any information about the private life of
Pericles, Cleon, or any other politician; and the
exception which he makes in the case of Alcibiades
only serves to show the reason for the rule; because
those sides of the life of Alcibiades which Thucydides notices had, in his view, distinct political
consequences in determining the attitude of the
Athenians towards him.   Further, he excludes the
internal history of the states with whose political
inter-relations he is concerned, except when the
internal affected directly, or was bound up with,
the external, as in the case of the plague and of
the domestic seditions.   He does not give any
information about the political parties at Athens,
though some of his statements imply their existence, till he comes to the oligarchical revolution.
His outlook, as Wilamowitz has observed, is not
bounded by the Pnyx, but by the Empire.

There are, of course, digressions in Thucydides,
but with hardly an exception they are either
closely relevant or introduced for some special
purpose.

The history of the growth of the Athenian
empire is in form an excursus; but we might
fairly say that it properly belongs to the prolegomena; it is distinctly relevant to the subject
of the book, and had the special purpose of supple-
menting and correcting Hellanicus.   The digression

on the fortunes of Pausanias is also a relevant,
though certainly not necessary, explanation of the
Athenian demand that the Lacedaemonians should
expel a pollution ; but the account, which follows,
of the later career of Themistocles is wholly
unconnected with the Peloponnesian war. I
will however show hereafter that the author
had a special motive in introducing it. The
valuable chapter on early Athens, with its archaeological evidence,[1] is strictly to the point, for its
purpose is to illustrate the historian's acute remark
that the distress of the country people at coming
to live in the city was due to habits derived from
the early history of Attica. A sketch of the early
history of Sicily was almost indispensable for the
elucidation of the narrative ; a knowledge of the
island and its cities could not be taken for granted
in the Athenian public. The description of the
Odrysean kingdom of Sitalces[2] was unquestionably
due to the author's personal interest in Thrace ;
but it had the object of suggesting a contrast
between the power and resources of Thrace and
Scythia with those of the Greek states.

The story of the fall of the Athenian tyrants
(in Book VI.), which is an excursus in the true
sense of the word, was introduced to correct popular
errors. The other passage in which Thucydides
seems for a moment non-Thucydidean is where
he sketches the history of the fair of Delos, quotes

[1] A part of it would naturally have appeared in a footnote, had footnotes been then in use.
[2] ii. 96-7 ; cp. ii. 29.

from a Homeric hymn, and deviates into the history of culture. I cannot help suspecting that here too he is correcting some current misapprehension. If he may legitimately be criticized for turning aside from his subject to correct errors which may seem trivial enough, and if he is sometimes reprimanded for having elsewhere captiously noted a couple of small blunders in Herodotus, it must be remembered that it was of importance to illustrate his doctrine that tradition cannot be taken on trust, and that the facile methods of current historiography inevitably led to inaccuracy.

The digressions then in Thucydides which can fairly be called digressions are different in character from the digressions and amplitudes of Herodotus. The critic Dionysius considered it a point of inferiority in Thucydides, as compared with Herodotus, that he pursued his subject steadily and kept to his argument, without pausing by the way and providing his readers with variety; and he supposed that in "the two or three places" where the historian did digress, his motive was to relieve the narrative by a pleasant pause. The criticism would have been more elucidating if Dionysius had pointed out that, while Herodotus was influenced by the epic, the artistic method of Thucydides must rather be compared with that of the drama. Thucydides adheres as closely to his argument as a tragic poet, and such variety as was secured in tragedy by the interjection of choral odes, he obtains by the speeches which he intersperses in the narrative.

His first consideration was accuracy; he had to follow events and not to mould them into correspondence with an artistic plan, and his strict chronological order excluded devices of arrangement. But occasionally we can detect deliberate management for the sake of a calculated effect. It may be pointed out that the long section on the origin and growth of the Athenian empire, placed where it is, between the two Assemblies at Sparta, has the effect of interrupting a series of speeches which coming together would have been excessively long. Again, it has been well shown by Wilamowitz-Möllendorff how the delays of Archidamus, in the first invasion of Attica, in the hope that Athens might give in at the last moment, are reflected in the form of the narrative, which is arranged to produce the impression of a slow and halting march; and the archaeological deviation into the early history of Athens has the value of assisting in this artistic effect.

§ 3. *Modern criticisms on his competence*

In common with other ancient historians, Thucydides may be taken to task for not having recognised the part played in human affairs by economic facts and commercial interests. That he was not blind to economic conditions is shown by the leading significance he attributes to want of material resources in the early Greek communities; and he fully realises the importance of finance. But it may be said that he should have furnished a detailed explanation and analysis of the commercial basis on which the Athenian power rested, and of the mercantile interests of other states which were affected and endangered by her empire.   It is however only in quite recent times that economical and commercial factors in historical development have begun to receive their due, and, perhaps it may be said, rather more than their due.   They have come so much to the front that some writers are tempted to explain all historical phenomena by economic causes.   This illustrates how the tendencies of the present react upon our conceptions of the past.   These factors, of such immense importance in the present age, certainly did not play anything like the same part in the ancient world, and if the ancient historians considerably underrated them, we may easily fall into the error of overrating them.   We may be sure that the interests of Athens presented themselves to statesmen, as to Thucydides, primarily under the political, and not the economical, point of view. Thucydides created political history ; economic history is a discovery of the nineteenth century.

Perhaps the gravest accusation which has been brought against the competency of Thucydides is that he misunderstood, if he did not intentionally misrepresent, the causes of the Peloponnesian war. The charge has been formulated and pressed in different ways by a German and by an English scholar.[1]   Their indictments do not appear to me

[1] H. Nissen and F. M. Cornford.

to be successful. The historian's account, which can only be refuted by proofs of internal discrepancy or of insufficiency, seems to be both consistent and, with certain reserves, adequate.

It will not be amiss to make a preliminary observation on two words which Thucydides uses in the sense of cause — $airia$ and $\pi\rho\acute{o}\phi a\sigma\iota\varsigma$. $airia$ has almost the same history as the Latin equivalent, *caussa*. Its proper sense was "grievance" or "ground of blame," "charge," and in Thucydides it generally [1] either means this or, even when we can most appropriately translate it by cause, implies a charge or imputation. $\pi\rho\acute{o}\phi a\sigma\iota\varsigma$ is an alleged reason, which may be either true or false; ultimately it became virtually restricted to a false or minor reason, and so equivalent to "pretext." In Thucydides it is not so restricted; he employs it in both ways. And from meaning an alleged reason, it is evident how easily it could come to mean a reason, whether alleged or not; in other words, a "motive" or an "occasion," so that here it approximated very closely to the sense of "cause." This various use of the word does not imply any confusion of thought; we use the word "reason" with similar elasticity; the context decides the sense.

When a war breaks out, there are two things to be explained which must be kept distinct: why the aggressors go to war at all, and why they go to war at the time they actually do. This distinction

---

[1] But cp. iv. 87. 4.

is crucial, for instance, in the case of the outbreak
of the Franco-Prussian war of 1870. In some
cases, the answer to both questions is the same ;
there may be no reason for the war, beyond the
particular circumstances which lead immediately to
its declaration. In the case of the Peloponnesian
war, Thucydides is careful to insist that this was
not so. There was a permanent motive for
hostility, of such a kind that war, sooner or later,
might be counted on as a certainty ; there were
also particular transactions which determined its
actual outbreak at a particular moment. When the
Lacedaemonians took steps to break the peace, of
course they did not mention the permanent and really
impelling motive, namely, jealousy of Athenian
aggrandisement, but rested their declaration on
certain recent actions on the part of Athens.
Thucydides puts it thus : " The true motive ($\pi\rho\acute{o}$-
$\phi\alpha\sigma\iota\varsigma$), though it was not expressed in words, I
consider to have been the fear which the growth of
the Athenian power caused to the Lacedaemonians ;
but the publicly alleged grounds of complaint
($\alpha\grave{\iota}\tau\acute{\iota}\alpha\iota$) which provoked the war I will proceed to
explain," and he enters upon the stories of Corcyra
and Potidaea. Thucydides accepted the convic-
tions expressed both by the Corcyraean ambassador
in his speech at Athens and by Pericles that a war
was unavoidable, and that it was merely a question
how long it might be postponed ; and we certainly
cannot prove that this judgment was wrong.

The distinction then between the real motive

of the Lacedaemonians, in the absence of which
they would not have declared war, and the particular actions which brought matters to a head and
determined the beginning of a war at a certain
date, is perfectly clear and valid. The further
question can be raised, whether in his account of
the affairs which moved the Peloponnesian alliance
to hostile action at a given moment, Thucydides
estimated rightly their proportional gravity. The
charge is that he has not given its due importance
to the Megarian business, whether failing to realise
its meaning, or deliberately keeping it in the background in order to devolve the responsibility for
the war from the shoulders of Pericles who was
responsible for the Megarian policy. The second
insinuation I need not consider; for I will show
hereafter (in the next Lecture) that the historian's
attitude to Pericles and his policy is detached. I
will only observe here that if he had wished to
shield that statesman from the alleged responsibility, it was clumsy of him not to suppress or
explain away the fact that in the final negotia-
tions the Lacedaemonians made Megara the test-
question, and said they would be satisfied if Athens
yielded on that point.

This ultimatum of the Lacedaemonians may
indeed appear, at first sight, inconsistent with the
subordinate rôle which the Megarian grievance
plays in the historian's narrative of the circumstances which led to the war; and it has been
urged that instead of keeping it in the background

he ought to have assigned it the most prominent place in the foreground. But a careful examination will show, I think, that the narrative is completely consistent, and embodies a closely reasoned account of the causes and motives at work.

The most casual reader receives the unmistakable impression that the Corinthians were the prime instigators of the war, driving the Lacedaemonians into action. The two affairs in which their interests were exclusively involved, the affair of Corcyra and the affair of Potidaea, are those which the author designates as the direct occasion of the war; and the leading part taken by Corinth is emphasized by the reproduction of two Corinthian speeches, voicing Peloponnesian dissatisfaction. If the deepest concern of Corinth was the action which Athens had taken in regard to Megara by excluding her from the markets of the Athenian empire, and thereby threatening her with economic ruin, then it must be allowed that Thucydides was entirely misinformed. In their speeches at Sparta, the Corinthian envoys do not mention the Megarian name, and the author expressly states that their eagerness to have war declared immediately was due to their anxiety for Potidaea. Can we discover any proof as to the real interest of Corinth in the Megarian question?

When the Corcyraean affair occurred, Corinth was so far from being anxious for war that she did all she could to secure the goodwill and neutrality of Athens. And she did not come with her hands empty. She did not merely urge her claims on Athenian gratitude for past services. She proposed a deal (433 B.C.). Some time before this, Athens had already initiated new designs on Megara by a decree excluding Megarian wares from Athens itself. Corinth now said to her in effect: Leave us a free hand in dealing with Corcyra, and we will leave you a free hand in dealing with Megara. The Corinthian ambassador put this diplomatically, at least in his speech before the popular Assembly.[1] He did not say: You have improper designs on Megara, and we will connive. He said: Your conduct in regard to Megara has been open to suspicion; you can allay these suspicions by doing what we ask. It came to the same thing.

This proposition on the part of Corinth shows that in her eyes the independence of Megara was not of crucial importance. Her interests there weighed much less than her interests elsewhere. It was the alliance of Athens with Corcyra, followed by the affair of Potidaea, that determined the collision of Corinth with Athens, and it was this collision that precipitated a war which would in any case have come later. The Megarian decrees did not determine the action of Corinth, and it was Corinth's action which was decisive. On the other hand, once war was decided on by Corinth and the war-party at Sparta, the grievance of Megara formed an imposing item in the

---

[1] i. 42. 2.

list of Peloponnesian complaints and the general
indictment of Athenian policy. In this indictment,
the alliance of Athens with Corcyra, though it had
been the first of the effective causes which led to
the war, could not appear at all; it could not be
represented as either illegal or immoral. The
attack on Potidaea could form a count; but it
arose out of a complicated situation, and a great
deal could be said on both sides. It was therefore
an obvious stroke of diplomatic tactics to move the
Megarian question into the foremost place, and
represent the cruelty of Athens to Megara as the
principal of her offences. The Lacedaemonians
said: Yield on this question and there will be no
war. It was a demand which no proud state, in
the position of Athens, could have granted, and
concession would have been simply an invitation
for further commands. The reply was: We deny
your right to dictate; but we are perfectly willing
to submit all your complaints to arbitration in
accordance with the instrument of the Thirty
Years' Peace.

This is a perfectly consistent and intelligible
account of the origin of the war; is there any
reason for supposing that it is not true? The
only positive evidence to which an appeal can be
made for rejecting it is that of Aristophanes, who
attributes the outbreak to the second Megarian
decree. This was the natural, superficial view, on
account of the prominence which had been given
to that decree in the final negotiation; and it is

not inconsistent with the Thucydidean account, in so far as that, if Athens had yielded, the war might have been avoided, or rather postponed. Further: in evaluating the statement of the comic poet, which doubtless reflected the current opinion of the Athenian market-place, we must not leave out of account the Athenian feeling against the war a year or so after it had broken out, a feeling which sought to lay the entire blame on Pericles and wove legends round the Megarian decree.[1] But the popular opinion, expressed by Aristophanes, does not really contradict the causal perspective of Thucydides. It was precisely the notion which in the given circumstances was most likely to be left in the popular mind, if the occurrences were such as Thucydides represents them.

There is another consideration which must not be neglected. Unless we hold the doctrine that all the speeches are entirely free inventions of his own, as purely Thucydidean throughout in argument as they are in style,—a doctrine which is untenable in face of his express statement,—and that he adapted the speeches of the first Book to a preconceived construction of his own, the speeches were a most important part of his material for forming his conclusion as to the causes and motives of the war. He probably heard those delivered at Athens; he was informed of the tenor or heads of those de-

---

[1] We do not know whether the Megarian business figured in the *Dionysalexandros* of Cratinus (430-29 B.C.), which satirised Pericles as being the cause of the war. See the Argument of the play, recovered by Grenfell and Hunt, *Oxyrhynchus Papyri*, iv. No. 663.

livered at Sparta; and he has reproduced the drift of these important pieces of evidence. Both in what they say, and in what they do not say, they bear out the justice of his construction and his perspective.

It is a distinct question, What were the guiding motives of the Athenian policy in regard to Megara? Thucydides does not consider it, because it did not seem to him to have determined the outbreak of the war, and was therefore, in a narrow sense, irrelevant; a modern historian would not venture to treat it in this way. The object of Athens was undoubtedly to recover control of the Megarid which she had in recent times won and lost; and, to do this without violating the Thirty Years' Peace, she resorted to economical pressure which would starve her neighbour into voluntary submission. Megara had a double value. Her control would give Athens the power of blocking the land route between the Peloponnesus and Boeotia, and would also secure to her a direct access to the Corinthian Gulf, for her commerce or her troops.[1] We cannot say which of these consequences of the geographical position of Megara counted more with Athenian statesmen, in their unarmed aggression against a neighbour with whom their relations had long been un-

---

[1] F. M. Cornford has ably explained the geographical importance of the Megarid as a commercial route between East and West, taking as his text what he calls Bérard's "law of isthmuses"; and those who do not accept his inferences as a criticism of Thucydides must recognise the value of his investigation.

friendly ; whether they were actuated rather by the "long view" of the use of a port on the Corinthian Gulf, for adding a western to their eastern empire, or by the more obvious view of erecting a barrier against the Peloponnesus. At Sparta, we may be sure, it was the second danger which would create more alarm. But however this may be, there is nothing to show that if there had been no affair of Corcyra and no affair of Potidaea, the Megarian question by itself would have caused the outbreak of the war at the time.

But the criticism to which Thucydides has been exposed illustrates the disadvantages of his method, when it is pressed too far. His principle is to mention only effective policies, and to mention them for the first time when they begin to become effective. If Megara was a pawn in Athenian schemes of aggrandisement in western Greece, it was never moved ; and in saying nothing of this aspect of the Megarian question, the historian is true to his method. If, in 433 B.C. or before, some Athenian politicians had their eyes on Sicily and Italy, the policy had no results till 427 B.C., and therefore in passing over with a bare mention the fact that Athens, in accepting the Corcyraean proposals in 433 B.C., recognised Italy and Sicily as within the range of her interests, he is again true to his method.

§ 4. *His treatment of non-contemporary history*

Thucydides not only showed Greece how contemporary history should be studied and recorded ;
he also gave a specimen of a new way of handling
the history of past ages.   He prefixed to his work
a general sketch of the history of Hellas which
Dionysius of Halicarnassus, who by no means
appreciated its merits, justly described as equivalent to an independent work.   This sketch is
amazing in its power and insight.   We must remember that it is confined strictly to one side of
the historical development.   It is intended to
answer a definite question : how it was that
before quite recent times no large and powerful
state had arisen in Greece ; and to explain the
small scale of the military and political enter-
prises of the past.   It does not touch on constitutional history at all, and the "period of the
tyrants " is only emphasized because their non-
aggressive policy was a relevant point in the
exposition.   Within the limits to which it strictly
adheres, this outline is a most closely reasoned
argument and was the revelation of a totally new
way of treating history.   We cannot endorse it
all ; and of the Homeric and pre-Homeric civilisation in Greece we have come to know within the
last thirty years more than Thucydides could
discover.   But criticism of details is not to the
point ; his sketch remains a shining example of

sheer historical insight and grasp. Rising with easy mastery over the mass of legends and details which constituted the ill-ordered store of Greek tradition, he constructs a reasoned march of development, furnishing the proofs of his conclusions. He draws broad lines of historical growth, elicits general and essential facts from the multitude of particulars, and characterizes periods by their salient features. He calls attention to the importance of considering conditions of culture, and suggests the text for a history of Greek civilisation. He turns the daylight of material conditions on the mythical period, and discovers in the want of resources the key to certain sides of the development of Hellas.

He accepts, of course, like Herodotus and every one else, the actual existence of heroes such as Pelops, Agamemnon, Minos, for whom the genealogies seemed to vouch.[1] He did not question the fact of the Trojan war; but he

---

[1] He takes a matter-of-fact account of the establishment of the Pelopid dynasty in Argolis from some previous writer, i. 9. 2 λέγουσι δὲ καὶ οἱ τὰ σαφέστατα Πελοποννησίων μνήμῃ παρὰ τῶν πρότερον δεδεγμένοι (where Πελοποννησίων depends on οἱ). A Peloponnesian on ancient Argive history suggests Acusilaus. We should expect a man interested in history like Thucydides to have read all or most of the historical works which then existed. The only particular works he mentions (besides Homer) are the συγγραφὴ Ἀττική of Hellanicus and the *Apology* of Antiphon; but he refers generally to the works of poets and prose writers (λογογράφοι, i. 21) on early Greece, and of prose writers he was here thinking chiefly of Herodotus, whom he admittedly criticizes elsewhere. It has been conjectured with much probability that in writing the early chapters of Book vi. on the colonisation of Sicily he used the history of Antiochus of Syracuse (Wölfflin). He cannot have failed to know the books of Ion of Chios and Stesimbrotus, which must have been read with avidity at Athens.

inferred that such a fact meant the eminence of a leading state in Greece at the time, and showed that an examination of the traditions about it pointed to a general lack of resources. He accepted Minos; and his instinct in emphasizing the Cretan thalassocracy seems to be justified by the recent discoveries in Crete. When he comes to a later time, he seizes with a sure eye as the greatest and most important fact of the two centuries before the Persian war the revival of nautical powers and the growth of navies.

In his acute arguments he employs methods which may be called modern. For instance, he points to the culture of backward parts of Greece as a survival of a culture which at one time in the past prevailed generally. He quotes Homer as a witness for the conditions of his own age without any reserve; but when he quotes him in evidence for facts about the Trojan war, he adds a clause of caution. His proof of a Carian population in the islands is not literary but archaeological — Carian tombs which were discovered in his own day when Delos was purified.

The outline of the growth of the Athenian empire after the Persian wars is an exercise of a different kind. No history of this period existed except what was furnished by the brief chronicle of Hellanicus. The account of Thucydides is an original contribution and embodies the results of his own inquiries. He comments on the work

of Hellanicus, noticing its inadequacy and alleging
that it was chronologically inaccurate.   Hellanicus,
as we saw, found a place for every event in an
archon year, and I gave an instance of the errors
into which he fell through pretending to know
too much.   Thucydides gives no absolute dates
and very few chronological indications of any
kind.   It looks at first sight as if Hellanicus
might have retorted on Thucydides that he had
a curious notion of chronological precision.   But
the point of the Thucydidean criticism was just
this, that there were no certain or sufficient data
for such precision, and that the chronological
exactness of Hellanicus was an illusion.   We
may suspect further that in the order in which
he placed some of the events, he corrected
his predecessor.   How far his corrections, for
which he must have relied on the memories of
older men, were right, we cannot say.   But in
any case, here too, he gave his contemporaries
a salutary lesson in scepticism.   He pointedly
abstains from referring at all to the archon
years.[1]   In his view the archon years, which ran
from July to July, were inconvenient and unsuitable for a chronicle of military events, and

[1] In the Pentekontaëteris.   He is careful to mark the beginning of the
Peloponnesian war (ii. 2) by the archon, the Spartan ephor, and the
Argive priestess of Hera (this last dating, which he puts first, shows
the influence of Hellanicus, which has also been conjectured in iv. 133).
Similarly, when he starts afresh after the Ten Years' War, the date is
marked by archon and ephor, v. 25.   But we may legitimately criticize
him for not having indicated formally the chronology of the four years
(435-2) which are treated in Book 1.   A date is obviously wanted in
c. 24.

liable to lead to serious inaccuracies. For this reason he based his own military history on the natural division of the year into summer and winter. That strict chronology was indispensable for accurate history, Thucydides was fully convinced. He proved it by casting his own work into the form of annals. He was an artist, and he could not have failed to see as clearly as his critics (like Dionysius of Halicarnassus) that the annalistic frame was an awkward impediment to any plan of artistic construction. The two claims of chronological accuracy and a pleasing literary arrangement are not irreconcilable, as other historians, like Gibbon, have shown; but Thucydides did not attempt to combine them, and it was characteristic that he should have preferred the demand of historical precision to the exigencies of literary art. His artistic powers were displayed not in the architecture of his work, but in a certain dramatic mode of treatment which will be considered in the next lecture.

LECTURE IV

THUCYDIDES (*continued*)

§ 1. *The Speeches*

THE historian has to do more than chronicle events. It is his business to show why things happened and to discover the forces which were at work. In order to understand the meaning of historical facts, he has to measure the characters and penetrate the motives of the actors, as well as to realise the conditions in which they acted. A psychological reconstruction is thus always involved in history, a reconstruction carried out in the mind of the individual historian, and necessarily affected by his personal temperament and his psychological ability. Some one has said that a writer who could draw a perfectly true and adequate portrait of Napoleon's complex character would be a man whose own soul was a counterpart of Napoleon's. This of course is an extreme way of putting the case, for there is such a thing as psychological imagination. But the subjective process can never be eliminated. It has different aspects in the cases of contemporary and non-contemporary historians. The contemporary historian lives in the same milieu, in the same sphere of ideas, and thus has more points of common sympathy with the political actors of his time ; but, on the other hand, he cannot generally avoid the bias of personal views of his own. The historian of a past epoch may hope to be more impartial, but he cannot hope to divest himself, beyond a certain point, of the standards and measures of his own age ; they are inwoven in the tissue of his mind and they must affect his attempts to reconstruct the past.

Thucydides has concealed this inevitable subjective element by his dramatic method. The persons who play leading parts in the public affairs which he relates reveal their characters and personalities, so far as is required, by their actions and speeches. The author, like a dramatist, remains in the background, only sometimes coming forward to introduce them with a description as brief as in a playbill, or to indicate what men thought about them or the impression they made on their contemporaries. His rule is to commit himself to no personal judgments, and to this rule there are very few exceptions.

The characters of some of the political personages are partly indicated in the speeches, of which I must now speak. They are an essential feature of the Thucydidean art. Herodotus had set the example, but Thucydides used speeches for different purposes and on a different scale, and adapted them to a different method. He states explicitly how

the speeches are to be taken and what they represent. In some cases he heard speeches delivered,
but it was impossible for him to remember them
accurately ; and in other cases he had to depend on
the oral reports of others. His general rule was
to take the general drift and intention of the
speaker, and from this text compose what he might
probably have said. It is clear that this principle
gave great latitude to the author, and that the
resemblances of the Thucydidean speeches to those
actually spoken must have varied widely according
to his information. They are all distinctly Thucydidean in style, just as the various characters in a
play of Euripides all use similar diction. Homogeneity in style was a canon of most ancient men
of letters ; they shrank from introducing lengthy
quotations or inserting the *ipsissima verba* of documents. Occasionally Thucydides has probably
indicated personal mannerisms. For instance, in a
speech of Alcibiades there are one or two expressions
which are intended to suggest his characteristically
" forcible " style.[1] But this has been done with
great reserve. Thucydides in his portraiture does
not depend on mannerisms. The speeches of
Pericles produce the effect of the lofty earnestness
of a patriotic statesman who is somewhat of an
idealist ; the speech of Cleon is that of a bullying
pedagogue. But the diction is the same. So in
Aeschylus, the nurse maunders, though she speaks

---

[1] vi. 18 οὐκ ἔστιν ἡμῖν ταμιεύεσθαι ἐς ὅσον βουλόμεθα ἄρχειν, and στορέσωμεν
τὸ φρόνημα,—noted by the scholiast as κατ' Ἀλκιβιάδην.

Aeschylean; and the *naïveté* of the policeman in
Sophocles is sufficiently revealed though he does
not speak a policeman's language.

But though Thucydides is always Thucydides,
yet within the compass of his style there are
remarkable variations. It is outside my scope to
enter upon this subject in any detail; to do justice
to the styles of the writers who come before us
would require another set of lectures. But in the
case of Thucydides, I suspect that his different
styles have a certain meaning for the treatment of
his subject. It is patent to any reader that there
is a difference between the narrative and the
speeches, and that there are marked differences in
the speeches themselves. Obscurity is a reproach
which has constantly been brought against him
and of which he cannot be acquitted. But it is
not true of his work as a whole. The narrative is
generally clear and straightforward. If it stood
alone, we should never dream of describing him
as obscure. Nor is this description true of the
speeches indiscriminately. Some are lucid and
simple; others excessively obscure; in others again
we have perfectly simple passages beside sections
which, with Dionysius, we may designate as
conundrums or as darker than dark sayings of
Heracleitus.[1] I have taken obscurity and difficulty
—difficulty which the Greeks felt no less than we

---

[1] It has been rightly pointed out by Mahaffy that it is a misapprehension to explain the obscurities of Thucydides as due to condensation of
thought. He is "condensed in expression but not in thought" (*Greek
Literature*, ii. 1. 112).

—as a rough test of distinction. But on what does this difficulty depend? It depends on stylistic technique. There is no doubt that Thucydides was influenced by the rhetorical school of Gorgias, though he was not dominated by it. He modified it by peculiarities of his own; but the affinity is unmistakably shown in the artificial balancing of clauses, the artificial verbal antitheses, the poetical phrase. Generally he keeps this tendency well in hand, but in some passages he deliberately allows it to run riot, and then he becomes obscure because the grammatical constructions have to be twisted unnaturally to subserve verbal effects. Some of these crooked passages produced upon a Greek ear almost the effect of dithyrambs released from the bonds of metre. Dionysius in his instructive criticism takes two passages as conspicuous for this fault (as he considered it),—the dialogue of the Athenian and Melian diplomatists, and the re-flexions upon the psychological and social aspects of civil sedition. Both might be described as elaborate studies in this kind of technique—the "obscure and contorted style." It is unnecessary, nor have I time, to illustrate it at length, but I will give one brief example. It is said in the Funeral Oration of Pericles, about soldiers who had fallen in battle:
οἷς ἐνευδαιμονῆσαί τε ὁ βίος ὁμοίως καὶ ἐντελευτῆσαι ξυν-εμετρήθη.[1] To express the meaning in tolerable English we have to render somewhat like this: "Whose days were so measured that the term of

their happiness was also the term of their life."
But this is a paraphrase, and it does not give the
effect of the Greek. The literal translation is :
"For whom life was made commensurate, to be
happy in and to die in, alike." (Even this fails to
bring out the force of the aorist tense ἐνευδαιμονῆσαι
which suggests the familiar Greek saying, that a
man's life cannot be judged happy till after his
death.) But if the English is obscure and intoler-
able, to a Greek ear, such as that of Dionysius, the
Greek was hardly less so.

Now is there any significance in this remarkable
variation in style ? Is it purely capricious ? Does
Thucydides break into dithyrambic prose just
when, and simply because, he is in the mood ?
Such caprice would not be artistic, and it would
not be Greek. If the difference in style corresponded to the distinction between narrative and
speeches, the explanation would be ready. The
speeches, in any case, serve the artistic purpose of
pauses in the action ; they introduce the variety
which Herodotus secured by digressions ; they
fulfil somewhat the function of choruses in the
drama. And so we should not be surprised to
find a corresponding variety in the diction and
technique. But the difference in style extends
into the speeches themselves.

The explanation which I would submit to you
is that when Thucydides adopts what we may
fairly call his unnatural style, when he is involved
and obscure, he is always making points of his

own. In support of this view, I allege the following considerations. (1) The meditation on the
party - struggles in Greek states, though not a
speech, belongs to this category. It interrupts
the action ; it is, in fact, a speech of the author.
And it is one of the flagrant examples of the
unnatural style, and is commented on, as such, by
Dionysius. Here then the author undisguisedly
adopts this style for his own reflexions. (2)
Secondly, take the Melian dialogue. Now whether
we think, as some do, that such a conference was
never held, or believe—and this is my opinion—
that it was held, all agree that the actual conversa-
tion is in the main fictitious. I will return to this
dialogue in another connexion. I would point out
now that it is a clear case in which the unnatural
style is employed for a political study of the
author. Contrast it, as Dionysius contrasts it,
with another dialogue, that between Archidamus
and the Plataeans. This is in the natural style,
and obviously gives the simple tenor of what
passed on the occasion. (3) My third proof lies
in the contrast between two of the speeches of
Pericles. The speech he delivered before the war
is so lucid and straightforward in style as to have
satisfied Dionysius ; and at the same time it is
perfectly appropriate to the situation, and no
doubt gives the general drift of the Periclean
argument. On the other hand, the speech which
he delivers in self-defence, when he became unpopular, is marked in part by those obscurities

which excited the censure of Dionysius, and is also distinguished by unsuitable statements which could not have been addressed by any statesman to a public whose favour he desired to recover.[1]

I infer that when Thucydides writes in the unnatural style, he intends the reader to understand that he has here to do with the author himself—that the author is making points. When he writes in the natural style, he is producing documentary evidence. The speech of Pericles on the eve of the war is virtually a document.

Let me make an application of this inference, which I think has some interest. The *Epitaphios* of Pericles is composed on the whole in the unnatural style.[2] It enshrines, as I believe, some utterances of Pericles himself; but the style is generally contorted and obscure, though we forgive, or may even find a certain pleasure in, this, so lofty is the spirit and so fine the thoughts. Now it is to be noted that, unlike other speeches, this funeral address does not cast any direct light on the events of the war, and that its tone is out of keeping with the occasion.[3] There was no great action, no conspicuous deed of valour, in the first year of the war, yet this oration over the Athenians who fell in it is pitched in a key

---

[1] I point out in the Appendix that it was composed or wrought over after the end of the war.

[2] The epigram of the Thucydidean Pericles on the virtue of women (ii. 45) may have been suggested by a saying of Gorgias. Wilamowitz-Möllendorff, *Hermes*, ii. p. 294.

[3] This was observed by Dionysius.

which would be appropriate to the burial of the heroes of a Thermopylae. My view is that Thucydides has seized this occasion to turn the light on Pericles himself. The Athens which Pericles here depicts is an ideal; and the purpose of the historian is to bring out the fact that he was an idealist. The very incongruity between the occasion and the high-pitched strain of the orator heightens the calculated impression that Pericles, along with his political wisdom, possessed an imagination which outranged realities.

If you were asked to translate into ancient Greek "he is an idealist," you could not, I think, find a more exact equivalent than ζητεῖ ἄλλο τι, ὡς ἔπος εἰπεῖν, ἢ ἐν οἷς ζῶμεν. This expression is applied by Cleon (in his speech about Mytilene[1]) to the Athenians in general, to whom it was hardly appropriate; it was, I take it, a covert hit at the *éthos* and character of Pericles. Now both this speech of Cleon and the counter-speech of Diodotus are, by my criterion, largely composed of matter which is purely Thucydidean. The speech of Diodotus contains, you remember, reflexions on the general theory of punishment— the earliest discussion of the subject in literature; and we know from other evidence that this was a question which had a special interest for Pericles. I venture therefore to think that one of the points which Thucydides wishes to make in these speeches is, that the more lenient treatment of the

[1] ii. 38. 7.

rebels of Mytilene was in accordance with the *spirit* of Periclean policy. With the spirit; but it might have been argued that it was not in accordance with the letter and the logic; and this, I think, is one of the points which Cleon's speech is intended to suggest. It is notable that while the speaker makes, as I think, an oblique hit at Periclean idealism, and strikes an anti-Periclean note in his dispraise of knowledge and criticism, at the same time he iterates phrases which occur in the Periclean speeches: "Empire means tyranny"; "Do not play the virtuous." Thucydides is here studying not only the contrast between the two politicians, but also the difficulties inherent in the Periclean imperialism.

§ 2. *Dramatic treatment of the* historiae personae

The speeches in general served two purposes. In the first place they were used by the author to explain the facts and elements of a situation, as well as underlying motives and ideas. In some cases the speech was only a dramatic disguise of a study of his own. Thus, the characters of the two protagonist cities, Athens and Sparta, are delineated in a speech of a third party, the Corinthians: the author of this famous comparison was unquestionably Thucydides himself. But in other cases he uses the actual expositions of politicians,—genuine political documents so far as the main tenor went,—as the most useful means of explaining a situation. The comparative advantages of the two contending powers for the coming war are stated in two speeches from opposite points of view.[1] The prospects and difficulties of the Sicilian expedition are set forth by the same means.

The speeches had the second function—and here I return to the point from which I set out—of serving the objective dramatic method of indicating character which Thucydides chose to adopt.[2] The speeches of Pericles, Cleon, Brasidas, Nicias, and Alcibiades, taken in conjunction with their actions, reveal as much of their characters as seemed to the author necessary for the matter in hand; that is, those sides of their nature which in his opinion governed their public actions or affected their political influence. The general plan was that the men, as well as the events, should speak or be made to speak for themselves, with little or no direct comment from the writer.

This method produced the illusion that the actors showed themselves to the reader independently of the author. It really meant that the author had framed a psychological estimate of them, as a dramatist constructs his characters: an estimate founded on his knowledge of their actions, but nevertheless no more than his own subjective interpretation. The reader is here almost as completely in the author's hands as in

[1] In the second speech of the Corinthians and the first of Pericles.

[2] Bruns (see Bibliography) was the first to study systematically the methods of the ancient historians in depicting character. I am much indebted to his well-known book.

a drama. He has not the means of forming a corrective judgment for himself; for he does not know how the historian has arrived at his results.

The application of the method may be observed in the cases of Cleon and Nicias. Thucydides held a distinct view of the character of Cleon as a politician. He allows us to see it reflected from Cleon's actions and from the opinions of people about him. When he describes Cleon as an influential leader of the demos, who was very violent, namely in manner and speech, he only states a fact which was undoubtedly notorious and admitted. The oration of Cleon on the Lesbian question exhibits his fashion of rating the people like a pedagogue. The drastic judgment that, if Cleon's command at Pylos ended in disaster, this would be a great blessing, for it would rid the city of Cleon, is not recorded as the historian's own sarcasm; it is mentioned as the opinion of some people at Athens. But as the people who thought so are called "sensible" (σώφρονες), the disguise is here very thin; the writer permits his own assent to be visible. No reader of the scenes in which Cleon appears would be left in any doubt that Cleon in the author's estimation was a pestilent demagogue; but in one passage [1] Thucydides entirely abandons his dramatic reserve and ascribes the worst motives to the politician for his unwillingness to bring the war to a close.

The portrait of Nicias, the conscientious patriot,

[1] v. 16. 1.

an embodiment of respectability, cautious and experienced, but unendowed with first-rate talent, afraid of responsibility, afraid of the Ecclesia, is perhaps the most successful achievement of Thucydides in dramatic art. All this comes out in his actions and speeches. But in this case too the author once comes forward himself and directly construes the motives which actuated Nicias in working in the interests of peace. They were of a selfish nature : he thought of his own reputation ; he desired " while he had suffered no reverses and was held in repute, to preserve his good fortune ; he wished for rest himself as well as to give the people rest; he hoped to leave his name to posterity as of one who had never brought calamity on the city ; and he thought that the best means to secure this was to trust as little as possible to fortune and to keep out of danger, which would be avoided by peace."[1] The irony is unmistakable. Again, in the last scene, when Nicias has been executed at Syracuse, the historian appears before the curtain for a moment and pronounces an epitaph, the point of which posterity has frequently misunderstood. It is generally taken as an encomium ; it is really *malice*. In my opinion, says Thucydides, Nicias deserved such an end less than any other Athenian, considering his conventional virtue.[2] In other words, a man of such conventional virtue was unsuited for such an unconventional end. That

---

[1] v. 16. 2 (Jowett's translation).
[2] νενομισμένη. This interpretation is favoured by F. Cauer.

is irony of a kind in which Thucydides rarely indulges ; behind it lurks the suppressed judgment that Athens was unfortunate in the trust which she reposed in Nicias, the model of irreproachable respectability.

In the case of Alcibiades the historian dwells on the extravagance and display of his private life, because they had a direct influence on the feelings of the Athenians towards him, and affected his public career and the course of the war. But here too the character is revealed in actions and words ; insolence and ambition come out in his orations, and, as I have already observed, some strong phrases seem to be characteristic of his manner. Thucydides refrains from commenting on his character, but points out his services and shows that the Athenians regarded him with a suspicious apprehension which prevented them from profiting by his ability.

In the cases of Themistocles, Pericles, and Antiphon, the author departs from his usual practice, and gives characterising judgments of his own. In the case of Themistocles this might be considered a necessary exception, as he does not come into the main narrative and cannot reveal himself dramatically. The same reason might be held partly to apply to Pericles, since the greater part of his lifework was over when he comes on the stage. The favourable notice of Antiphon's ability might also be explained by the fact that he had hardly appeared in the political arena before the year of the revolution, and his appearance then was so brief. The eulogy on Antiphon indeed has a personal note, which betrays perhaps a friendship. It is, however, futile to seek to explain or explain away these exceptions. The truth is that in general Thucydides is dramatic, but he has not carried his method to extremes.

It is noteworthy that nearly all the judgments which he pronounces concern intelligence and political ability. This is the case with Themistocles, Pericles, Antiphon, Theramenes, and Hermocrates. They all receive greater or less praise for political capacity, which in the case of Themistocles is said to have amounted to genius.

The case of Hyperbolus demands a few words, because it illustrates the method of Thucydides and his political leanings. In the years between the Fifty Years' Peace and the Sicilian Expedition, the division of parties under the opposing leaders Nicias and Alcibiades paralysed the foreign policy of Athens and hindered continuity of action. The situation was so serious that the only way out seemed that proposed by the demagogue Hyperbolus—a trial of ostracism, which would expel one of the rivals and secure unity. Alcibiades frustrated this device by combining, if not with his rival, at least with a sufficiently large oligarchical faction, to procure the ostracism of Hyperbolus. Thucydides does not say a word about this affair, though of course he was perfectly aware of the facts, and though they had an immediate bearing on the foreign policy of Athens. We must suppose that as the purpose of the ostracism was defeated and the relative positions of the two leaders were not altered by the vote, he considered it super-fluous to record the occurrence. It will be admitted, however, that a modern historian who allowed himself such an omission or carried his principle of exclusion so far, would not escape censorious criticism. But in another connexion, Thucydides refers to the ostracism, without dating it, or in any way suggesting its significance. Hyperbolus was killed in 411 B.C. at Samos. Thucydides records this and mentions that Hyper-bolus had been ostracized. This is the only place where he names the demagogue, who in the years following Cleon's death had been one of the most influential speakers in the Ecclesia. We might suspect that in ignoring this politician, just as he ignored men of the same type like Eucrates and Lysicles, he exercised a reserve which was equi-valent to an adverse criticism, a negative expression of contempt; but no doubt is permitted by the words in which he paints his memory black. Hyperbolus was ostracized, we are told, not because he was esteemed dangerous, but because he was an unprincipled scoundrel and a disgrace to the city. The same epithet ($\mu o \chi \theta \eta \rho o s$) is here applied to Hyperbolus which was applied to him by Aristophanes.[1] We may note how Thucydides violates here his own principle of relevance. At this moment, Hyperbolus is not interesting or

---

[1] *Knights*, 1304.

important, and in holding up his character to
reprobation the historian is deviating from his
narrative. Again, what he says of the cause of
the ostracism is untrue. Hyperbolus was not
ostracized because he was a disgrace to the city,
whether he was so or not. He would not have
been ostracized if the supporters of Alcibiades had
not been instructed to write his name on the sherds
instead of that of the virtuous Nicias. We know
very little about Hyperbolus; but this judgment
of Thucydides cannot be taken as objective or
impartial. It is quite clear that he had a profound
antipathy to popular leaders like Cleon and Hyperbolus, and that he was incapable of doing them
whatever justice they deserved. And such antipathy is sufficient to account for the treatment
of Cleon, without invoking a further motive of
personal resentment for any part Cleon may have
taken in procuring the condemnation of the
historian.[1]

§ 3. *Rationalistic view of history*

It is by his practice of allowing his characters to
reveal themselves by their actions and words, while
keeping himself in the background, although he
does not adhere to this plan with pedantic consistency, that the art of Thucydides may be
appropriately called dramatic. The description of
"dramatic" has indeed been claimed for his history

---

[1] F. M. Cornford touches on this point in his *Thucydides Mythistoricus*.
I think he is right. The hypothesis of personal spite is superfluous.

on another ground. It has been thought that he viewed the whole war under the scheme of a tragedy, in which the Sicilian expedition was the *peripeteia* or "reversal" of fortune for Athens. This idea has recently been developed in a new shape by Mr. F. M. Cornford, in a brilliant study which seeks to establish that the historian read Aeschylean conceptions into the events of the war and mounted it, like a tragedy, with the dark figures of Tyche, Hybris, Peitho, and Eros, moving in the background and prompting the human actors. That such a conception should be read by an ingenious scholar in a work which impresses the ordinary reader as entirely matter of fact in its treatment of political transactions, illustrates what a wonderful book the history of Thucydides is. The truth is, I think, that the style of Thucydides was influenced by the Attic drama, no less than by the rhetoric of Gorgias, and it is one of the merits of Mr. Cornford's monograph to have illustrated this influence. But that the tragic phrases and reminiscences, and the occasional use of tragic irony, cannot be held to have more than a stylistic significance, and that Thucydides did not intend to cast the war into the typical scheme of a tragic development, will be apparent if we consider his own clear statements.

His view of the causes of the collapse of Athens displays the difference between his own outlook on human affairs and that of Herodotus. The older historian pourtraying the collapse of the Persian power discerns, in the development of the plot, imminent above the actors a superhuman control and the occult operation of nemesis. The only external influence recognised by the younger writer appears in the form of the incalculable element which he calls *Tyche*, Chance. Herodotus interpreted history and life, in the sense that the decline of a state or of a man from a post of commanding eminence was due to the action of a supernatural power which would not tolerate the exaltation which invariably leads to immoderate elation of soul and often to acts of insolence and rashness. In one of the speeches in Thucydides this anthropopathic idea is translated into the dry formula : " It is the nature of human things to decline." But it can hardly be said that he believed unreservedly in this principle (which may be found in Ionian philosophers) as a certain fact. And his analysis of the course of the war and his explanation of its issue show that the operation of the incalculable element of chance need not be decisive. It contributed to the decline of the Athenian power, but that power might have survived and defied its outrages, if it had not been for human mismanagement.

In the early stage of the war there were two cases of the play of the incalculable. There was first of all the plague. But though severe, maiming and weakening more than anything else the offensive power of the State for years to come, it was not crushing, it did not spell doom ; one of its

gravest consequences was the psychical effect upon
the Athenians, for which Pericles suffered. The
other surprise of fortune was a kind one, the
combination of circumstances which helped the
Athenians to their stroke of luck at Pylos. This
elated them, as the pestilence had cast them down.
Instead of grasping the opportunity of making
advantageous terms and bringing to an end a war
which they would gladly have concluded on any
terms a few years before, they were incited to
hopes of new conquest. But the consequences
were by no means disastrous; the Peace of 421
B.C. left the balance of power much the same.

They had recovered from the effects of the
plague and the war when they undertook the
conquest of Sicily in 415 B.C. The catastrophe of
that enterprise was the beginning of a gradual
decline, which was determined by domestic dissensions in Athens, and afterwards by the intervention
of Persia. A modern historian has designated the
Sicilian expedition as an act of insanity, an instance
of a whole people gone mad, analogous to the case
of England in the Crimean war. But this was
not the opinion of Thucydides. He says, and he
is speaking in his own name, that it was not an
error of judgment in the design or in the calculation of strength, and would have been a success, if
it had been properly supported and carried out.
The verdict of the modern writer was influenced
partly by ethical considerations; the verdict of
Thucydides did not take ethics into account; he

only contemplates the question whether, judging
the strength of Athens and the resistance offered
to her, the ambition of extending her empire to
Sicily was reasonable or foolish. The failure of
the enterprise and the reverses of the ensuing years
he imputes to the dissensions at home; and in the
same way he explains mismanagement in the earlier
period of the war by the jealousies of rival politicians. In other words, the key to the decline of
Athenian power was the fact that Pericles had no
successors. The city began to fall away from her
eminence when her government was no longer
controlled by an able leader.

Even after the Sicilian expedition, the situation
might have been retrieved; for there was a man
marked out to be a leader like Pericles, if the
Athenians had trusted him. This was Alcibiades.
That this was the view which Thucydides formed
of Alcibiades can, I think, admit of little doubt.
The distrust of the Athenians, he says, contributed
heavily to the fall of the city; Alcibiades conducted the war with masterly ability.[1] In other
words, things would have turned out very differently, if the conduct of affairs had been
entrusted to him. The distrust is attributed to
the somewhat insolent display and splendour of his
private life, which excited envy and the suspicion
of tyrannical designs. Nicias taunts him with this
λαμπρότης, Alcibiades glories in it.[2] Now the career
of Alcibiades had remarkable points of resemblance

---

[1] vi. 15.　　　　[2] vi. 12; 16.

with that of a great Athenian statesman of a former
age, Themistocles.   They were both banished from
Athens ; both conspired with her enemies against
her ; and Alcibiades like Themistocles became a
trusted adviser of the Persians.   But another
point of likeness is indicated by Thucydides, λαμπρότης.   It is not for nothing that he describes
Themistocles and Pausanias as the most magnificent or luxurious of the Greeks of their time
(λαμπροτάτους).   That was a weak point in the case
of Themistocles as in that of Alcibiades ; it led to
the suspicion of tyranny.   This parallel suggests
that one motive of the digression on Themistocles
was to point it.   At all events it throws light on
the view of the historian.   Athens produced three
men who had the faculty, which cannot be learned
by study, for guiding the affairs of a great state,
Themistocles, Pericles, and Alcibiades.   Two of
them fell into the snare of luxurious splendour,
which ruined their careers.   Pericles avoided that
pitfall, and won and retained the public confidence.
This contrast, I would observe, gives special point
to a famous phrase in the *Epitaphios*.   Pericles
himself was φιλόκαλος μετ᾽ εὐτελείας, he was not
λαμπρός, he indulged his private tastes without
undue or obtrusive expense.

This analysis, which is furnished by the historian's own comments, eliminates entirely the
dim superstitious notions of doom and nemesis,
which do duty for Providence in Herodotus and
dispense the spectator from any deeper study of

the course and causes of events. Thucydides deals
with purely human elements; human brains bear
the ultimate responsibility. There is nothing
mysterious about the fact that events cannot be
foreseen. The course of events, says Pericles, may
sometimes be as incalculable by reason as the
thoughts of a man's mind. Thucydides does not
regard the plague as a divine dispensation. It
was simply an occurrence which could not be foreseen, exactly as you may not foresee the moves of
your enemy. Herodotus credits the oracles with
mysterious knowledge; Thucydides occasionally
refers to oracles, but their sole significance for him
lies in the psychical effect they produce on those
who believe them. Of the oracle which predicted
that the war would last twenty-seven years, he drily
observes that it is the only one to which people
who put their faith in oracles can point as having
been certainly fulfilled. Here he was at the same
standpoint as Anaxagoras and Pericles.[1] The
philosophers who had established the reign of law
had not written in vain for Thucydides.[2] Chance
means for him the same kind of thing that it
means for us; it does not signify the interference
of an external will or caprice; it simply represents
an element which cannot be foretold. He recognises the operation of the unknown; he does not
recognise the presence of "things occult." And

---

[1] He speaks indeed strangely of the frequency of solar eclipses during
the war (i. 23. 3), as if they had some significance for the human race;
we may wonder what comment Anaxagoras would have made.

[2] Cp. Gomperz, *Griechische Denker*, i. p. 61 (on Heracleitus).

he reduces the unknown to its minimum of significance for human life. The great philosopher, Democritus of Abdera, had said : "Chance is an idol which men fashioned to excuse their own mental incapacity. As a matter of fact chance seldom conflicts with wisdom. In most affairs of life, an intelligent mind can exercise clairvoyance with success."[1] These words of Democritus might serve as a motto for Thucydides.

The elements for the conception of the war as a tragedy, in the proper sense of the word, were absent from his interpretation of the course of history. There was no mysterious controlling force, no doom or retribution, no inevitable decree of fate, no moral principle at stake. The lessons which the catastrophe conveyed were not moral or cathartic. The war was full of instructive lessons for statesmen and generals ; but those lessons were assuredly of a very different order from the lessons of Aeschylus and Sophocles. And the occasional use of phraseology, which the tragedians charged with meaning, should not mislead us. Just as a writer of the present day who is completely innocent of any traffic with the supernatural may employ such terms as fate, doom, nemesis, so Thucydides could borrow the personified abstractions of tragedy for purposes of expression, without meaning to suggest anything occult. If I say that

---

[1] Democritus, in Mullach, *Frag. Phil.* 167. Thucydides observes *sub persona Hermocratis* (iv. 62. 4) that in war the incalculable element has its uses ; it is the same for both and conduces to caution and prudence.

I have been prompted to do something by an imp of mischief or by a demon of unrest, you will not impute to me a belief in demons or imps. If Thucydides has sometimes expressed psychological observations in the language of tragic poets, this does not prove that he looked at history from a tragic poet's point of view.

§ 4. *Political analysis*

Attempts have inevitably been made to peer behind the scenes and discover the personal political views or tendencies of this singularly reserved historian. Dionysius, a critic who is usually instructive though never profound and often obtuse, stigmatizes in Thucydides a lack of patriotism so marked as to amount to positive ill - will both towards Greece and towards Athens. " He began at a point where the Greek world had begun to decline. A Greek and Athenian should not have done this, especially one who was no outcast but had been honoured by the Athenians with high command. He was so malicious that he imputed to his own city the open causes of the war, though he might have found means to attach the responsibility to other cities. He could have *begun* not with the Corcyraean affair but with the supreme successes of his country after the Persian war, and could have shown that it was through jealousy and fear, the consequence of these successes, that the Lacedaemonians, alleging other reasons, began the war."[1] When this criticism is examined, it will be found that it mainly touches the *arrangement* of the first Book,[2] but it shows that the narrative produced upon Dionysius the impression that Thucydides was unpatriotic.

On the other hand, it is held by some modern critics that the account of the beginnings and first years of the war is virtually a defence of the policy of Pericles, and it is even insinuated that the author manipulated facts, concealing some and mitigating others, with the purpose of presenting that policy in a favourable light. This view evidently contradicts that of Dionysius; it implies that Thucydides sympathized with Athens during the Periclean régime and at the outbreak of the war.

The fact that the narrative can convey two such contradictory impressions is a certificate of the author's critical impartiality. The censure of Dionysius is based on the conventional principle of later times that it is a historian's duty to be patriotic at all costs, to sacrifice his critical judgment; and it is superfluous to refute his charge of ill-will. On the other hand, the theory that Thucydides was an unreserved admirer of Pericles and deliberately intended to exalt and defend his policy, almost as a partisan, has some *prima facie* plausibility, and, as it has a direct bearing on the writer's

---

[1] *Letter to Pompeius*, 3. 9.

[2] But he also blames Thucydides, 3. 4, 5, for the choice of his subject. The war was οὔτε καλὸς οὔτε εὐτυχής, and therefore should be forgotten and ignored by posterity.

attitude to history and politics, we must consider it more particularly.

We have seen how Thucydides speaks in the highest terms of the political ability of Pericles, and was convinced that, if he had lived or had a successor as able as himself, the war would have terminated favourably for Athens. But this general conviction would be quite compatible with discriminating criticism. The tribute which he has paid to Pericles does not imply that he saw eye to eye with the statesman in all things or held his political faith. There are proofs, in my opinion, that he exercised here, as in other cases, a cold independent judgment, and had no scruples in exhibiting weak points.

The speeches of Pericles claim our special attention. I may begin by pointing out that the praise which Pericles bestows in the *Epitaphios*[1] on the democratic constitution of Athens, implying that it was an ideal form of government, is not in accordance with the view of Thucydides, who expressly states that in his opinion the short-lived *politeia* which was established in Athens after the fall of the Four Hundred was not merely superior to democracy, but was the only good constitution that Athens had enjoyed in his lifetime.[2] In other words, he did not consider democracy a good constitution. In the second place, we may feel con-

---

[1] ii. 37.
[2] viii. 97 καὶ οὐχ ἥκιστα δὴ τὸν πρῶτον χρόνον ἐπὶ γ' ἐμοῦ Ἀθηναῖοι φαίνονται εὖ πολιτεύσαντες. Is the reserve ἐπὶ γ' ἐμοῦ simply cautiousness, or is it an allusion to the πάτριος πολιτεία of early times?

fident that the eloquent and fascinating portrait of Athens, drawn by Pericles, did not in the historian's opinion correspond to reality. It was the Periclean ideal. And Thucydides knew perfectly well that the claim that Athens was the school of liberal education for Greece would have been scouted by other states; and, as a matter of fact, it did not become anything of the kind till after the Peloponnesian war. Again, it seems more than doubtful whether Thucydides approved of the Periclean policy of bringing all the inhabitants of Attica into the city. The length at which he dwells on the unpleasant consequences of this arrangement, his pains in showing how distasteful it was to the people, suggest that he considered it a measure of highly questionable wisdom.

He certainly looked on Pericles as the most successful statesman who had recently guided the counsels of Athens. But he saw him, like all his other *dramatis personae*, in a dry light, and, as I have suggested, he has presented one side of the statesman's mind with a certain veiled irony.

The dramatic detachment of Thucydides readily produced the impression that he was unpatriotic. He allows every party to state their case as strongly and persuasively as possible. But while he wrote not as a patriot but as a historian, it is Athens, not Sparta, the Athenian Empire, not the Peloponnesian Confederacy, in which the interest of the narrative centres throughout. As to the questions at stake and the issues involved in the war, what we may hope to discover is not what political views the historian held, but *what was his attitude of mind in observing political events.*

His interest centres in the Athenian empire. In the passage in which he offers a general explanation of the result of the war he writes from the Athenian side entirely. Now as to the nature of the Athenian empire he has no illusions. In the first Book he unfolds the unscrupulous way in which it was acquired, with perfect candour. He states that it was generally unpopular, and he allots a speech to an indictment of it by one of the subject states. That it was a despotism based not on right but on might is not merely alleged by the opponents of Athens but is emphasized by Athenian speakers. The Athenian diplomatist who spoke at the Congress of Sparta characterizes it without any reserve as having been won from motives of self-confidence and ambition; and the justification assigned is that it is a law of human nature that the weaker should be constrained by the stronger. Pericles is still more candid and emphatic. "The Empire you possess," he says, "is a tyranny; it may have been unjust to acquire, it is perilous to relinquish it." Again: "That man is truly wise who incurs odium for the highest stakes. Hatred does not balance the present magnificence and the future fame." Here power, wealth, and glory are assigned as a justification of an unjustly gotten and unpopular empire. Arguing against the peace-party — οἱ ἀπράγμονες — who have scruples about

justice, Pericles takes the same line, though with
more cynicism, as a modern British chauvinist con-
temptuous of those whom he calls the Little Eng-
landers. He sneers at their conscience, which, he
suggests, is a cloak for cowardice. Alcibiades in
advocating the Sicilian expedition points out the
necessity to imperial states of an active and aggressive policy. Hermocrates, the enemy of Athens,
does not complain of such a policy on grounds
of morality; he says: "I can fully pardon the
Athenians for their grasping policy; I do not
blame those who seek empire, but those who are
ready to submit; for it has always been the natural
instinct of man to rule him who yields and to resist
the aggressor."

The excuse which both Hermocrates and
Athenians urge for the acquisition of empire is
the instinct of human nature. But Pericles also
attempted what may be called a justification on
higher grounds. In the Funeral Oration he draws
a picture of the grandeur and the *culture* of
Athens. There, he so much as says, is the ideal
which our city, by winning power and wealth,
through an empire which was certainly *not* built
on foundations of justice, has realised for the
admiration and imitation of Hellas. Such things
cannot be achieved by timid justice and stay-at-
home piety. This is the *leit-motif* of the Funeral
Oration.

Thus the historian kept before himself, and
keeps before us, the fact that the empire cannot be

defended on grounds of justice, that it could not be maintained except by *force majeure*, and that if slavery was an extreme word for the condition of the subject states, they were generally reluctant under the yoke. It is further to be observed that when Thucydides makes occasional reflexions of his own, he never takes justice or morality into account, from which we may infer that in his estimation those conceptions did not illuminate the subject. He recognised that the ideal of justice was an actual psychological force and could not be neglected by statesmen, any more than popular religion. But he did not consider it worth while to apply the standard of justice in estimating political transactions, just as he did not ask whether an action was pleasing to the gods.

The speech of Diodotus, advocating lenient treatment for the rebels of Mytilene, is interesting in this connexion. As the speaker played no part in history except here, the harangue must be introduced solely for the sake of its arguments. Its chief interest is that it repudiates the intrusion of justice into the question; the speaker reproaches Cleon for having dragged in so irrelevant a consideration, and bases his own view entirely on reasons of state. Thucydides with his usual reticence abstains from comment, though the tone of his narrative suggests that he sympathized with the lenient policy; but the fact that he chose these speeches of Cleon and Diodotus for working up, and that he has worked them up largely in the style which he employs when he is not documentary, shows that *his interest lay in the logic of policy*.

In the light of the debate on Mytilene we may consider the notorious debate of the Athenian and Melian representatives. Melos, you remember, was an independent state. Athens had made an attempt to force her into her empire in 426 B.C.; the idea was not resumed till 416 B.C., but in the meantime the relations of the two states had been hostile. When the expedition reached the island, the generals sent envoys to demand submission. They were admitted to a round-table conference with members of the Melian government, and Thucydides gives in the form of a dialogue what purposes to be the tenor of the debate. That such a conference was held, there cannot be a reasonable doubt, nor is it improbable that Thucydides had something to work upon. There is no difficulty in supposing that he might have heard enough from some one who knew to furnish him with a text.

The note of the dialogue is the elimination of justice from the discussion, by the Athenians. "Lass unsern Herr Gott aus dem Spass." The field of the argument is confined to policy and reason of state. When the Melians essay to find an issue from this restricted ground by observing that, being innocent of wrong, they expect a heaven-sent chance to intervene in their favour, the Athenians retort that gods as well as men recognise it to be a law of nature that the weaker should be ruled by the stronger. Now this is nothing more than what had already been said by Hermocrates and the Athenian envoy at Sparta. The attitude of the Athenians on this occasion is exactly the same as that of Diodotus in arguing for leniency towards Mytilene. Both alike are ruthlessly realistic; both alike refuse to consider any reason but reason of state. The conscience and feelings of the readers of Thucydides have been shocked by the tone of the Athenians at Melos because they sympathize with Melos; whereas they are not shocked by Diodotus because they sympathize with Mytilene. Yet Diodotus in 427 B.C. regarded Mytilene just as Athens in 416 B.C. regarded Melos, merely as a pawn in the game of empire. It is also important to observe that the discussion in the Melian council-chamber before the siege has nothing to do with the rigorous treatment of the people after the capture of the city. A few years before, Athens had meted out the same treatment to Scione; all the adult males were killed, the women and children enslaved. Thucydides makes no comment in either case. But if Athens had contented herself with reducing Melos to the condition of a tributary, the notorious dialogue would have been equally to the point. The policy of annexing Melos was one thing, the policy of punishing was another; Thucydides does not express his views on either. But it has been supposed by various critics that he introduced a cynical dialogue for the purpose of holding up to obloquy the conduct of Athens, and even of making it appear an ill-omened prelude to the disastrous expedition against Sicily. This theory will not, in my opinion, bear examination. Thucydides, as we have seen, did not consider that the Sicilian expedition was ill-advised in principle, and he does not hint that any consequences, bad or good for Athens, ensued from the conquest of Melos.

The truth is, I think, that Thucydides took the opportunity of the round-table conference to exhibit, pure and unvarnished, the springs of political action. The motives and arguments of the Athenians, whether wisely or unwisely applied in this particular case, were nothing new; they were the same which lay at the foundation of all their empire-building. This was the first case of a new annexation since the outbreak of the war, and it was the first occasion offered to the historian to analyse imperial policy from the point of view of aggression; he had already examined it from the point of view of preservation. The Melian dialogue only develops more undisguisedly and expressly— and the circumstance that no public was present gave the author the artistic pretext for candour— what is to be found in all the argumentative speeches : that not justice but reason of state is the governing consideration which guides the action of cities and claims the interest of historians.

We are now in a position to understand the attitude of Thucydides. *His object is to examine and reveal political actions from an exclusively*

political point of view. He does not consider moral
standards; his method is realistic and detached;
he takes history as it is and examines it on its own
merits. This detached analytical treatment is illustrated by the earliest political prose pamphlet we
possess, written by a contemporary of the historian
in the early years of the war; I mean the short
tract on the Athenian Constitution. The author
was an oligarch and declares without reserve his
personal hostility to the democracy; but it is not a
polemical work. He detaches himself from his
own feelings, places himself at the point of view of
democrats, and examines democracy exclusively in
this light. Applying his acute logic, he demonstrates that the institutions of Athens could hardly
be improved upon. The writer is intellectually
allied to Thucydides in the detachment of his attitude and the logical restriction of the issue under
a particular point of view.

Now when Thucydides offers reflexions *in
propria persona* on events, his criticisms, on the
policy of Athens, for instance, or on the value of an
Athenian politician, are generally determined by
the consideration whether they were conducive to
success or failure in the war. In his appreciation
of Brasidas, he places himself at the point of view
of Sparta, and recognises that this general's conduct, policy, and character were conducive to the
extension of Spartan power in competition with
Athens. He takes the objects of the conflicting
states as given, without approving or condemning;

and in recording acts and methods his rare verdicts
of praise or blame are confined to the question
whether those acts and methods were calculated to
achieve their object; just as in characterizing a
man he refers only to his intellectual powers.   He
offers no opinion whether the aims were justifiable
or admirable; he applies no ethical standard to
policies or politicians.

Of course, he was fully conscious of ethical
questions which arise in connexion with high
politics, and these questions raise their heads in
the dramatic parts of the work.   In the speeches,
justice and expediency are frequently distinguished
and opposed.   A speaker, for example, according
to circumstances, is concerned to show that a
course which is just is also expedient, or that
expedience ought to be preferred to justice.
Sometimes the consideration of justice is briefly
dismissed as irrelevant.   It appears as a psychical
factor actually operative in international transactions, a principle to which at least homage of the
lips was paid, by which praise and blame were
popularly awarded, and which therefore had to be
taken into account.   But its rôle was slight and
subordinate : the dramatist could not ignore it,
though he allows it as small a range as he can ; the
thinker dismissed it.

There is not, so far as I can discover, any reason
for believing that Thucydides thought or intended
to suggest that an uncompromising policy of self-
interest conduced to the fall of the Athenian

empire, or that her wrong and unwise actions were wrong and unwise because they were guided by considerations of expediency alone. There is no ground for supposing that he would have had a thought of censure, if he had lived in our own days, for statesmen like Cavour and Bismarck and Disraeli, who were guided exclusively by reason of state, and are therefore blamed by moralists for having debased the moral currency in Europe. If, instead of a history, Thucydides had written an analytical treatise on politics, with particular reference to the Athenian empire, it is probable that he would occupy a different place from that which he holds actually in the world's esteem; he would have forestalled the fame of Machiavelli.

Thucydides simply observes facts; Machiavelli lays down maxims and prescribes methods; but the whole innuendo of the Thucydidean treatment of history agrees with the fundamental postulate of Machiavelli, the supremacy of reason of state. To maintain a state, said the Florentine thinker, "a statesman is often compelled to act against faith, humanity, and religion." In Thucydides, reason of state appears as actually the sovran guide in the conduct of affairs. But the essential point of comparison is that both historians, in examining history and politics, abstracted from all but political considerations, and applied logic to this restricted field. Machiavelli—the true Machiavelli, not the Machiavelli of fable, the *scelerum inventor Ulixes*

—entertained an ideal : Italy for the Italians, Italy freed from the stranger : and in the service of this ideal he desired to see his speculative science of politics applied. Thucydides had no political aim in view ; he was purely a historian ; his interest was to investigate the actual policy of Athens in maintaining and losing her empire. But it was part of the method of both alike to eliminate conventional sentiment and morality.

A certain use of the term ἀρετή by Thucydides has an interest in this connexion. It is sometimes said that he did not assign great importance to the action and rôle of individuals. This seems to me a mistake, due to the circumstance that he does not draw personal portraits in the manner of subsequent historians. For it is evident that he considered the brains and wisdom of him whom he calls "the first man" as largely responsible for the success of Athenian policy before the Peloponnesian war. We can read between the lines that in his view the Peisistratids, Themistocles, and Alcibiades were also forces which counted for a great deal. The pre-eminent significance of the individual was a tenet of Machiavelli and his contemporaries (a classical feature of the Renaissance) ; it was a prince, an individual brain and will, to which he looked for the deliverance and regeneration of Italy. Both writers conceived the individual, as a political factor, purely from the intellectual side. Now Thucydides has used ἀρετή in his notice of the oligarch Antiphon, to express the intelligence, dexterity, and will-power of a competent statesman, in sharp contradistinction to the conventional ἀρετή of the popular conception. The only appropriate equivalent by which we can render in a modern language this Thucydidean ἀρετή is a key-word of Machiavelli's system, *virtù*, a quality possessed by men like Francesco Sforza and Cesare Borgia.[1]

It must be understood that this attitude of Thucydides only concerns international politics, the subject of his work. Domestic politics lie, except incidentally, outside his scope. When he turns aside to describe the disintegrating influence of party faction on the internal conditions of Greek states, he recognises the important operation of ethical beliefs and religious sanctions in holding a society together. But where national aims are at stake and international rivalries are in motion, no corresponding beliefs and sanctions appear, possessing the same indefeasible value for the success and prosperity of a state. There is irony in his remark that the Lacedaemonians, after the first war had come to an end, ascribed their own want of success to the fact that they had refused the Athenian proposition to submit the Peloponnesian grievances to arbitration, in accordance with the Thirty Years' Peace. It is noteworthy that in the Funeral Oration of Pericles,

---

[1] Since writing this paragraph, I observe that Murray had already compared this ἀρετή to *virtù* (in his chapter on Thucydides, *History of Greek Literature*).

where he pourtrays the qualities of his countrymen, there is not a single word about those conventional virtues in which Nicias shone. The Athenians are praised for their political intelligence and versatility, for their adventurous activity, for enlightened freedom in their intercourse with strangers, and for other excellent things. Not a word is said of their piety, and they were certainly pious. We are told that they have accomplished much and reached the heights by their own talents and their own toil. There is not a word, not a single perfunctory phrase, of assistance or favour from heaven. Of religion, or of morality in the conventional sense, there is not a syllable from the beginning to the end of this brilliant speech. Pericles could hardly have avoided at least some conventional reference to the gods, in the speech he actually delivered at the sepulture ; that Thucydides overlooked it is significant.

If this appreciation of the historian is sympathetic, I hope you will not suppose that I belong to the band of devotees who make a cult of Thucydides and can see no defects in their idol. Such devotees existed in ancient as well as in modern times, and the historian's ancient indiscriminating admirers received a very proper rebuke from Dionysius of Halicarnassus. I have already suggested that he carried his method of exclusion and omission too far. His treatment of individuals displays a more serious limitation in his idea of historical reconstruction. Thucydides does not seem to have grasped fully that in estimating the action of an individual in history his whole character must be taken into account; he is a psychical unity, and it is not possible to detach and isolate certain qualities. Psychological reconstruction is one of the most important as well as delicate problems which encounter the historian, and Thucydides failed to realise all that it means. In his impatience of biographical trivialities, he went to the extreme of neglecting biography altogether. Take, for instance, his silence concerning the personality of Pericles. This statesman was one of the forces which operated in bringing about the war, and to understand his actions we want to know more about his personality. Thucydides is content to note his consummate political ability and his indifference to money, and to indicate his idealism. This does not enable us to realise what manner of man Pericles was; we still feel, and modern criticism illustrates this, that he is in many respects an unknown or at least ambiguous quantity.

The work of Thucydides has limitations which we must beware of underrating; but it marks the longest and most decisive step that has ever been taken by a single man towards making history what it is to-day. Out of the twilight in which Herodotus still moved wondering, he burst into the sunlight where facts are hard, not to wonder but to understand. With the Greeks historical study never acquired the scientific character which it was reserved for the nineteenth century to

impress upon it. But within the limits of the task
he attempted Thucydides was a master in the craft
of investigating contemporary events, and it may
be doubted whether within those limits the nineteenth century would have much to teach him. If
he had admitted his readers into the secrets of his
workshop, if he had more clearly displayed his raw
material and shown how he arrived at his conclusion, if he had argued and discussed, he might have
exercised a greater influence than he did on the
methods of subsequent Greek historians. His incomplete work, posthumously published, had an
immediate and far-reaching result in establishing
political history ; and in the next lecture we shall
see how men of the younger generation received a
stimulus from him. But, although the value and
greatness of his work were at once recognised,
and he always remained the one and undisputed
authority on the period he had treated, yet, for
several centuries after his immediate successors,
his history seems to have been little read except
by scholars ; he was a great name, not a living
influence as a teacher or a model. His style, with
its " old-fashioned and wilful beauty,"[1] repelled, and
other ideals of history, sharply opposed to his,
came into fashion. It was not till the first century
B.C., with the return to Attic models, that the
interest in his work revived ; and from that time
we can trace his influence on leading writers[2] down

---

[1] ἀρχαϊκόν τε καὶ αὔθαδες κάλλος, Dionysius, περὶ συνθ. ὀν. 165.
[2] Dexippus and Procopius are instances.

to one of the latest Byzantine historians, Crito-
bulus. But this influence was of a superficial kind ;
it concerned style and phraseology ; it was generally
a mere mechanical imitation.[1] And the historians
whom he would himself have most esteemed were
not those who came under his own influence.

[1] The servile imitation of Thucydides is ridiculed in Lucian's πῶς δεῖ
ἱστορίαν συγγράφειν ;

LECTURE V

THE DEVELOPMENT OF GREEK HISTORIOGRAPHY
AFTER THUCYDIDES

§ 1. *The generation after Thucydides*

THUCYDIDES had set up a new standard and
proposed a new model for historical investigation.
He taught the Greeks to write contemporary
political history ; this was the permanent result
of his work. But the secret of his critical methods
may be said to have perished with him ; it has
been reserved for modern students fully to appreciate his critical acumen, and to estimate the
immense labours which underlay the construction
of his history but are carefully concealed like the
foundation stones of a building. Influences came
into play in the fourth century which drove history
along other paths than those which he marked out ;
the best of the principles which his work had
inculcated did not become canonical ; and his
historical treatment was not sympathetic under
the new intellectual constellations.

The age succeeding his death was perhaps not
favourable to the composition of political history.[1]

---

[1] This is an observation of von Wilamowitz-Möllendorff.

The engrossing intellectual interest was then
political science, and the historical method had
not been invented. The men who might otherwise have shone as historians were engaged in
speculations on the nature of the state. They
were eagerly seeking an answer to the speculative
question : What is the best constitution ? Only
three historians of note arose in this period ; they
were more or less under the influence of Thucydides, but at long intervals behind.

Of these the only name familiar to posterity is
Xenophon, who was probably the least meritorious
of the three. To the circumstance that he is one
of the very few classical Greek historians whose
work has survived, he owes a prominence to which
his qualities do not entitle him.[1] In history as in
philosophy he was a dilettante ; he was as far
from understanding the methods of Thucydides as
he was from apprehending the ideas of Socrates.
He had a happy literary talent, and his multifarious
writings, taken together, render him an interesting figure in Greek literature. But his mind
was essentially mediocre, incapable of penetrating
beneath the surface of things. If he had lived
in modern days, he would have been a high-
class journalist and pamphleteer ; he would have
made his fortune as a war-correspondent ; and

---

[1] The preservation of his works is due to the overestimate which was
formed of him under the Atticistic revival ; he was canonized by literary
judges, with Thucydides and Herodotus. Cp. Lucian, πῶς δεῖ 4, "Every-
body wants to be a Thucydides, a Herodotus or a Xenophon " (Θουκυδίδαι
καὶ Ἡρόδοτοι καὶ Ξενοφῶντες).

would have written the life of some mediocre
hero of the stamp of Agesilaus. So far as
history is concerned, his true vocation was to
write memoirs. The *Anabasis* is a memoir, and
it is the most successful of his works. It has the
defects which memoirs usually have, but it has
the merits, the freshness, the human interest of
a personal document. The adventures of the Ten
Thousand are alive for ever in Xenophon's pages.

He took up the story of the Peloponnesian war
where Thucydides had left it, and he carried down
the history of Greece from that date to the fall
of the Theban supremacy, in the work which we
know as the *Hellenica*. By this work his powers
as a historian must be judged. Some of its
characteristics are due to the superficial lessons
which the author learned from the founder of
political history. In the first portion of the book[1]
he employed strictly the annalistic plan of Thucydides. He adopted the device of introducing
speeches, and the objective method of allowing the
actors to reveal themselves in their acts and words.
He does not himself pourtray their characters, as he
pourtrays Cyrus and the generals in the *Anabasis*.
But he never goes down below the surface of
events ; he never analyses the deeper motives ; and
he writes with little disguise of his own predilections.
His history is an apotheosis of Agesilaus ; he does
not conceal his strong philo-Laconian leanings or
his hatred of Thebes ; he pointedly ignores Epami-

---

[1] B. i. and B. ii. to iii. 10.

nondas. His ideas about historical happenings were
those of the average, conventional Athenian; and
he ascribes the fall of the Spartan supremacy to
divine nemesis, avenging the treacherous occupa-
tion of the Theban citadel. He cannot resist the
commonplace attraction of commonplace moralising; he tells anecdotes which his austere predecessor would have disdained; but he has learned
from Thucydides to keep to the matter in hand.

Other works of Xenophon had more influence
than the *Hellenica*, on subsequent historiography;
or, as it would probably be safer to say, reflected an
interest which was to become not only permanent
in literature but a conspicuous feature in history.
I am referring to biography. Interest, deliberate
and serious interest, in individual personalities, had
been awakened by the sophistic illumination; and
Euripides probably did as much as any single man
to heighten and deepen it. A new branch of
literature, biography, emerged; and the word βίος,
life, acquired a new meaning, charged with the
whole contents of a man's actions and character.
Biography was founded by Isocrates and the pupils
of Socrates. The earliest biography we possess is
the *Evagoras* of Isocrates, and it is to this model
that we owe the second, the *Agesilaus* of Xenophon. In other works of Isocrates also there are
biographical sketches, and perhaps the portraits in
the *Anabasis* were due to his influence.[1] We can

---

[1] They remind us of the character-portraits of the dead Argive leaders
in the *Suppliants* of Euripides (861 sqq.).

see too that the original personality of Socrates, which made a deep impression on his disciples, was effective in helping to establish this kind of literature ; most of them used their pens ; and the incidental portraiture of Plato, and the *Memoirs* of Xenophon, which are not a Life, have their significance for the rise of biography. I have not to follow its further development or to show how it was stimulated by the Peripatetic school.[1] As a literary art ancient biography reached its highest perfection in Plutarch's gallery of great men. That series is invaluable to us, because the author consulted many books which are now lost ; but he was not a historian ; his interest was ethical. What we are here concerned to note is that, after Xenophon and Isocrates, historians generally considered sketches of character and biographical facts to be part of their business. It was a feature which was flagrantly liable to abuse, and often led to irrelevancies, which would have shocked Thucydides. But although, in practice, ancient character-portraits tended to be conventional and uninstructive, it was in principle an important advance to recognise that the analysis of character and personality has historical value, and cannot be confined within the limits which Thucydides had allowed.

The continuation of Thucydides was taken up by another writer who seems to have had a truer

[1] For these remarks on the rise of biography I have used F. Leo's admirable work *Die griechisch-römische Biographie* (1901).

calling than Xenophon to exercise the historian's
trade. Cratippus was one of the obscurest figures
in literature, and till a few months ago we had not
even a fragment to indicate the character of his
work. But a passage of Plutarch might suggest
that his history possessed more than ordinary
merit. "If there were no men of action," Plutarch
observes,[1] "there would be no historians. Abolish
Pericles, Phormio, Nicias, and the rest, and you
eliminate Thucydides. Abolish Alcibiades, Thra-
sybulus, and Conon, and you abolish Cratippus."
Here Cratippus is singled out as the leading
historian of Athens for the years subsequent to the
termination of Thucydides, and as one whose loss
would be acknowledged to be an impoverishment
of historical literature. The passage also leads us
to infer that Cratippus carried his continuation as
far as the naval victory of Cnidus, 394 B.C., which
enabled Athens to win back an independent and
eminent position in the Greek world. Egypt,
which has yielded so many invaluable relics of
classical literature to the indefatigable explorations
of the eminent Oxford scholars, Grenfell and
Hunt, has recently enriched us with a treasure,
which, I have little doubt, is a portion of the
work of Cratippus. This substantial fragment
covers a part of the year 396 B.C. and most of the
year 395, so that it may represent more than
a twentieth part of the whole history. Some
eminent scholars claim for it the authorship of

---

[1] *De Glor. Athen.* ad init. (ed. Bernardakis, ii. p. 455).

Theopompus; but the weight of evidence, in my opinion, is entirely against that theory; while there is nothing inconsistent with the authorship of Cratippus (the only other admissible claimant[1]), which was advocated by Blass. As no relics of the work of Cratippus have been preserved in literature, we have no direct positive evidence for the identification. The case rests (1) on the argument by exclusion; the claims made for other candidates cannot be reconciled with the character of the fragment; (2) on the circumstance that the few things we know about Cratippus correspond to the indications of the new text. The narrative bears the stamp of an original composition by a contemporary (like that of Thucydides, and

---

[1] The only other; for the claim put forward for Androtion by G. de Sanctis (see Bibliography) is obviously out of court. It is enough to say here that the narrative of the campaigns of Agesilaus could not possibly have appeared in Androtion's Attic history.—The case against Theopompus, who is considered to be the author by Wilamowitz-Möllendorff and E. Meyer, has been stated impartially by Grenfell and Hunt, who, however, incline to this theory, and has been forcibly presented by De Sanctis. I will not go over the arguments which they have put so well. But I would emphasize that the few positive indications of contact between the papyrus and fragments of Theopompus may be otherwise accounted for (as Theopompus would naturally have used Cratippus); that what we know about the life of Theopompus, unsatisfactory as it is, renders it highly unlikely that he wrote his *Hellenica* before 350 B.C. ; and that the hypothesis—to which the advocates of his authorship are forced to resort—that the *Hellenica* was entirely different in the style of treatment from the *Philippica*, is contradicted by a passage of Porphyrius (Eusebius, *Praep. evang.* x. 3, cited by De Sanctis in his tract, p. 9) and by the way in which Dionysius (in his appreciation in the *Letter to Pompeius*, 6) associates both works closely together and describes the character of his "historiography" without the faintest suggestion that the earlier work presented a radical contrast to the later. [Since the above was written, papers have appeared by W. A. Goligher, in the *English Historical Review*, April 1908, and W. Rhys Roberts, in the *Classical Review*, June 1908, arguing against the Theopompus theory.]

even more so than Xenophon's *Hellenica*), not compiled from books. We can see that it was written without knowledge of Xenophon's work. The lower limit of its date can hardly be later than about 350 B.C.[1] Now Cratippus, we know, was a younger contemporary of Thucydides,[2] and his literary activity must have been subsequent to the death of Thucydides (c. 396 B.C.) whose work he continued; so that chronology as well as subject accords with the hypothesis of his authorship. There are no speeches, and one of the things we know about Cratippus is that he disapproved of the speeches in Thucydides and considered the absence of them in the last Book a proof that Thucydides had come to regard them as undesirable.[3] The narrative is lucid and simple, unadorned by rhetorical phrases and free from didactic commonplaces. It is also extremely dull; but it would be illegitimate to judge from this particular section that the work as a whole could not have evoked the praise implied by Plutarch. If nothing were left to us of Thucydides but, say, the last thirty chapters of the third Book, with the tedious account of the Acarnanian operations of Demosthenes, what a dull writer we should esteem him. We can see that the author was not given to passing personal criticisms; no hard words are said of any one; a slight approbation is accorded to an act of Conon; and one much-mutilated

---

[1] E. M. Walker thinks it was written before the end of the Phocian war.

[2] Dionysius, *De Thucydide*, 16.

[3] *Ib.*

passage contains apparently a characteristic of a statesman, whose identity can hardly be determined.[1] This evidence does not enable us to decide whether Cratippus adopted the objective method of Thucydides in regard to the personalities of the historical actors. But in other matters at least he condescended to his readers. He explains the relations and actions of political parties; he traces the growth of anti-Spartan feeling in Greece; and of the constitution of Boeotia he gives as clear an account as could be desired in a handbook, an account which shows us that we were ignorant of its real nature. The general impression I gain from the fragment is that if the work had survived it would occupy a distinctly higher place than the *Hellenica* of Xenophon, though the author did not possess Xenophon's technical knowledge of warfare.

The discovery of Grenfell and Hunt has added to our knowledge of facts, but for our present purpose its interest lies in showing on what lines the writing of contemporary history, founded by Thucydides, might have developed in the hands of men, not endowed with his brain-power and originality, but competent and diligent, if it had not been diverted from an independent path by forces which I will presently notice.

[1] The passage, on which nothing persuasive has been suggested, is in col. x., where οὐ γὰρ ὥσπερ ο[ἱ(?)πλεῖστοι τῶν δυ]ναστευόντων and δη[μο]τικωτ are the slight clues. Could it possibly be Dionysius of Syracuse? That Sparta was interested in some of his proceedings described by Diodorus, xiv. 7. 8, might conceivably have led to a mention of him here and a digression on his policy.

The influence of Thucydides was probably more marked in another contemporary historian, who moved in another part of the world and had a different horizon, Philistus of Syracuse. Like Thucydides, he had experience of public affairs, and suffered exile, and lived to be recalled. He did not confine himself to contemporary history, as Thucydides did, for he related the story of Sicily from the very beginning down to the time of his own youth—he had been an eye-witness of the Athenian expedition. But his more important work was the history of the two tyrants Dionysius, father and son, a record of events in which he had himself played an active part both as politician and military commander. He enjoyed the posthumous distinction of being the only historian whose works followed Alexander, along with the great poets, to Further Asia, and, as Freeman says, "the reason of the choice is plain enough. Nowhere could Alexander find reading more to his taste than in the history of Dionysius, the first man who carried on war on a scale and after a fashion at all approaching to his own."[1] Philistus made Thucydides his model,[2] not by a slavish imitation of his style, but rather in temper and method, and we may suspect that of all Greek historians he was most Thucydidean. He

---

[1] *History of Sicily*, iii. 63.
[2] Dionysius, περὶ μιμήσεως, 426 (Usener and Radermacher, p. 208); Cicero, *De Orat.* ii. 13. The differences in style between Thucydides and Philistus are explained by Dionysius, *Letter to Pompey*, 5. The style of Philistus was tediously uniform.

is thus appraised by Cicero, who, though he lived in a day when other styles of history were in fashion, had a keen literary sense. "Philistus," he writes to his brother Quintus, who was engaged in reading the Sicilian author, is "a writer of the first rank, pithy, sagacious, concise, almost a miniature Thucydides."[1] Cicero's portrait suggests that Philistus displayed Thucydidean qualities beyond conciseness and the faculty of keeping strictly to the point; and this we know from other evidence. The court of the old fox (*veterator*) Dionysius the Elder, of whom he was an intimate confidant before his disgrace, was a school of statecraft and political casuistry, in which the imitator of Thucydides could well learn to study political phenomena from the non-moral attitude of his exemplar. But the mere fact that Philistus undertook to write in detail the early history of Sicily raises a presumption that he was less sceptical than the Athenian; and as a matter of fact he did not disdain to record wonders and omens, such as the appearance of a swarm of bees alighting on the mane of a horse, which was taken to presignify the reign of Dionysius.[2]

§ 2. *The influence of rhetoric*

During the period in which these three historians, Philistus, Cratippus, and Xenophon, wrote,

---

[1] "Capitalis creber acutus brevis paene pusillus Thucydides": *ad Q. fr.* ii. 11. I give the renderings of Tyrrell and Purser, vol. ii. ed. 2, p. 136.
[2] Cicero, *Div.* 1. 33 = fr. 48. Cp. fr. 57.

the educated Greek world was succumbing to the
spell of two influences, towards which Thucydides
had been detached and independent. I refer to
rhetoric and philosophy. You are all familiar with
the immense influence which Isocrates exerted on
literature and education. He was not a man of
genius, yet at no age, perhaps, can we find a single
man who in this sphere held such a magisterial
position. Greeks from every part of the world
repaired to his school at Athens, and his rules for
style were canonical. I need not illustrate this,
but will go on to show how he affected the development of historiography and especially through two
eminent admirers, Ephorus and Theopompus.

And first of all I may point out how the
political view of which Isocrates was the most
conspicuous exponent affected history. The rise
of Macedon in the middle of the fourth century,
and the gradual fulfilment of the aspiration for
the union of Greece, under Macedonian direction,
brought to the front what was virtually a new
conception of Hellenic history. Hitherto, history
had been either sectional, the histories of particular
states or groups, or had been concerned with
particular episodes, such as the joint efforts of the
Greek states against the Persian or inter-Hellenic
wars. But the idea of Greek unity preached by
Isocrates, and taking the special form of unity under
Macedonian leadership against Persia, reacted upon
history, and no fewer than three works were
written in the days of Philip and Alexander,

which were inspired by the idea of the unity of
Greek history. Two of them have vanished,
leaving not a trace except the mere record of
their existence. One was by Zoilus, whose name
is better remembered for his carping criticisms
of Homer which earned him the nickname of
Homero-mastix, Homer's scourge.[1] The other was
by his pupil Anaximenes, who was one of the
teachers of Alexander. Both these historians were
submerged in oblivion by the success of the third,
Ephorus of Cyme. He is said to have been a
pupil of Isocrates, but I do not think that this is
established.[2] The work to which he devoted his
life, beginning with the mythical origins of Greece
and embracing the barbarian peoples with which
the Greeks came into contact, was probably
intended to terminate with the year 334, when
Alexander crossed into Asia, but only reached
as far as 356, in consequence of the author's
death. It became and remained one of the
standard works of antiquity, and established what
has been aptly described as "the vulgate of Greek
history." It is usual to designate this book, which,
although it has perished, is inwoven in the narratives of our later authorities, so that we know a
good deal about it indirectly, as the first universal
history; and so it is described by Polybius. But
it is important to discriminate the precise sense in
which we can admit this description. We must

---

[1] His work came down to Philip's death.
[2] Cp. Schwartz, art. "Ephoros," in Pauly-Wissowa.

always remember that the Greeks had never formed a nation; they were never united even in an all-embracing federation; they had no national history in the proper sense of the word. The bond of community among them was the general homogeneity or unity of their civilisation. Now the novelty of the work of Ephorus lay in this, that, recognising this unity of culture which contained potentialities of a real Hellenic nation, he brought together the particular histories of all Greek-speaking communities, and thus produced what might be called a quasi-national history. But it was distinctly a history of Greece, *Hellenica*, not a history of the world; non-Greek peoples only came in so far as they were connected with Greek history; and the title "universal" can be applied, not on the ground that the author, like Herodotus, comprised portions of non-Greek history, but in the limited sense that all the Greeks were embraced. To some extent the chronicles of Hellanicus had been an anticipation of this idea of Ephorus and his contemporaries.

It became the fashion at this time to divide large works into books. The history of Ephorus consisted of twenty-nine Books, of which each was a unity in itself and had a preface of its own.[1] Thus it was not constructed on the annalistic

---

[1] A thirtieth Book was added by the author's son, coming down to the siege of Perinthus, 340-339 B.C. The treatment must have been considerably more summary than in the work of Ephorus himself, whose last ten Books seem to have covered not more than thirty-four years (since 390 B.C. was treated in Book XIX.). See Schwartz, *op. cit.* pp. 5, 6.

method. The author seems to have had a wide acquaintance with the whole range of historical and geographical literature, and he did not copy uncritically. He was fully conscious of the value of first-hand information, and we may note his acute observation, wondering how far he applied it, that in the history of modern times the most detailed accounts are the most credible, but for ancient history those who profess to know most particulars are the least worthy of belief. His critical principles led him formally to throw over the purely mythical period and begin with the return of the Heracleidae; but he did not carry out consistently this counsel of wisdom; in the course of his narrative he introduced myths and indulged in the crude methods of rationalising which had been initiated by the Ionians.

I cannot enter into a detailed account of the work of Ephorus, and must be content just to mention characteristics for which the influence of Isocrates is responsible. Among them may be noticed the interruption of the narrative by moralising platitudes; the introduction of elaborate Isocratean speeches, even when an army was facing the enemy; and the passion for panegyrics. These features, and his conventional battle-scenes, which conformed more or less to a model scheme, manifest the same tendency to sacrifice truth to effect. History is becoming epideictic, like oratory and poetry, and desires to show off. And this is what is meant by saying that historiography was

drawn under the pernicious influence of rhetoric.
One does not mean by that, the cultivation of
a clear, agreeable, and rhythmical style; one means
the tendency to seek first of all and almost at any
cost what may be called rhetorical effects.

The other famous historian of the Isocratean
school, Theopompus, continued the work of Thucydides in his *Hellenica*, which covered the same
period as Cratippus and for which he must have
derived his material mainly from older works, such
as those of Cratippus himself and Xenophon.
His more important effort was the *Philippica*, a
history of Greek affairs in the time of Philip, and
here he was in the full sense an original contemporary writer.[1] He, too, was affected by the
national idea of Isocrates; he saw in the Macedonian power a unifying principle, and he made
it the pivot of his contemporary history. But it
is notable that he called that history, not Mace-
donica, but Philippica. It was a new thing to
treat a period as "the age of Philip."

He was probably the most interesting historian
of the fourth century. But some have even
pronounced him truly great, worthy to rank near
Thucydides. The evidence is sufficient to disprove
such a claim.[2] The Isocratean features which were
common to him with Ephorus are decisive. And
if we observe that he was more concerned with

---

[1] This work (which was not published before 324 B.C., cp. frags. 108,
334) consisted of fifty-eight Books.

[2] See Wachsmuth, *Einleitung*, 537 sqq.

the private morality of men of action than with their political or military capacity, that he served up miracles and fables, and related a figment of his own invention concerning the imaginary land of Merope beyond the ocean, where the golden age is still a reality,[1] we may see that any comparison with Thucydides is almost ludicrously inappropriate. He seems to have been a man of restless vanity, endowed with what we might call an epideictic temper. While Ephorus devoted his life to study without personal ambition, Theopompus travelled about, eager to cut a figure in the world, like Gorgias and others of the early sophists. He had a "temper," revealed in his writings and infusing a spice, which was lacking in the flavourless works of Ephorus and Cratippus. He was a psychological analyst, and he was more inclined to be censorious than panegyrical. The critic Dionysius says that his great aim was to dive into the profundities of the human soul and discover the secret wickedness almost invariably lurking beneath the semblance of virtue.[2]

In judging these new tendencies to which history succumbed under the Isocratean régime, we must bear in mind that they responded to the taste of the public which Isocrates did much to educate. In old days Homer and the epic poets satisfied the

---

[1] He said expressly that in myths he would outdo Herodotus, Ctesias, and οἱ τὰ Ἰνδικὰ συγγράψαντες. Strabo, i. 2. 35.

[2] *Letter to Pompey*, 6, 7. "I suppose," adds Dionysius, "that the mythical judges in Hades conduct their trials of the dead with the punctual severity of Theopompus."

requirements of a large public. Herodotus similarly appealed to public taste and public interest. Thucydides had a different object in view. He formed a standard of historical truth, and deliberately renounced the idea of making his book a popular success. We may conjecture with high probability that the works of his successors Cratippus and Philistus had a very small and select circle of readers. Ephorus and Theopompus determined to win the public ear. It was not enough to write; they wanted to be read. From this point of view they represented a reversion to the days before Thucydides. But they had a different audience to please from that which listened to Herodotus, and they captured votes by accommodating history to the rhetorical effects for which the public cared. This was a natural instinct of self-preservation. At all events, the craving for the achievement of popular success dominated historiography henceforward; the exceptions to the rule are few.

Under Isocrates, Athens had been the educational and literary centre of Greece. The primacy passed away from her in the greater Greece created through the conquests of Alexander; she was no longer the arbitress of taste or the leader of intellectual fashion. In the field of history, Timaeus of Tauromenium illustrates the transition from Attic to Hellenistic literature. He lived through vast political changes. Born two years before Chaeronea, he survived the outbreak of the First Punic war. Driven from Sicily by Agathocles for political

reasons in his youth, he found a new home at
Athens, where he devoted the rest of his long life[1]
to a history of Sicily and Italy. He not only
ransacked literature, but travelled for the purpose
of his work, sparing neither time nor money to
gain accurate information about the ill-known
western nations, Iberians, Celts, and Ligurians.
He made a special investigation of chronology, and
was the first to introduce into Greek historiography the clumsy, inconvenient method of
reckoning time by the Olympiac years. His work
(in thirty-three Books) came down to 320 B.C., but
he continued it in a history of Agathocles, and in
a later book which reached to 264 B.C. and included the campaigns of Pyrrhus. Timaeus was
not only used extensively by subsequent historians,
especially by Diodorus, but his history was recognised as an authoritative storehouse of information
by the scholars and poets of Alexandria, such as
Apollonius, Lycophron, Callimachus, and Eratosthenes. The material furnished by this means has
enabled Geffcken to restore the general construction of the first two Books of his chief work, dealing with the mythical history and geography of
Sicily and Italy. For us his merit lies in his industrious collection of ethnographical facts and
local legends, material which is still of value; but
this merit would never have sufficed to secure him
the popularity and authority which he enjoyed for
many generations after his death, if his history had

---

[1] 340-256 B.C. ; exiled 317 B.C.

not possessed other features which we should mark
as his weak points. When he came to Athens he
studied rhetoric under a pupil of Isocrates, and his
work had characteristics which we expect from the
Isocratean school, such as speeches packed with
commonplaces, and the conventional administration
of praise and blame. He had also weaknesses of
his own. He was a thorough pedant, without
sense of proportion or the faculty to discriminate
weighty from trivial things; interested in disconnected details; fond of fables and marvels. He
was also something of a mystic. He sought to
show, for instance, that to every sinner punishment, unmistakable as such, was meted out, and
that coincidences of date had a transcendent significance; he was ever on the watch for the revelation
of mysterious or daemonic influences in historical
events. Again, his history of the contemporary period
must have been far from impartial. His extravagant admiration of Timoleon was the counterpart
of his failure to recognise any but the worst qualities
of Agathocles, whom he hated on account of his
own banishment, which had embittered his mind.

Living in the Attic atmosphere and trained in
Isocratean rhetoric, we should expect to find Timaeus
conforming to the canons of Attic style. But it
appears that he adopted a new kind of writing
which bade farewell to the traditions of Attic taste.
It is impossible to decide whether he struck out
this new way for himself, or came under the
influence of Hegesias of Magnesia, who is always

designated as the founder of the famous school of style which came to be known as the Asianic. As we do not know the precise dates of the life of Hegesias, we cannot say whether he and Timaeus were independent of each other. The literary parentage of this new style is to be sought in the prose of the elder sophists, like Gorgias and Alcidamas; but it outdid anything that Gorgias in his most frigid moments had been tempted to essay. It produces the impression of a bacchic revel of rhythms and verbal effects. This Asianic movement triumphed; the general public lost the power of appreciating Attic measure and Attic sanity; and the new style was predominant for two hundred years. Nor did it disappear when the reaction came and Attic models again came into fashion. On the contrary, as Norden has shown, the two styles, the archaic and the modern, contended for mastery throughout the ages of the Roman Empire. For instance, in the fourth century A.D. we have a great archaic rhetorician, Libanius, thrilling Antioch with his eloquence, while a great modern sophist, Himerius, was teaching the art of style at Athens.

Of the modern style, in its early or Asianic period, we have very few specimens, but we know that it comprised two distinct kinds—the pretty style and the bombastic style. The bombastic suited the taste of grandiose Hellenistic princes, and it so happens that the one considerable example we possess of it is a long inscription of Antiochus

of Commagene (discovered in 1890), in which the
King describes his achievements.   It is, as Norden
says, a prose dithyramb.   But the other, the pretty
style, was the more popular and more important;
it was the style in which Timaeus experimented
and which Hegesias established.   It is not easy to
reproduce the effect of this style in a modern
language, because it depends so much on rhythm;
but in order to show the sort of thing you would
find in the most popular works of the lost literature of the third and second centuries B.C., I will
quote a passage of Hegesias, who wrote a history
of Alexander the Great.   The historian makes the
following comment, shall I call it? or dirge, on that
monarch's destruction of Thebes:[1]

> In rasing to earth Thebes, O Alexander,
> Thine hand a deed has done,
> Such as Zeus would do
> Were he to cast the moon utterly
> Out from yon heaven's section;
> For the sun as a fitting symbol I keep for Athens.
> Verily these cities twain were visual orbs of Hellas;
> So that now for the one of the pair in pain I travail.

---

[1] Fr. 2 (ed. Müller, *Scr. rer. Alexandri Magni*, p. 140):

> ὅμοιον πεποίηκας Ἀλέξανδρε
> Θήβας κατασκάψας,
> ὡς ἂν εἰ ὁ Ζεὺς
> ἐκ τῆς κατ' οὐρανὸν μερίδος
> ἐκβάλοι τὴν σελήνην.
> τὸν γὰρ ἥλιον ὑπολείπομαι ταῖς Ἀθήναις.
> δύο γὰρ αὗται πόλεις
> τῆς Ἑλλάδος ἦσαν ὄψεις.
> διὸ καὶ περὶ τῆς ἑτέρας ἀγωνιῶ νῦν.
> ὁ μὲν γὰρ εἷς αὐτῶν ὀφθαλμὸς ἡ Θηβαίων
> ἐκκέκοπται πόλις.

See the rhythmical analysis in Norden, *Griechische Kunstprosa*, i. 136.

For Hellas hath lost half her vision, one eye knocked out,
Even the Theban town.

This means in plain language : Athens and
Thebes are in Greece what the sun and moon are
in the sky ; or they may be likened to the two
eyes of Greece, and Alexander in destroying
Thebes has deprived Greece of one eye. I have
made an attempt to imitate the rhythm, though it
is indeed impossible to catch the effect in another
language, or perhaps to appreciate it even in the
Greek. But the example will illustrate the
poetical character of the Asianic style. Is not
this passage what one might look for in the
chorus of a third-rate historical tragedy ?

The popularity which Timaeus enjoyed for a
couple of centuries mirrors the public taste, and he
would hardly have enjoyed it if he had adhered to
the canons of Attic style, which drew a sharp line
between poetry and prose. But there was another
school of historical art bidding for public favour in
the days of Timaeus. It was initiated by Duris
of Samos, a pupil of Theophrastus. He became,
through some stroke of luck, tyrant of Samos, and
he wrote a history of Greece from 370 B.C. to 281,
a biography of Agathocles, and a chronicle of his
native city. He declared war on what I may call
the conventional school of Ephorus and Theopompus, asserting that these writers failed to excite
the pleasure which history, differently treated, is
capable of affording. They lacked, he said,
mimêsis. *Mimêsis* is the nearest Greek equivalent

of "realism"; and we shall not be far from the mark if we say that what Duris demanded was realism, and if we call his school the realistic school. Duris was intensely interested in the theatre; he wrote books on tragedy and the history of art; and it was this interest in drama that inspired him with the idea that historians should aim at producing the same kinds of effect as dramatists. He required, for instance, that they should introduce their personages dressed in the costumes appropriate to the time and circumstances. But his chief point of insistence was that the feelings of the readers should be moved and harrowed by highly wrought pathetic scenes, conjured up by the writer's imagination; while they were also to be entertained by anecdotes and gossip and amorous stories. He achieved a success with the public, and naturally his success was followed up by others. For example, Phylarchus, who wrote an important history of the years 272-220 B.C., is blamed by Polybius as "feminine" because he aimed at moving his readers to tears.[1] That was the influence of Duris.

There was a good deal to be said for the instinct of Duris in his reaction against conventionalism. The power of realising and vividly describing scenes of the past is a high merit in a historical writer, provided he has the material necessary for constructing a true picture. But this proviso is

---

[1] We must remember that Polybius was disposed to be unfavourable to Phylarchus as a partisan of Cleomenes.

sure to be overlooked when the writer's first consideration is not truth, but effect. And so it was with Duris. His school, like the conventionalists, subordinated history in the Thucydidean sense to literary art. The conventionalists appealed to taste, the realists appealed also to the emotions. The former edified, the latter excited. But for both alike history was simply a branch of rhetoric.

We may regret this corruption, as we call it, of history. But it is more to the purpose to understand the Greek point of view. It is not easy for us to realise the importance which the art of rhetoric possessed for the Greeks, as a purveyor of aesthetic pleasure. Indeed, the history of Greek rhetoric testifies, perhaps as impressively as the history of Greek plastic, to the large part which aesthetic pleasure played in Greek life. For the later Greeks, the declamations of rhetoricians, which we find intolerably tedious to read, had as intense an aesthetic value as the Homeric poems for their remote ancestors, and were listened to with as eagerly attentive and as critical ears. People went to hear a rhetorical display just as we go to hear a symphony. And this interest lasted down to late Graeco-Roman times. Greek prose was always an art in as full a sense as the poetry from which it sprang, regulated by principles and canons, which have no counterpart in modern languages, even in French, and required prolonged study and practice. And rhetoric came to fulfil for Greek audiences the same rôle which had been

once fulfilled by the epics. Just as the historians, or
as we should say mythologers, of the Homeric age
were epic poets, so the later historians were rhetoricians. If the historian were not trained in the school
of the rhetorician he would have had few readers.

Again, history and geography were the great
field from which light reading was provided for the
educated public. The later historians helped to
satisfy the same need of entertainment which had
formerly been met by the tales of the epic poets
or the historical anecdotes of the sixth and fifth
centuries. There was no special literature yet of
romances and novels, and the functions of our
modern novelists were to a great extent fulfilled by
the historians. History had to answer the purpose
now answered by fiction, and it is not surprising if
it tended to partake of the nature of fiction.

The knowledge of strange lands won by the
conquests of Alexander the Great stimulated the
appetite for marvels and provided abundant food.
It was not necessary to imagine, as Theopompus did, a land of Merope; there was now an
actual background and there were actual adventures; history could appear without excuse as
romance, and romance could mask as history.
The sober and veracious relations of Alexander's
achievements, the political Memoir of Aristobulus
and the military Memoir of Ptolemy, fell dead;
and four centuries elapsed before the excellent
Arrian composed the first history of the Macedonian hero's conquests that was based on these

and some other trustworthy sources,[1] with a rigorous rejection of the literature which was written πρὸς ὄχλον καὶ θέατρον, not only, I am afraid, as we say " for the gallery," but for the stalls too. The great popular success was won by Cleitarchus, a rhetor of Colophon,[2] who made the most of the possibilities of his theme and captured his public by fantastic descriptions of the gorgeous East. This quasi-historical work became the standard book on the subject, and seems to have exerted a deep influence on the traditional history of Alexander.

But while such romances captivated the public, those plain veracious reports of Ptolemy, Aristobulus, and Nearchus have an important place in the development of historiography. They founded a new branch of historical literature,[3] which in the next generations was represented by the Memoirs of Pyrrhus and of Aratus, to be succeeded in Roman days by the Commentaries of Julius Caesar, the Memoirs of Corbulo, and Trajan's history of his Dacian wars. The Commentaries of Caesar fulfilled indeed, in a most subtle way, the function of political pamphlets, but the plain businesslike, unadorned relation has its literary parentage in the memoirs of the generals of Alexander. And it is

---

[1] Especially the work of Nearchus on his voyage in the Indian Ocean.

[2] He wrote about the end of the fourth century. From the criticisms of Longinus and Demetrius, it appears that his style was marked by features which heralded the Asianic school.

[3] We may indeed compare parts of Xenophon's *Anabasis*. And the work of Nearchus may remind us of the report which Scylax made for Darius.

not, I think, unreasonable to conjecture that these
memoirs were the model or inspiration of an exceptional work of this period, which fulfilled, as it
would appear, the demands which Thucydides
made on historiography. Hieronymus of Cardia,
a soldier and statesman, who had served under
Eumenes and Antigonus Gonatas, wrote a history
of the Diadochi and Epigoni from the death of
Alexander to about 266 B.C. His sole concern
seems to have been to record facts accurately ; he
used official despatches, and in general he told only
what he knew of his own knowledge or from
credible information. But his style was careless ;
he disdained rhetoric. The Greeks would not read
what did not gratify their aesthetic sense ; and a
work like that of Hieronymus had no more chance
in competition with Duris than the Memoir of
Ptolemy against the sensational and rhetorical
story of Cleitarchus. Speculating on what we
casually learn about this lost book, we may
suppose that if it had survived we should regard
Hieronymus as a third in a triumvirate of Greek
historians, along with Thucydides and Polybius.

We saw in the first lectures how the Persian
conquest of Asia Minor and invasion of Greece
played a determining part in the rise of history.
Similarly, the Greek conquest of the Persian
empire had a decisive influence on its development. I have pointed out some of the ways in
which this second great stimulus from the Orient
operated. Just as it was in consequence of

the destruction of Miletus and the Persian war
that the intellectual primacy in Greece passed
from Ionia to Athens, so it was a consequence of
the expansion of Hellas by Alexander that the
primacy passed away from Athens to Alexandria
and other places—passed back, we might say, to
the East; and this affected history as well as other
branches of literature. Again, the opening up of the
distant countries of Asia stimulated and ministered
to the romantic history which gratified the popular
appetite for sensation. On the other hand, the
reports and "blue-books" of Alexander's generals
founded a new kind of history which eschewed
rhetoric, addressed no appeal to the public, and had
very few exponents. Another result of Alexander's
work was the rise of the idea of the *oecumene*,—the
realisation of the inhabited world as a whole of
which account must be taken.[1] This idea had
indeed no immediate influence on history. We
can trace its influence in the Stoic philosophy, and
it gave rise to the conception of the Romans that
their dominion was potentially conterminous with
the *orbis terrarum*. As a historical principle, it
then began to become effective, as we can see in
the universal histories of the first century B.C., and
it prepared the way for the Christian conception
of world-history.

[1] Compare J. Kaerst, *Die antike Idee der Oekumene in ihrer politischen
und kulturellen Bedeutung*, 1903.

§ 3. *The influence of philosophy and the rise of antiquarianism*

I have traced the influence of rhetoric on history; we must now consider the influence of philosophy. In the first half of the fourth century, a period of intense practical, as well as theoretical, interest in problems of government and social organization, we find, beside Isocrates the sophist, who wrote for the hour, Plato the philosopher, who wrote for the ages. Different as they were, they both represented from different sides the same interest in political speculation, and both alike gave it an ethical direction, the effects of which were permanent. Both these masters, the man of genius and the man of talent—the programmes of the one and the ideals of the other — set historical tasks to the next generation. While Isocrates set in motion Theopompus, Ephorus, and Androtion, the greatest pupil of Plato found it necessary, in investigating political philosophy, to trace the histories of the political constitutions of Hellenic states.

We should understand many points in the political speculation of Plato as well as in the political pamphlets of Isocrates if we possessed the mass of political literature which inundated Athens during the period of the Peloponnesian war. Of that literature we have one early specimen in the anonymous book on the Athenian Constitution. We have only a few fragments of the publications of Antiphon, Thrasymachus, and Critias,

the most distinguished names. Some papyrus fragments of the *Apologia* of Antiphon have been published the other day by Nicole, but, welcome though
they are, they do not amount to very much.[1]

It has been happily observed by Wilamowitz[2]
that these political pamphlets, of which the book
of Stesimbrotus was one of the first, were the
prose successors of the Elegies of Solon and
Theognis. The most effective and important
flysheets emanated from the men who were dissatisfied with the democracy and desired to substitute oligarchy or polity; they were dealing with
burning questions and they did not spare persons.
The book of Stesimbrotus, which seems to have
been entitled *Concerning Themistocles, Thucydides,
and Pericles*, had struck the personal note. The
Athenian history of the fifth century was per-
verted by these writers into a history of demagogues; and this perversion had a decisive influence
on Athenian thinkers of the following century.
The pupils of Socrates were only too ready to
adopt a view which held up to obloquy the
democracy which had taken the life of their
master. We have the scheme of the Athenian
demagogues in Plato's *Gorgias*, in the *Politikos* of
Antisthenes, in the *Dialogues* of Aeschines, in the
Philippika of Theopompus, in the *Athenian Constitution* of Aristotle. It was somewhat as if the

---

[1] *L'Apologie d'Antiphon, ou λόγος περὶ μεταστάσεως*, 1907 (Geneva-Bâle).

[2] The same scholar has made it probable that one portion of the
Panegyric of Isocrates was aimed against the pamphlet of an Ionian who
(*c.* 404 B.C.) wrote against the Athenian supremacy and in favour of
Sparta.

sources of the American history of the nineteenth
century were lost, and a reactionary publicist
wrote a book to make out that a series of dema-
gogic Presidents was the key to the history of
the United States.

This literature, contemporary with Thucydides,
must have had a considerable effect in creating an
interest in Athenian history. It corrupted history,
but it also quickened it. It was the object, for
instance, of Theramenes and his followers to prove
that polity, the form of government which they
desired, was not an innovation but the true and
original Athenian constitution, the πάτριος πολιτεία,[1] and that the existing democracy was a
perversion which had been generated and fostered
in the interests of demagogues. The historical
question, what was the nature of the πάτριος
πολιτεία and the Solonian reform, thus became a
question of burning political interest. We may
illustrate it by the controversies, not yet extinct,
as to the nature of the Reformation in England,
between Church parties which, in the interests of

---

[1] To the literature on this subject belong the συμβουλευτικός of Thrasymachus (411 B.C.); the pamphlet from which Aristotle derived much material
for his 'Αθ. π.; then, later (403 B.C.), Lysias, περὶ τοῦ μὴ καταλῦσαι τὴν πάτριον
πολιτείαν 'Αθήνησι. [The puzzle of the περὶ πολιτείας, vulgarly ascribed to
Herodes Atticus, has been discussed in a minute and careful study by
E. Drerup, 1908 (*Studien zur Geschichte und Kultur des Altertums*, ii. 1,
Paderborn). His solution is very interesting. From a variety of indications he concludes that it was written in the summer of 404 B.C. by an
Athenian belonging to the party of Theramenes, and is a political
pamphlet concerning the Athenian politics of the hour, Thessaly, the
nominal subject, being merely a disguise. So an Irish patriot might put
a plea for Home Rule in the mouth of a Bohemian. If Drerup is right,
his further inference that the "speech" of Thrasymachus ὑπὲρ Λαρι-
σαίων was a brochure of the same sort seems probable.]

their own ecclesiastical views, place different interpretations upon historical events.

Aristotle's *Constitution of Athens* may itself be regarded from one point of view as belonging to the political literature of the fourth century. To describe it as a pamphlet [1] is as absurd as it would be so to describe the work of Herodotus. Its main purpose was scientific; but the author was deeply interested in the politics of the day, and his book had an intentional bearing on the contemporary situation. [2] It was due to his own views as a politician, and not to his curiosity as a historian, that he used as authorities flysheet literature, especially a polemical pamphlet dating from the last years of the fifth century and expressing the anti-democratic conception of Athenian history which prevailed in the circle of Theramenes.

But the *Constitution of Athens* is only one of 158 Greek constitutions and some not Greek, which were compiled by Aristotle or under his direction. Their purpose was to supply actual material for a scientific study of political phenomena. And thus Aristotle possesses the great significance that he was the founder of constitutional history, the precursor of Waitz and Stubbs. The *Constitution of Athens*, the only one of the collection we possess, was the one most likely to be affected by Aristotle's political prejudices. Its weaknesses are evident. It consists of two parts— a sketch of the constitutional changes to the end

[1] As Nissen has done. [2] Compare Bauer, p. 274.

of the fifth century, and a description of the existing constitution. His main thread in the former was the local history of Athens as described by Attic chroniclers who came after Hellanicus;[1] just as his main guides for other states were probably the local histories which had been industriously consulted by Ephorus. So far, so good; and he also displayed historical instinct in using the poems of Solon for his account of the economic conditions of that statesman's time. But he completely neglected the material on which a modern historian would base his investigation, the stones and the archives. And it is clear that he did not comprehend the working of the constitution in the fifth century; his critical faculty did not resist the spell of the polemical literature of the extraordinarily clever publicists who had invented their own version of Attic history. When he has recorded the overthrow of the Council of the Areopagus, instead of pointing out that the actual power and government were in the hands of the Council of Five Hundred, he intimates that the conduct of the state rested entirely with Pericles. The truth is that Aristotle

---

[1] One of the important results of the discovery of the Ἀθηναίων Πολιτεία is the light gained for the lost historians of Athens who stood on the shoulders of Hellanicus, and who formed a principal source of Aristotle. It is notable that some at least of these chroniclers were religious *exêgêtai τῶν πατρίων*, who are the nearest analogy at Athens to the pontifices of Rome. Cp. Wilamowitz, *Aristoteles und Athen*, i. 280 sqq. We know the names of Cleidemus, Melanthius, Phanodemus (? Anticleides); Androtion is more than a name. The series was continued by Demon and closed by Philochorus, an *exêgêtês*, the last and greatest, whose work eclipsed its predecessors. The recovery of Philochorus would mean a greater addition to our historical knowledge than the Ἀθηναίων Πολιτεία. Some new fragments are contained in the Commentary of Didymus on the Philippics of Demosthenes.

seems to have reflected very little on the subject,
or rather to have confined his reflexions within very
narrowly drawn lines. The formalism of his conception is most evident in the way in which he
treats, or fails to treat, the Athenian empire. To
a modern student, who should undertake to write
a constitutional history of Athens, one of the most
important problems would be to examine how the
democracy governed the empire and how the
empire reacted on it. Aristotle dismisses the
empire in about four lines (c. 24). Moreover,
although he has traced the constitutional changes
in relation to the political crises which brought
them about, he has, in general, his eye merely on
the dead machinery ; he tells us the names of the
parts, but he does not show how the machine
worked. Even when we come to the democracy
of the fourth century, we get only a full account
of the official organization and the formal procedure ; no effort is made to gain an insight into
the political efficiency of the institutions. It is
doubtful whether even here he consulted the laws
themselves, or rather used an analysis written by
somebody else.[1] And if in this historical treatise
he fails to show the actual working of the constitution and to explain the unwritten *Staatsrecht*,
his scientific treatise, the *Politics*, does not supply
this want.

Plato troubled himself little with history, but
it is not improbable that one of his speculations

[1] See Wilamowitz, *op. cit.* i. c. 7.

suggested the idea of the first history of civilisation. In the *Laws*, where he descends to lower heights, nearer to the actual conditions of terrestrial society, Plato has sketched a reconstruction of the development of the human race. It is governed by the idea of cataclysms, such as deluges or pestilences which wiped out the human race, leaving only a remnant, which had to begin at the very beginning and weave civilisation, like the web of Penelope, all over again. The latest of these periodic cataclysms was a deluge, and the few survivors who had gained safety on the tops of high hills found themselves without the means of travelling and without arts; the metals had disappeared and there were no means of felling timber. "The desolation of these primitive men would create in them a feeling of affection and friendship towards one another; and they would have no occasion to fight for their subsistence; for they would have a pasture in abundance"; also abundance of clothing, bedding, and dwellings, and utensils; so that they were not very poor. And they were not rich, as there was no gold or silver. But "the community which has neither poverty nor riches will always have the noblest principles; there is no insolence or injustice, nor, again, are there any contentions or envyings among them."[1] Plato draws here the picture of an age which is ethically golden; although he does not use the

[1] *Laws*, 678-9, transl. Jowett. The cycle of degenerate states in *Republic* viii. is a sequence in thought, not in time.

expression. He then sketches the patriarchal government of primitive societies, appealing to Homer's description of the Cyclôpes; the rise of agriculture and of city-life; the beginnings of legislation which became necessary when men who had different laws in their separate life came to live together. He shows how this gathering into large communities suspended patriarchal rule and brought about a monarchical or aristocratic government.

Up to this point we suppose that we are reviewing the general development of mankind throughout the whole earth. Then suddenly, by a sort of legerdemain, the philosopher changes this universal scene to the plain of Troy, and continues the imaginary record from the foundation of Ilion. The rest is a curious commentary on the history of Greece. It turns on the idea that the Heracleidae missed a great opportunity. The object of the Dorian institutions which they introduced was, Plato alleges, to protect the entire Hellenic race against the barbarians, and, if they had only legislated with more far-sighted wisdom, they might have secured a permanent union or confederacy of the Hellenic world, strong to resist all assaults of the barbarians. As history, this is absurd; the interest lies in Plato's reflexion of the national Hellenic idea which was preached by Isocrates. Nor indeed does Plato intend it to be taken more literally than the previous imaginary reconstruction of the progress of man from his primeval conditions.

This slight sketch, which represents the primitive age as ethically golden, but materially rudimentary, must, I fancy, have been present to the mind of Dicaearchus when he decided to compose the earliest *Culturgeschichte* or history of general civilisation, his Βίος Ἑλλάδος in which, starting from conditions like those indicated by Plato, he traced the progress of Greece in public and private institutions and in the arts. It is remarkable how the speculations of the Greeks on primitive civilisation were bounded by that tradition of a decline from a golden age, which Hesiod expressed in his scheme of the Five Ages.

But if Dicaearchus found his text in Plato, his work was a characteristic product of the Peripatetic school to which he belonged. It was the merit of that school to promote specialism, and it produced a considerable historical literature on all kinds of special subjects, such as the history of philosophy, the history of drama, the biographies of sculptors. Demetrius of Phaleron played an active part in establishing in the Greek world the Peripatetic idea of collecting and classifying facts of every order. For it was largely due to his stimulus and influence, after he retired from Athens to Egypt, that under the auspices of Ptolemy I. books were collected at Alexandria which formed the nucleus of the two great libraries formally founded by Ptolemy II.[1] Political history indeed was not much written by the savants of Alexandria, whose great achievements

---

[1] Susemihl, i. 6.

were in the sphere of philology ; but the antiquarian
tastes which found their fullest satisfaction there,
and afterwards at Pergamon also, in the shadow of
large libraries, were introduced by the Peripatetic
movement, and did not fail to affect historiography. We can notice this influence in the work
of Timaeus, who, though he was thoroughly incapable of philosophical ideas and made scurrilous
attacks on Aristotle, shared with the Aristotelian
school the passion for collecting facts of all kinds,
and was so trivial in its indulgence that he was
called an "old rag woman" (γραοσυλλέκτρια).

The creation of antiquarian study is one of the
numerous precious services of the Greeks to the
progress of human culture. Its distinction is that,
apparently and in its immediate aspect, it is disinterested. The Greeks described it as πολυπραγ-
μοσύνη, attending to what is not one's business, a
singularly felicitous phrase for a sphere which has
no relation to human life. The Roman word for
antiquarianism had a similar significance: *curiositas*,
superfluous care for what is practically unimportant,
or, in fact, the love of useless knowledge. But
although *curiositas* came to be an instinct in men
who could not have assigned any reason of utility
for their pursuits, it must be remembered that it
sprang from a certain side of the general philosophical theory of Aristotle, and, thus having a place
in a system, had originally a justification outside
itself. It may be called useless in a narrow sense
of the term, but from another point of view, as I

will show in a subsequent lecture, it has a human
value and is therefore ultimately not disinterested.

Although the ancient antiquarians tended to be
rather learned than critical, and in criticism to be
rather minute and finical than luminous, there were
brilliant exceptions ; such as Eratosthenes, the
greatest and most original geographer of the ancient
world.   His studies in physical science helped him
to prosecute his antiquarian researches with freshness of insight.   I would, in particular, point out
his attitude to Homer.   One of the most serious
impediments blocking the way to a scientific
examination of early Greece was the orthodox
belief in Homer's omniscience and infallibility—a
belief which survived the attacks of Ionian philosophers and the irony of Thucydides.   Eratosthenes
boldly asserted the principle that the critic in studying Homer must remember that the poet's knowledge was limited by the conditions of his age, which
was a comparatively ignorant age.[1]   This was an
important step in historical criticism.

Ancient antiquarians did not work out principles
of method, nor did they, beyond the collection of
libraries, provide facilities for research, like the
bibliographies and innumerable works of reference
which are compiled for the convenience of modern
students.   It is somewhat surprising that archives
were not systematically transcribed, and official
documents collected.   The idea was not unknown.
Craterus, who seems to have been a contemporary

---

[1] Strabo, vii. 3. 6 ; cp. also 1. 23-25.

of Theophrastus, compiled a corpus of the Attic decrees of the fifth century, arranged in chronological order. The traveller, Polemon of Ilion, was such a diligent copyist of inscriptions that he earned the name of stone-rapper (*stêlokopas*). Among the Romans, Mucianus, the friend of the Emperor Vespasian, collected and edited a large corpus of official documents, probably including reports of the proceedings of the Senate (*acta senatus*) during the last age of the Republic.[1] As this collection included reports of public speeches by leading orators and statesmen, the motive of Mucianus in compiling it may have been an interest in oratory rather than in history. Such labours were in any case exceptional.

Greece did not create scientific philology any more than scientific history. But the movement set on foot by the Peripatetic school was invaluable, both for preserving the records, and exploring the recesses, of the past; and however uncritical or crude the methods of ancient antiquarians may appear to us, they represent a prominent stage in the advance of knowledge. But while their disinterested passion for research affected the reconstruction of past history, contemporary history was composed by men who subordinated truth to rhetorical effect. There were few exceptions, conspicuously Hieronymus, whom I have mentioned, and Polybius, to whom the next lecture will be devoted.

[1] Tacitus, *Dial.* 37.

LECTURE VI

THE life of Polybius covered about the first eighty years of the second century B.C. (*c.* 198-117 B.C.)—the period of the great political process which linked together the destinies of Greece and Rome. He was born in the Hellenistic world, a noble representative of its civilisation, to become the herald of the new Graeco-Roman world into which he witnessed the Hellenistic system passing. You will remember that having played a public part in the politics of the Achaean League of which his father Lycortas was then the leading statesman, and having served as a commander of cavalry, he had been taken with other hostages, after the battle of Pydna (168 B.C.), to Rome, where he was placed in the house of the victorious general Aemilius Paullus. There he enjoyed the intimate society of Scipio Aemilianus, and had exceptionally good opportunities of gaining a first-hand knowledge of Roman affairs and of studying the character of the governing class and the working of the constitution. There he became reconciled to the fate of his country. He lived sixteen years at

Rome before he was allowed to return to Greece, and during that time he conceived the idea of his work and wrote a considerable part of it (at least fifteen Books). His original design was to relate the history of the advance of Roman conquest, through a period of fifty-three years from the eve of the Second Punic war (220 B.C.) to the Roman conquest of Macedonia (168 B.C.). He explains very fully why he chose his starting-point. There broke out almost at the same moment three great conflicts : the war of Rome with Carthage, the war of the Leagues in Greece (in which the Achaeans and Philip were ranged against the Aetolians), and the war in the East between Antiochus and Ptolemy Philopator. Up to that epoch, events happening in the various quarters of the world were unconnected and did not bear upon each other either in their purposes or in their issues. But from this time Italian and African affairs begin to come into relation with Asiatic and Greek affairs, and history begins to assume the form, not of strewn *disiecta membra*, but of a single organic body ($\sigma\omega\mu\alpha\tauο\epsilon\iota\delta\hat{\eta}$ [1]).

But, while Polybius marks this date as the proper beginning of his work, he goes back farther in a long introduction, filling two Books, in which he sketches the earlier history of the relations of Rome with Carthage, including the First Punic

---

[1] i. 3. 4. This unity does not become clear till after the defeat of Carthage ; but the Eastern events during the Second Punic war went to determine the subsequent intervention of Rome.

war and the previous history of the Achaean League. Thus, so far as the lands of the Western Mediterranean are concerned, his history began where Timaeus had left off, as he expressly notes.[1]

He signalises the *motif* of his work in imposing phrases. " Our own times have witnessed a miracle, and it consists in this. Fortune moved almost all the affairs of the world towards one quarter and constrained all things to tend to one and the same goal. And so it is the special note of my work to bring under one purview for my readers the means and the manipulations which fortune employed for this end. This idea was my principal motive and stimulus. It was an additional reason that in our time no one had attempted a universal history."[2]

Subsequent events, the fall of Carthage and the annexation of Greece in 146 B.C., led Polybius to extend his plan and fix this later year as the term of his history. In its augmented form it reached the considerable bulk of forty Books, of which only the first five have been preserved completely, though of many of the others we possess long excerpts. He seems to have finished the composition of the whole work about the year 134, but he continued to insert many additions and corrections up to 120 B.C. These supplements are often in contradiction with other passages, for he died without submitting the book to a systematic revision. Indeed, he had allowed the original

[1] i. 5. 1.   [2] i. 4. 1.

introduction, which expounded the first scheme of his history, to remain unchanged, and simply inserted a statement of his revised plan.[1] Of the later additions the most interesting are those which were suggested by the author's visit to Spain about 133 B.C.,[2] and those which allude to the revolutionary movement of the Gracchi. Of the latter I shall have something more to say.

I have observed that the history of Polybius follows on to that of Timaeus, and it is to be noted that in his chronological arrangement he has adopted the awkward reckoning by Olympiads which Timaeus introduced, but he supplements it by the years of the Roman Consuls and other marks of time.[3] In the first portion of his work, up to the year of Cannae (216 B.C.), he pursues continuously the history of each of the various states without interruption ; but after that, he adopts the annalistic method and synchronizes events in different parts of the world under the same year.

[1] Old plan i. 1-5 and iii. 1-3 ; new plan iii. 4-6.

[2] It has been shown that in his description of New Carthage Polybius was in error as to the orientation. After he had seen the place he inserted (x. 11. 4) a correction of current statements as to the circumference, but left the other errors uncorrected. See Cunz, *Polybius*, 8 sqq., and Strachan Davidson, *Selections*, Appendix.

[3] The beginning of the Polybian year, however, did not coincide with that of the Olympiad (July), but fell some three months later (*c.* Oct. 1). This division seems to have been determined by the fact that the autumn equinox and the beginnings of the official years of the Achaean and Aetolian *stratêgoi* fell about the same time. See Nissen, *Rheinisches Museum*, 26. 241 sqq. He calls attention to a passage, xii. 11. 1, which suggests that Timaeus may have been partly responsible for this system.

The arrangement of his immense work displays
conspicuous skill; but whether the forty Books can
be reduced to the scheme of a symmetrically
grouped work of art, like the history of Herodotus,
is a question which we can hardly answer with
confidence, considering that of many of the Books
we possess only a few fragments. Nissen has
attempted the discovery of a symmetrical plan.[1]
He holds that it was divided into seven parts,
each of which contained six Books, except one
which contained four. These groups, he thinks,
correspond to definite stages in the development
of Roman dominion: "The first group," he says,
"contains the introduction; the second the cul-
minating years of the contest between Rome and
Carthage; the third begins with the war in Africa,
and ends with the destruction of the Macedonian
hegemony; the fourth traces the history of the
Roman hegemony, and the fifth its transformation
into an empire of client states; the sixth (which
is the exceptionally small division) forms the transition to the last rising of the Mediterranean states
against Rome, which is the subject of the seventh."
In support of this design, he points out that three
Books which are devoted to long digressions—VI.
on Roman Institutions, XII. on the work of
Timaeus, XXXIV. on Geography—come each at
the end of one of these main divisions. Moreover,
the addition of a fortieth Book, containing a *résumé*
of the contents, is urged as an argument in favour

---

[1] i. *op. cit.* The theory is favourably entertained by Susemihl, ii. 125.

of the alleged construction, on the ground that it was required to complete the last hexad. The theory has a certain plausibility, but we have to remember that Polybius changed and enlarged his plan in the course of its composition, and I find it difficult to believe that, if he had deliberately adopted a definite scheme of this kind, he would have failed to draw attention to it in the preface to his first or third Book. His solicitude that the reader should fully grasp his plan and arrangement is hardly reconcilable with his silence on such a leading point. The symmetry is not clearly convincing as in the case of Herodotus.

But whether this incomplete symmetry is due to the design of the author or only to the discernment of an ingenious reader, Polybius has shown a fine artistic sense of propriety in fixing the place which he chose for his account of the institutions of Rome. The third Book concludes with the defeat of Cannae, which set the mistress of Italy face to face with the prospect of the extinction of her power. How was it that, brought to bay, she baffled the triumphant invader, recovered Italy, and conquered Carthage? The historian emphasizes the problem. Of course, the measures her government adopted after the disaster were wise. But a sagacious policy at the last moment would not have availed if Rome had not been what she was. The explanation lay, Polybius believed, in her institutions. And so he interrupts the narrative of the Punic war at this point to describe the

institutions which saved Rome.[1] He has seized
the instant at which the reader's interest is most
fully prepared and awake to learn the lessons
which those institutions have to give.

Polybius is not less express than Thucydides
in asserting the principle that accurate representation of facts was the fundamental duty of the
historian. He lays down that three things are
requisite for performing such a task as his : the
study and criticism of sources; autopsy, that is,
personal knowledge of lands and places; and
thirdly, political experience. He was himself a
man of action, and had acquired political and
military experience before he became a historian,
so that he fulfilled the third condition ; and he
was most conscientious in endeavouring to satisfy
the two other self-imposed requirements. He possessed a wide acquaintance with historical literature, and criticized the authorities whom he used
with fearless independence of judgment. He was
not taken in by "authority," and he declined to
render unreserved credit to a writer on the ground
that he was a contemporary or a man of character.
For instance, he criticizes the views of the Roman
historian Fabius on the causes of the Punic war.
"There are some," he observes,[2] "who think that
because he lived at the time and was a Roman
senator he should be believed without more ado.
Whereas I consider his authority high, but not

---

[1] In Book vi.   The intervening Books iv. and v. deal with synchronous
events in Greece.   See iii. 118.   [2] iii. 9.

absolute or such as to dispense the reader from forming his own judgment on the facts themselves."

Polybius was also a traveller, and he travelled for the purpose of historical investigation in accordance with his belief that topographical autopsy was a primary qualification for writing history. He passes severe criticisms on Timaeus, who, he says, always "lived in one place," and on Zeno of Rhodes, for the blunders they committed through ignorance of geography. He was intimately acquainted with Greece itself ;[1] his description of the battle of Sellasia was censured by Delbrück, but has been successfully defended by Kromayer. He travelled in Italy and Sicily ; he visited Africa in an official capacity ; he went with Scipio to Spain, and explored the coast of the Atlantic, returning to Italy by Southern Gaul and the Alps.

The historians of whom Polybius seems to have most highly approved were Ephorus and Aratus. The Memoirs of the Achaean statesman naturally appealed to him as an Achaean politician, but also because they satisfied his doctrine that history is a practical and not an antiquarian study. Written by a man of action, whose interests were directly practical, they gave the kind of instruction which it was the main function of history, in the esteem of Polybius, to give. On the other hand, Ephorus

---

[1] There is indeed, in xvi. 16. 5, a curious statement as to the position of Mycenae relative to Corinth.

appealed to him as a universal historian, "the first and only writer who undertook to write universal history."[1]   Thus Aratus and Ephorus displayed severally the two great features of the work of Polybius, on which he constantly insists.   His view of history is *pragmatical* and it is *universal.* The word pragmatical (πραγματικός) has been some-times misunderstood.   By a pragmatical man he means a practical politician, and by pragmatical history he means history which bears on political actualities and furnishes practical instruction.   In an interesting passage he says[2] that this kind of history has always been useful, but is more than ever opportune now, "because in our times science and art (ἐμπειρία καὶ τέχνη) have made such great advances that theoretical students can deal, as it were on methodical principles, with the situations that occur."   He insisted very strongly on the point that, in order to serve such pragmatical uses, a mere narrative of events is inadequate, and the historian must investigate and explain the causes and the inter-connexions.   The whole value of history, he said, lies in a knowledge of causes. Some exponents of Polybius have applied the term "pragmatism" to his work, in the particular sense that he investigated the causal nexus of events. This is a misuse of the word, and is not countenanced by his language.   "Apodeictic" is the term which he uses of his history in so far

[1] v. 33.
[2] ix. 2. 5.   This is one of the rare passages in which an ancient writer betrays a sense of " progress."

as it traces causes.[1] His history is pragmatical, and because it is pragmatical, it is also apodeictic.

Now, what does Polybius understand by causes? He is careful to enlarge on the distinction between cause and beginning (αἰτία and ἀρχή), and he illustrates it by examples. For instance, while the beginning of the Persian war of Alexander the Great was his crossing over into Asia, the causes are sought by Polybius as far back as the expedition of Cyrus and the wars of Agesilaus.[2] But it cannot be said that he goes very deep into the question of historical causes. He conceives causation in an external and mechanical way, and he does not proceed beyond the idea of simple one-sided causation to the idea of reciprocity, or of action and reaction, which is often required to express adequately the relations of historical phenomena.

The view of Polybius on causation in general is more interesting than his applications of it to particular cases. Until he was well on in years and had virtually completed his work, he shared the popular belief that, apart from the regularly operating natural and human causes, a superhuman power, which men call Tyche, exerts a control over events and diverts them in unexpected ways. This popular view had been presented in a quasi-philosophical dress by Demetrius of Phaleron, whose treatise Περὶ τύχης [3] doubtless made a deep

---

[1] ii. 37. 3; cp. iii. 1. 3. [2] iii. 6.

[3] It is not preserved, but its general argument and contents were transferred by Plutarch into his *Consolation to Apollonius.* Consult the work of von Scala (see Bibliography).

impression on the mind of Polybius, for its
influence on a number of passages in his work
has been proved by von Scala. The event of
167, the fall of the Macedonian monarchy, the
new step in the resistless advance of the western
world - power, in whose chariot wheels Polybius
himself and his country were caught up, might
well seem a powerful confirmation of the theories
of the wise man of Phaleron. Though Polybius
traces the causes of the success of Rome to its
history and constitution, he writes as follows in
the preface to the original plan of his work :
"Fortune has caused the whole world and its
history to tend towards one purpose—the empire
of Rome. She continually exercises her power
in the lives of men and brings about many changes,
yet never before did she achieve such a labour as
she has wrought within our memory."[1] Thus the
Roman conquests produced upon Polybius the
same impression which the Macedonian conquests
had produced upon Demetrius. Elsewhere Polybius quotes the very words which Demetrius had
used.[2] "Fortune, who exhibits her power in
compassing the unexpected, is even now, I think,
displaying it to the world, having made the
Macedonians the inheritors of Persian prosperity.
She has lent them these blessings, till she forms
a new resolution on their destiny." In many
other places, too, Polybius recognises the active
operation of Fortune, and comments on her

---

[1] i. 4. 5.   [2] xxix. 21. 5-6.

instability, her paradoxes, her caprices, quite in the tone of Demetrius.

But there are other passages in which Polybius sounds a very different note. Thus he finds fault with writers who ascribe public calamities or private misfortunes to Fortune and Fate, and only allows that when it is impossible or difficult for man to discover causes, as in the case of storms or droughts, he may in his embarrassment refer them to God or Fortune, "but when you can discover the cause of an event it is not, in my opinion, admissible to impute it to God." [1] Before you pray for rain, it is wise to look at the barometer. Again, he deprecates the practice of ascribing to fortune or the gods what is due to a man's ability and prudence. These and other similar observations are not perhaps ultimately inconsistent with the doctrine of Demetrius, but the note is different; they show a desire to restrict the operation of the external power within as narrow limits as possible. But there are other assertions which are directly opposed to that doctrine. When he inquires into the causes of the power and eminence attained by the Achaeans, a people who were not numerous and lived in a small country, "it is clear," he says,[2] "that it would be quite unsuitable to speak of Fortune ; that is a cheap explanation ; we must rather seek the cause. Without a cause nothing can be brought about, whether normal or apparently abnormal." When he wrote this, he had reached

---

[1] xxxvi. 17. 1-4.   [2] ii. 38. 5.

a point of view diametrically opposed to that
which he had learned from Demetrius. Further,
he applied his new doctrine to the empire of
Rome. If, in the words which I quoted a few
moments ago, he had claimed Rome's successes
as a supreme illustration of the mysterious dealings
of Fortune, he now, with equal confidence, repudiated the theory that Fortune had anything
to do with the making of Rome's greatness. "It
was not by fortune, as some of the Greeks think,
nor causelessly, that the Romans succeeded; their
success was quite natural; it was due to their
training and discipline; they aimed at the hegemony
and government of the world, and they attained
their purpose." [1]

Thus it appears that Polybius, having originally
started with the conception of an extra - natural
power, directing the world and diverting the
course of events from its natural path, was led
by wider experience of life and deeper study of
history to reduce within narrower and narrower
bounds the intervention of this *deus ex machina,*
until he finally reached the view that it was superfluous for the pragmatical historian. But it would
be rash to assert that he ultimately embraced a
theory of pure naturalism. All we can say is
that he came to entertain the view that nothing
happens without a natural cause, and the operation of Tyche or chance is, in general, an invalid
assumption.

[1] i. 63. 9.

It is probable that Stoicism had something to do with his change of view. It is certain that he came under the influence of the new school of liberal Stoics, through intercourse with Panaetius, who, like himself, was an inmate of the house of Scipio at Rome. "I remember," says a speaker in Cicero's *De Republica*,[1] "that you, Scipio, often conversed with Panaetius in the presence of Polybius, two Greeks the most deeply versed in politics" (*rerum civilium*). Polybius did not become a Stoic, but he assimilated some Stoic ideas, as in his earlier life he had been influenced by the Peripatetics.

In his actual treatment and presentation of historical events, the fluctuation in his views on this question probably did not make much difference. A change in his views as to the freedom of the will would have affected his treatment far more deeply. I know for myself that on days when I am a determinist I look on history in one way, and on days when I am an indeterminist, in quite another. Polybius was an indeterminist, like most Greeks; he believed in free-will. The particular Stoic influences to which he submitted did not touch this doctrine. For Panaetius did not share the doctrine of Chrysippus and older Stoics, that the world is governed by laws of iron necessity which exclude free-will.

We can see the results of his contact with Stoicism in the account which Polybius gives of

[1] i. 21. 34.

the rise and fall of political constitutions.[1] He
adopts the newer Stoic version of the theory of
a cyclic succession of forms of government.
When the human race is swept away (this has
happened, and may be expected to happen again)
through deluges, plagues, or famines, and a new
race takes its place, the work of civilisation has
to begin afresh; monarchy is the first form in
which society constitutes itself; this passes
through successive corruptions and revolutions
(tyranny, aristocracy, oligarchy, democracy) into
an anarchical democracy which Polybius calls
cheirocracy, the rule of might; from which a
dissolving society can only be rescued by a return
to monarchy, and then the cycle begins again.
In the interval between two cataclysms there may
be any number of such cycles. Polybius accepts
catastrophic occurrences not as a mere ancient
tradition or philosophical speculation, but as a
proved scientific fact.[2]

The theory of a recurring cycle of political
constitutions which comes from Plato and the
Stoics is an application of the cyclical theory of
the world-process which was propounded by early
philosophers. Such a theory is more or less implied by Anaximander and Heracleitus, but it was
clearly formulated, in very definite terms, by the
Pythagorean school.[3] You remember the passage
in Virgil's Fourth Eclogue where a new Argonautic

---

[1] In Book VI.   [2] VI. 5. 5.
[3] Cp. Gomperz, *Griechische Denker*, i. 46, 54, 113 sqq.

expedition is contemplated and a second Trojan war :—

> atque iterum ad Troiam magnus mittetur Achilles.

That is the cyclical doctrine, and logically it applied to small things as well as great. I may illustrate it in the vivid manner of the philosopher Eudemus. According to the Pythagorean theory, some day I shall again with this manuscript in my hand stand here in this hall and lecture on Polybius, and you each and all will be sitting there just as you are this evening; and everything else in the world will be just as it is at this moment. In other words, the cosmical process consists of exactly recurring cycles, in which the minutest occurrences are punctually repeated. We do not remember them—if we did, they would not be the same.

But the cyclical doctrine was not, perhaps, generally taught in this extreme form.[1] Polybius does not appear at first to have held even the universal validity of the law of growth, bloom, and decay. He considered that it holds good of simple constitutions, pure monarchy, for instance, or pure democracy, but he thought that the setting in of decay could be evaded by a judicious mixture of constitutional principles. He has submitted to a minute analysis the Spartan and the Roman systems of government, as eminent examples of

---

[1] It is interesting to observe that Dionysius (Περὶ τῶν ἀρχαίων ῥητόρων, 2) suggests periodicity as an explanation of the Attic renaissance : εἴτε θεοῦ τινος ἄρξαντος εἴτε φυσικῆς περιόδου τὴν ἀρχαίαν τάξιν ἀνακυκλούσης.

the union of the three principles of monarchy, aristocracy, and democracy, compounded in such a way that they balanced one another and mutually counteracted the separate tendencies of each to degenerate. The Spartans owed the idea of their mixed constitution to the happy divination of the genius Lycurgus, the Romans attained to theirs through the school of experience. In other words, the Spartan constitution was an invention, the Roman was a growth. From these premisses, which are largely untrue, Polybius deduced the exceptional permanence of the institutions of Sparta and Rome, and evidently thought that they defied the law of degeneration. It may be noticed that the superiority of a mixed constitution was not a new idea.

In other passages, however, Polybius speaks in a different tone. He sacrifices the theory that Rome owed everything to her mixed constitution, by admitting that her government was aristocratic when she reached her greatness in the time of the Second Punic war. It was a mechanical and wholly inadequate theory, even if the facts on which it was based had been correct — even if Rome *had* possessed a constitution in which the equilibrium of the three constitutional principles was maintained. In abandoning it Polybius was forced to recognise that the secret of life did not lie in a mechanical adjustment of the parts of the state, and to admit that there was no guarantee that Rome herself would not decline. But what

induced him to abandon it? Undoubtedly his
observation of the revolutionary movements in
the time of the Gracchi. These movements came
as a great surprise to him; nothing could have
seemed to enjoy a more secure stability than the
fabric of the Roman state in the days when he
began writing his book. But the Gracchan revolution opened his eyes. Its significance was brought
home to the friend of Scipio by Scipio's assassina-
tion. These stormy years flashed a lurid light
on the past, and Polybius could now look back
with illuminated vision and see in the agrarian
law of Flaminius (232 B.C.) the beginning of the
degeneration of the people.[1] Without touching
what he had written before, he introduced into
his work new paragraphs which meant the surrender of his former belief in the permanence of
the constitution. He now recognised that Rome,
too, was destined to decline, and he could con-
sequently accept unreservedly the principle of
anacyclosis. Stoic teaching may have gradually
prepared him for this change of theory; and
Scipio assuredly had not been blind to the signs
of the times. The revolutionary outbreak illustrated the melancholy prediction which he heard
from the lips of his friend on the ruined site of
Carthage :—

ἔσσεται ἦμαρ ὅταν ποτ' ὀλώλῃ Ἴλιος ἱρὴ
καὶ Πρίαμος καὶ λαὸς ἐυμμελίω Πριάμοιο.

[1] ii. 21. 8.

> Some time will come the day
> Of doom for Troy divine and Priam's sway,
> And Priam and his folk shall pass away.

More than an epitaph on Carthage, it was a prophecy on Rome.

Both Polybius and Thucydides, as I have already observed, held with equal conviction that the first obligation of a historian is to discover and relate facts as they actually occurred, and herein they both represented a reaction against the history which held the field. Each alike feels that the purpose of his work is to be instructive and not to be entertaining. Polybius is fully aware that for the majority of the reading public his work will have no attractions;[1] it is intended for statesmen, not for antiquarians or people who want to be amused. Just as Thucydides is conscious that his conception of how history should be written is opposed to that of Herodotus, so Polybius repudiates the fashion of historiography which was in vogue, and denounces the rhetorical effects or exciting sensations of the works which were most popular, such as those of Timaeus and Duris. He is severe upon Phylarchus for introducing into history effects which are appropriate to tragedy.[2] Phylarchus was always "forcing the note." He was ever attempting to arouse the pity and sympathy of the readers by pictures of despairing men and dishevelled women, children and aged parents, embracing, weeping and making loud lamentation,

[1] ix. 1.   [2] ii. 56.

in the extremity of woe. Tragedy and history, says
Polybius severely, have different objects. The aim
of tragedy is to move the soul; but the aim of
history is to instruct the mind. Again, just as
Thucydides ignores all the gossiping anecdotes
which memoir-writers like Ion and Stesimbrotus
collected, so Polybius condemns writers of a later
day for retailing what he calls the "vulgar babble
of a barber's shop"—what we should call the gossip
of the clubs, or the canards of the daily press.[1]

Polybius then represents a return, though not a
conscious return, to the principles of Thucydides
and a reaction against some of the most conspicuous tendencies which had marked historiography in
the interval. But Thucydides exercised no direct influence upon him, and the extant parts of his work
indicate that he was not one of the historians with
whom he was familiar. Polybius has been affected
by the speculations in political science and by the
schools of philosophy, no less than by the changes
in the political world which had come to pass since
the lifetime of Thucydides. Any one who turns
from one to the other is struck by the salient contrasts between their methods of treatment. Thucydides is an artist, Polybius is a teacher. Thucydides,
as we saw, employs the objective treatment of
a dramatist, and rarely comes forward himself to
address directly to the reader brief criticisms or
explanations. Polybius on the contrary is entirely

---

[1] iii. 20. 5 κουρεακῆς καὶ πανδήμου λαλιᾶς. Compare his criticism on the
insinuations of Timaeus against Aristotle, xii. 8. 5-6.

subjective. He is always on the stage himself,
criticizing, expounding, emphasizing, making points,
dotting the *i*'s and crossing the *t*'s, propounding and
defending his personal views. Thucydides did all
his constructive work beforehand, and presents to
the reader only the syntheses and results. Polybius takes the reader fully into his confidence, and
performs all the processes of analysis in his presence.
Thucydides states in a few sentences the plan of
his work, indicates in a few lines his principles of
historiography; and his rare criticisms on other
historians are confined to a word or two. Polybius
devotes pages to an exposition of the scheme of his
history, at the outset, and reiterates it in another
place. At the end of his work he gave a chronological scheme of the whole plan. He had commenced with the intention of supplying an epitome
of contents at the beginning of each Book, but
afterwards preferred to place at the beginning of
each Olympiad a summary of the events which
occurred in it.[1] He thus showed a kindly solicitude
that the reader should fully understand the construction of his work. He goes, at length, into the
proper principles and methods of history, frequently
returning to the subject, and he digresses into
elaborate criticisms of other historians, such as
Timaeus and Phylarchus, Ephorus and Theopompus. He is unsparingly didactic and his diffuse
explanations are often wearisome. This feature, as
to which he stands in marked contrast to the early

---

[1] The change was made after Book v. See beginning of Book xi.

historians, may partly be set down to the influence of popular philosophy, which tended to promote a didactic style. We might indeed say that the history of Polybius contains the material for a handbook of historical method; and this adds greatly to its value for us.

Like Thucydides and the ancients in general, Polybius believed in the eminent significance of the individual in history. He reiterates the platitude that one mind is more efficacious than a mass of men, quoting the saying of Euripides, "One wise plan prevails over many hands." [1] He takes a deep interest in the characters of the men who appear on his scene. On the other hand, he sees that there are potent forces at work besides great men. A student of the history of Rome, which had won her supreme position, unsteered by single men of transcendent powers, could not be blind to this. Polybius recognises the importance of national character. He considers the influence of climate upon it, and finds a key to a nation's character in its institutions and political life. We have seen the importance which he ascribed to the mechanism of political constitutions. But he had no idea of history as a continuous progress, no eye for what we call historical tendencies, no notion of the way in which historical changes are brought about by the innumerable and almost invisible activities of thousands and thousands of nameless people. He possessed a knowledge of the

[1] viii. 5. 3 ; i. 35. 3.

facts and conditions of his own age, and of the men
of his own age, to which we could not attain even
if we had his whole work in our hands. Yet, fragmentary as our knowledge is, we can say with some
confidence that we have a deeper insight than he
into the tendencies of his time, and of the time
immediately preceding, and a clearer comprehension
of the change through which the Roman state was
then passing and of the causes at work. He never
discerned how the new circumstances of Rome
in the latter half of the third century were altering
her commercial and economic condition, and were
already modifying the character of the state. We
owe our power of divining this to the enlarged
experience of the human race.

To return to his treatment of individuals.
While Thucydides leaves us to form our own
impressions from their public acts and from the
words which he makes them say, Polybius, in
accordance with his method, analyses and discusses
their qualities. But it is important to observe
that he does not, like Xenophon in the *Anabasis*,
and nearly all modern historians, attempt to draw
complete portraits of Philip or Hannibal or Scipio,
or any of the leading persons of his history, but
condemns on principle such a mode of treatment.
For, he says, men are inconsistent : they constantly
act in a manner which belies and contradicts their
real nature, sometimes under the pressure of friends,
at others on account of the peculiar complexion of
the circumstances. It is therefore misleading to

characterize a man when he first appears on the stage, or to infer his whole character from particular acts. The right method is to criticize his actions as they occur.[1] The same man must be praised as well as blamed; he is changed by vicissitudes of affairs; his conduct, for instance, may become better or worse.[2] Characters such as that of Philip III. of Macedon, which seems to have specially attracted him as a problem, impressed him with the necessity of adopting this principle; and in the treatment both of Philip and of Hannibal we must admire the conscientious fairness of Polybius in endeavouring to understand and estimate their characters.

Psychology indeed was a subject on which Polybius seems to have reflected much. We can see his interest in it, for example, in the account which he gives of the mental process of learning to read;[3] in his observation that in fighting those have an advantage who have a stronger will to conquer, so that a battle is in a certain measure a contest of wills;[4] in his insistence on the importance of personal experience ($a\dot{v}\tau o\pi \acute{a}\theta\epsilon\iota a$); or in such a remark as that change from one kind of activity to another is a relief. His psychological ideas have furnished material for a treatise to a German scholar. One principle must specially be noticed because he applies it to his own work: the importance of

---

[1] On this principle he only draws general portraits of subordinate persons who appear but once or twice. The preliminary account of Scipio in x. 2 is concerned only with his youth.

[2] xvi. 28.   [3] x. 47.   [4] Fr. 58.

connecting the unknown and remote with the known
and familiar. For instance, he considers it useless
to mention the names of strange places, which are
mere sound conveying no meaning, unless they are
brought into relation with the geographical knowledge which is familiar to the reader.[1] He does not
omit to make observations on the psychology of
the masses. Their chief characteristics he considers
to be ignorance and cowardice ; and therefore
religious feeling is important for them, because they
cannot endure surprises or face dangers without
hope from the gods.[2] The only use of mythology
is to preserve the religion of the multitude.[3] Polybius does not hold that religious belief has any
value for the educated person ; it would be superfluous in a state consisting exclusively of wise men.
But he certainly did not underrate its importance
in actual societies. He designates religion as the
keystone of the Roman state.[4]

In general, it may be said that Polybius is
large-minded in his judgments and aims at scrupulous fairness. While he applies ethical standards
to the conduct of public men, his broad study of
human nature inclines him generally to the more
indulgent view of their acts. Perhaps no ancient
writer was more impartial in temper than he, and
the prejudices which we can detect are exceptions
to the rule. These prejudices are chiefly to be
discovered where he deals with the affairs of
Greece. Here his patriotism has unquestionably

---

[1] v. 21 ; iii. 36.   [2] x. 2. 10.   [3] xi. 12. 9.   [4] vi. 56. 6 sqq.

coloured his account of Achaean politics, and he is
distinctly unjust to the Aetolians.   The danger of
such partiality did not escape him.   "A good
man," he says, "should be fond of his friends and
of his country, he must share in the hates and
affections of his friends.   But when he undertakes
to write history, he must forget these attachments,
he must often bestow the highest praises on
enemies when facts require it, and, on the other
hand, censure severely his most intimate friends
when their errors demand such censure."[1]   Elsewhere,[2] in censuring two Rhodian historians (Zeno
and Antisthenes) for twisting facts to the credit of
their country, he discusses the question whether a
historian should allow himself to be influenced by
patriotic feelings.   "Admitting," he says, "that
historians should lean to their countries, I deny
that they should make assertions inconsistent with
facts.   We writers must unavoidably fall into
many errors through ignorance, but if we write
what is false, for our country's sake or to please
our friends or to win favour, and measure truth by
utility, we shall discredit the authority of our
works and be no better than politicians."   The
indefeasible claim of historical truth cannot be
more explicitly expressed or emphatically enforced;
and the significance of these passages lies in the
challenge which was thrown down to the prevail-
ing practice of the rhetorical school of history.
But Polybius has not absolutely adhered himself

[1] i. 14. 4.   [2] xvi. 14.

to his admirable doctrine. He is disposed to make
their attitude to the Achaean League the measure
for judging other Greek states. On the other
hand, he is impartial towards Rome. The justification of Roman dominion is the *motif* of his
work, and the practical lesson for his fellow-Greeks
was acquiescence in that dominion. But if he
fully recognised the great qualities of the Romans,
his Greek sympathies secured him from being
blind to their faults.

Polybius, then, stands out among the few
ancient writers who understood the meaning and
recognised the obligation of historical truth and
impartiality. Belonging to no school, he opposed
the tendencies of the current historiography of the
day. But while he protests against straining after
pathetic effects and such bids for popularity, he
shows occasionally that he possessed the art of
telling a moving tale, as in his description of
Hannibal's passage of the Alps, and he can display
powers of realism in describing an insurrection at
Alexandria or the Mercenary war of the Cartha-
ginians. But there is no attempt at striking word-
pictures or purple passages; when he is effective,
he succeeds, like Herodotus, by the simplest means.
He followed the received usage of inserting
speeches, and laid stress upon their importance.
But he held that they should reproduce the tenor
of what was actually said, and he censures Timaeus
severely for having invented orations entirely out
of his own imagination. Some of the speeches

have a Polybian flavour, but we are bound to believe him that he had always evidence to work upon in their construction.

He was not indifferent to style; his care is shown in his scrupulous avoidance of hiatus. It is highly significant that in the Greek versions which he made of the Latin texts of the treaties of Rome with Carthage he neglected the rules of hiatus, the observance of which would have embarrassed or harmed the accuracy of the translation. He did not, so far as we know, follow literary models. To illustrate his diction and vocabulary we must look not to belles lettres but to the language of official-dom — decrees and despatches — and technical treatises on philosophy and science. Yet he had a wide acquaintance with literature and the classical poets. He quotes lyric poets, Pindar and Simonides, as well as Euripides. Like all educated Greeks, he was familiar with Homer, and the fragments of his thirty-fourth Book, which was concerned with the geography of the West, show that he was interested in Homeric criticism. The question was debated in ancient, as well as modern, times whether there was any real geographical background to the adventures of Odysseus. Do the islands of the Cyclops, of Circe, of Calypso, do Scylla and Charybdis, correspond to actual places on the Mediterranean coasts? Or are they "faery lands forlorn," and is it vain to seek their names on the traveller's chart? Eratosthenes held that Homer had here created a world of poetical

imagination, and that the places are as imaginary
as the people. "It is useless to look," he said,[1]
"for the scenes of the wanderings of Odysseus.
You will find those places when you find the man
who stitched together the bag of the winds."
Polybius did not agree with this view. He
accepted the common opinion that the poet's
geography was realistic, and did not hesitate to
identify the passage of Scylla and Charybdis with
the Straits of Messene. The work of M. Victor
Bérard has at least shown that in principle
Polybius was right.

But while rhetoric did not seduce Polybius, he
could not escape from the philosophical and ethical
tendencies of his age. A good deal of what I have
said will have shown that he regarded the application of moral standards and the pronouncement of
moral judgments as pertinent in history. His
ethical preoccupation is shown very clearly in his
study of political constitutions. The causes which
come into play in bringing about decay and change
are, according to his exposition, mainly ethical; he
ignores political and economical forces. Here
he is not thinking for himself; he is under the
sway of the speculations of philosophical schools.
Thucydides impresses us as more independent and
freer from the influence of speculative theory in
his criticism of facts. He was not imposed upon
by constitutional forms, and never ascribed to
them the significance which they possessed for

---

[1] xxxiv. 2. 11.

Polybius. Any superiorities which Polybius seems to enjoy over Thucydides are due to the richer experience of two and a half eventful centuries of which records had been kept, to the larger stage on which Mediterranean history had come to move, and to the inspiration of the world-power of Rome pointing to a new idea of universal history.

The positive value of the historical labours of Polybius, as a trustworthy source, can hardly be appraised too highly. I may quote the judgment of Mommsen, who was not attracted towards the personality of the author. " His books are like the sun, in the field of history; where they begin, the veils of mist, which still enshroud the wars with the Samnites and with Pyrrhus, are lifted; where they end, a new and if possible more vexatious twilight begins."

Of that part of the work which was most original because he wrote as a contemporary and had not to rely entirely on other writers, only fragments have been preserved, and of the last years which saw the destruction of Greek independence very scanty fragments indeed. But much of the material has passed directly or indirectly into the books of later historians; he became, indeed, for the period which he treats the chief ultimate source of information. If another Polybius, a man of his political experience and his historical faculty, had appeared in the next generation, our knowledge of the period of the great democratic movement, a period so critical for the Roman state

—from Tiberius Gracchus to the dictatorship of
Sulla—would have been far clearer than it is. The
task of continuing Polybius was, however, undertaken by a remarkable man of exceptional talent,
Poseidonius of Apamea (*c.* 235-151 B.C.), whose
wide influence as a thinker is becoming more and
more recognised—recognised even to exaggeration.
He was a pupil of the Stoic Panaetius; he taught
in Rhodes, where Cicero heard his lectures ; he was
a friend of Pompey, and well known to cultivated
circles in Rome. He travelled in western Europe,
and embodied his geographical researches in a book
On the Ocean, which was much used by Strabo.
Besides being a philosopher and a geographer, he
was a mathematician, an astronomer (he wrote a
book on the size of the sun), a student of natural
science, a meteorologist. He made an important
contribution to the study of tides in relation to the
phases of the moon. He had the encyclopaedic
interest and the encyclopaedic faculty of an
Aristotle or a Leibniz. History was only one,
and not the chief, of his many pursuits. His
historical work (in fifty-two or perhaps sixty-two
Books), beginning with 144 B.C. where Polybius
ended, appears to have come down to 82 B.C. We
have only a few fragments of it, but it is the source
of our knowledge of those times—the source from
which Livy, Diodorus, Appian, Plutarch, and
Josephus drew. The leanings of Poseidonius were
somewhat oligarchical, and he was partial to his
friend Pompey. Like Polybius he was a traveller,

and like Polybius he played a part in political life; it was a smaller part, and on the tiny stage of Rhodes. He once acted as ambassador of his city to Rome. Polybius was first of all a man of action; Poseidonius was first of all a philosopher and a savant, and he had a strain of poetical imagination and enthusiasm, a certain passion, which we do not find in Polybius. It is to be feared that for the vagueness of our knowledge on some of the important facts of this period Poseidonius himself is responsible rather than those who compiled from him. His mental attitude was certainly different from that of Polybius, and the difference does not conduce to confidence in Poseidonius. For in philosophy he did not follow the sobriety of his master Panaetius; his Stoicism was of a more mystical strain; in fact, it departed so far from the earlier tenets of the sect that it may be described as a theology. He believed in the mantic art, on which he wrote a treatise,[1] and in the significance of dreams; and he was thus disposed to accept what Polybius would have rejected as fabulous. On the whole, I think we may say that while Poseidonius exercised a wide and deep influence on the intellectual life of his day, and occupies a considerable place in the history of ancient learning, and while his historical work was the chief source of the records of his time, and its loss is deplorable, he cannot be said to have advanced the study of history by new

---

[1] Used by Cicero in *De Divinatione*, Book i.

principles or methods, and in some respects he represented a retrogression from Polybius. His fragments show that general *Culturgeschichte* was a conspicuous feature of his work; and he seems to have aimed at suggesting a contrast between the rude but fresh manners of barbarians like the Gauls and Parthians, and the decadent civilisation of Egypt and Syria. We cannot form any definite idea of his general treatment, but we may say with probability that Poseidonius had qualities which entitled him to be reckoned among those historians to whose works men go, not for rhetoric or sentiment, but for the illumination of the past by reasonable thought.[1]

[1] Some interesting aspects of the work of Polybius, on which I have not been able to touch in this lecture, are brought out in Mahaffy's valuable chapter on the historian in *Greek Life and Thought*.

LECTURE VII

THE political genius of Rome might lead us to expect that the Romans would have possessed a home-grown historiography of their own, reflecting their national character. But Greek influence intervened before they had time to discover a form of historiography for themselves; and in this, as in all branches of literature, they found Greek influence irresistible. Their history was moulded by the Greeks; in its methods and principles it is Greek.

Its birth from Greek history was undisguisedly proclaimed by the fact that its founders, aristocrats contemporary with the Second Punic war, wrote their Roman annals in the Greek tongue. The chief of these writers, and the only one of whose work we can form any idea, was Q. Fabius Pictor, whose book was consulted and respected by Polybius. Greek was at that time recognised as the language of the educated world; it was the Esperanto of those parts of the universe that counted; and this fact outweighed the strong national feeling which would have suggested Latin. You may remember that Frederick the Great wrote his *Memoirs* in French, and that Gibbon at first thought of composing his *Decline and Fall* in that polite and universal idiom.

To break the tradition required an unconventional man who carried his national feelings to the length of miso-Hellenism and who was determined to go his own way, M. Porcius Cato. He wrote his history of Rome, the *Origines*, in his native tongue. It expressed his own strongly marked personality, and mirrored his prejudices. Discarding the annalistic form, he introduced freely his own observations and opinions, and in fact *liberavit animam suam*. Its significance, for our present purpose, is that it was effective in breaking the tradition: his successors wrote in Latin.

But the change was only in the vehicle. The Romans remained completely under the influence of Greek methods and models. The worst tendencies of Greek history were exemplified in the *Annals* of Valerius Antias, which came down to the time of Sulla. He outdid *Graecia mendax* in audacious falsification; all claims of truth were sacrificed to national vanity. Wachsmuth calls his work "a historical romance and of the worst kind." On the other hand we have Sallust, who was a younger contemporary. He belongs to a triumvirate of Roman historians, in which some think that his true place is second, next to Tacitus and above Livy. But

unluckily of his chief book, dealing with a period
of twelve years, 78-67 B.C., only some speeches
and letters have survived. His monographs, the
Jugurtha and the *Catiline*, enable us to see that
his work was coloured to the core by a strong
personality; it sensitively reflected the deep mis-
givings and gloomy outlook which the experiences
of the Roman state in the days of Caesar and
Pompey suggested to a pessimistic observer. It
is significant that he was deeply attracted by the
most original of previous Latin historians, Cato
the Censor. But the writers who influenced him
most were Greeks, Thucydides and Poseidonius.
He came under the spell of Thucydides, but he
was of too different a nature to imitate him except
in superficial things.

Livy was inspired by the idea of giving to the
Romans a history of the growth of their nation,
which in the fulness of its treatment and the
magnitude of its scale should be adequate to the
theme. He rose to the majesty of his subject,
and triumphantly satisfied the ideal of historiography which was popular at the time. The
gentle and even flow of his style, his *clarissimus
candor* and *lactea ubertas* are irresistible. But he
had many of the deeply-rooted defects of the
rhetorical school, though his history is incomparably superior to that of his Greek contemporary,
the rhetorician Dionysius of Halicarnassus. He
wished to be accurate, but his standard was not
high and his methods were careless. Livy had

no notion of the austere methods of historical research pursued by Thucydides and Polybius. He entirely disdained the trouble of consulting primary sources such as inscriptions or the Pontifical Acts. In one of the few cases in which he refers to an inscription, his attention was called to it by the Emperor Augustus, who displayed great interest in the progress of the work. He did not take to heart the maxim of Polybius that personal knowledge of topography is necessary for a historian in narrating military events. He did not, for instance, take the trouble to visit the scene of the Battle of Lake Trasimene, and in his story of that action he has jumbled together two inconsistent accounts. On the whole, there is a great deal of truth in the Emperor Caligula's criticism that he was "wordy and careless," *verbosus et negligens.*[1]

As the work of Sallust reflected, in its temper, the stirring age of the Civil Wars, so Livy's history mirrored the calm which settled over the Roman world after the triumph of Augustus. He was a Court historian, and his work fitted into the system of the political ideals of the Emperor. With its unimpassioned optimism, it is inevitably far less interesting than the writings of his pre-

---

[1] It is to be noted that Professor Howard has successfully defended Livy against the charge that he was at first deceived by the extravagant statements of Valerius Antias, and, having afterwards become convinced of that writer's untrustworthiness, avenged his own credulity by holding him up to obloquy. Howard shows that the evidence is not there, and that Livy always used Valerius with caution. See his paper on the question, in *Harvard Studies in Classical Philology*, xvii., 1906.

decessor, who so mercilessly exposed the corruption of the Roman aristocracy, and of his greater successor, who painted the dark sides of the Imperial régime. Tacitus was not only a writer of far stronger individuality than Livy, but also a far greater historian. He was more critical, and was guided by a higher standard of what historical research required. Our distrust in reading him is not of his facts or of his use of sources, but of his innuendo and his illumination. Haupt said he was born to be a tragic poet, and his pages are saturated with his personality. The dominant note of all he wrote is expressed in those words of doom, *urgent imperii fata*. The historian who exercised most influence on him was undoubtedly Sallust, whose political and ethical pessimism was akin to his own. He outdid Sallust in *brevitas Sallustiana*; he resembled him too in solemn and deadly seriousness; in his passion for psychological analysis. But here he was also affected by the tendencies of the rhetorical schools of his own time; there, too, psychological analysis and epigrammatic brevity had come into fashion. Tacitus, though an accomplished student of rhetoric, is very careful and sparing in the use of rhetorical artifices, which he always reserves for the production of some definite effect. But in his descriptions of battles he sacrifices accuracy to style; his motive for describing them at all was not military, but rhetorical, interest.

It so happens that we have a means of testing

the relations of the speeches which Tacitus has
introduced, to those actually delivered. A bronze
tablet of Lyons preserves a considerable portion
of the harangue which the Emperor Claudius
addressed to the Senate when he conferred the
ius honorum on the inhabitants of Gaul. Tacitus
professes to reproduce this speech. A comparison
of his version with the original shows that he took
it as his basis, but remodelled it, rearranging the
order, adding some new matter, cutting down
tedious passages, adapting it to his own style, and
eliminating the Emperor's ungainly mannerisms.
For instance, Claudius in the middle of his speech
suddenly addressed himself: "It is high time,
O Tiberius Caesar Germanicus, to disclose yourself
to the Senate and show whither your oration
tends." This eccentric transition does not appear
in Tacitus. But the general tenor and argument
are the same. The case is highly instructive as
exemplifying how the best historians like Tacitus
and Thucydides constructed their speeches. When
an original speech had been published, historians
refrained from reproducing it. The literary canon
of homogeneity of style, which the Tacitean treatment of the oration of Claudius illustrates so well,
forbade them to transcribe it; and it would have
been obviously out of place to challenge comparison by a paraphrase. We can prove this rule
in the case of Livy, who expressly declines to give
a speech of Cato for the Rhodians, which Cato
had included in his own history, and in the case of

Tacitus, who similarly omits the dying discourse of Seneca on the ground that it had been already published. Exceptions were only made in favour of very short pieces. For instance, Tacitus reproduces verbally a brief communication of Tiberius to the Senate, just as Xenophon reproduced the laconic message of a Lacedaemonian admiral. Otherwise, the rule which the Roman historians inherited from the Greeks was never to reproduce documents or speeches in their original form, and to avoid reproducing at all such as had been published. Suetonius and Cornelius Nepos were exceptional in not obeying this rule; they could quote the example of Polybius.

Sallust had skilfully employed the Thucydidean method of exhibiting the motives and personalities of historical actors in speeches. But he had not confined himself to this method; he also freely pourtrayed characters himself; for example, his two contrasted pictures of Cato and Caesar are famous; and he had freely introduced personal comments of his own. Tacitus adopted the dramatic and indirect method, but he developed that method with such elaborate skill and refinement that it became a new thing in his hands. One of the simplest examples of his art is the portrait of Augustus, which he exhibits reflected in the mirror of men's judgments about him. It is managed just as a dramatist might make two people of opposite views meet in the street and argue over somebody's character, in order to show what manner of man he was.

But the *chef d'œuvre* of Tacitus is his *Tiberius*.
The author had psychologically reconstructed that
emperor on the assumption that the mainspring
of his character was dissimulation; he never discusses it as a problem, but simply reveals the man
in this light, interprets his acts and words in this
sense, and uses all the devices of innuendo, of
which he was so subtle a master, to bring it out.
The Tacitean method is illustrated by contrasting
the descriptions of Tiberius in Suetonius and
Velleius Paterculus, who collect together all the
traits of the Emperor and facts which attest them.
It is also evident that Tacitus has produced his
general effect by a limitation of his subject, by
emphasizing certain sides and omitting others.
The *Annals* are a history of Rome and the crimes
of the Julio-Claudian dynasty. The wars of the
period are indeed recorded, but it may be said
with virtual truth that the book ignores the
Empire. No reader of Tacitus would come away
with the smallest conception of the efficiency with
which the Empire as a whole was administered.

Tacitus, like Sallust, looked at history from
an ethical point of view, I mean from the point
of view of the morality which is valid for the individual. He judged actions by the ideals of virtue
and nobility; he was not prepared to take time
and circumstances into account, nor to acknowledge that the standard applied to private conduct
may be inapplicable to public transactions. In
this respect, he occupied the same ground as the

late Lord Acton, whose first principle in reading history was the application of the strictest rules of private morality to the actions of public men. It may be thought by some that this attitude in examining the past is somewhat futile. Sociology is still in its infancy, and it may be asked, Has the time come for verdicts? Is not Thucydides more reasonable, and is not his political analysis more instructive, than the ethical criticism of Tacitus? The predominating moral interest is of course one of the features which Tacitus shares with the rhetorical school. The ethical side had been emphasized, without passion, by Greek historians since the fourth century; with Tacitus it was a question of life and death.

I have still to refer to an illustrious Latin historian who stands altogether apart from the rest, in method and style, as well as in his own relation to the facts which he records. As a clear businesslike narrative of external events, told from the inside, by one who had fuller knowledge than any other man, the *Commentaries* of Caesar are a model of excellence. In reading them, indeed, we have to remember that it was not a purely historical interest that moved the writer to assume the historian's part. He had political purposes in view. The Memoir of the Gallic War was written to show the necessity of his actions and to prove or illustrate his competence. The history of the Civil War, which he left unfinished, was designed to shift the blame from his own shoulders. Thus the works are in a certain sense political pamphlets. In the story of the conquest of Gaul we cannot control the narrative; it is possible that much has been suppressed; and Caesar's artless simplicity may have been the instrument of most artful misrepresentation. Our present concern, however, is not the criticism of his facts, but his choice of that plain straightforward method of narration, which had been introduced by the men who had worked in the service of Alexander the Great. Of this genus of historical literature, Caesar's *Comment-aries* are the only extant specimen; we can have little doubt that they are the best which antiquity produced; but they were not an original growth on Roman soil; the Memoirs of Pyrrhus and Aratus were precedents. It is, however, significant that Caesar regarded his own work as merely material for the professional, that is, the rhetorical, historian to work up.

You see then that the most eminent Roman historians moved entirely within the limits of Greek traditions, in regard to principles and methods. For them all, history was, as Cicero considered it, a branch of the art of rhetoric. We may, indeed, say that from the beginning of the Empire the distinction between Greek and Latin historians has only a subordinate significance. In studying historical literature from the time of Livy and Dionysius of Halicarnassus, Greek and Latin writers must be considered together.

Rhetorical history remained in the ascendant, but antiquarian history also had some devotees. Rome has a distinguished roll of antiquarians to point to, such as Varro, Hyginus, Asconius, and it was the distinction of Suetonius to have written history which aimed simply at the industrious collection of facts, without any thought of rhetorical effects. His political attitude was very similar to that of Tacitus, but in his biographies, which (as Leo has shown) are built up on a conventional scheme, he keeps his own personal views in the background and lets the facts speak.

The development of the Graeco-Roman historiography under the early Empire, up to the time of Theodosius the Great, can now be studied in the elaborate work of Peter,[1] the special value of which consists in treating the Greek and Latin historians together, and in showing how the writing of history was affected by the Court and by the public. He has illustrated abundantly how a writer's freedom in treating contemporary history was limited by fears and hopes ; and how his scope was narrowed by the lack of interest of the public of these ages in any contemporary events except the scandals of the Court. Exceptions were few. We have been accustomed to think of Ammianus Marcellinus as the only Latin historian after Tacitus whose merits entitle him to a high place. Recently a new star has been announced, whom

---

[1] See Bibliography.

Kornemann, the discoverer, has named "the last great historian of Rome." This unknown writer is said to have supplied the authors of that ambiguous collection of imperial biographies known as the *Historia Augusta* with valuable material. Even if we accept the demonstrations, the place he holds among Latin historians will not be vacated by Ammianus for this anonymous author who flourished in the age of the Severi.[1]

I may say, finally, a few words about universal history, which became an established form of composition under the Roman Empire. It has often been noticed how the cosmopolitan doctrines of the Stoics, their creed of the brotherhood of men, gave a stimulus to the construction of comprehensive works embracing the annals of the known peoples of the world. The value of universal history, on the Stoic assumptions, has been stated impressively enough by Diodorus of Agyrion. "All men," he says, "living, or who once lived, belong to the common human family though divided from one another by time and space; and the universal historian who aims at bringing them all under a common view is a sort of minister of divine providence. That providence orders alike the stars and the natures of men, throughout the cycles of time, allotting to each its proper part; and those who have recorded the history of the

---

[1] E. Kornemann, *Kaiser Hadrian und der letzte grosse Historiker von Rom*, 1905; O. Th. Schulz, *Das Kaiserhaus der Antonine und der letzte Historiker Roms*, 1907.

world as if it were one town, have, in their
works, supplied mankind with a sort of bourse
for exchanging records of the past." Diodorus
himself, however, was quite unequal to the task.
There is no central idea in his work ; there is
no grasp of lines of development, no discernment
of interconnexion between the parts of his subject, no independent thought of his own. The
special histories of the various peoples rest side
by side in the framework of his forty Books
(was the number suggested by Polybius ?). His
history is a rhetorical compilation of excerpts
from older writers which he has paraphrased, and
its value for us lies in the circumstance that its
extant portions contain so much of lost writers
like Ephorus and Poseidonius.

Far superior in conception and grasp seems to
have been the lost work of Pompeius Trogus,
of which we know something from its Epitome
by Justin. It was a universal history of the
Hellenic and oriental world. Roman history was
excluded up to the point at which Greek and
Eastern peoples came into contact and collision
with Rome. It has been plausibly conjectured
that the author omitted Roman history because
it had been so fully treated by his contemporary,
Livy. But though its universal character was
thus limited, it showed a sense of unity and continuity, like that of Polybius ; and this was reflected in the title of the work, *Philippica*, which
indicated that Macedonian history was, more or

less, the guiding or binding thread.   Older history
had culminated in the Macedonian Empire, and
out of it had developed the great monarchies after
Alexander.   The work was thus an intelligent
development of Polybian ideas.

Such reconstructions helped to prepare for the
new framework into which history was compressed,
and the new meaning which was given to it, by
the Christians.   They undertook the task of synchronizing Graeco-Roman with Jewish records,
and constructing a universal history in theological
interests.[1]   The Church could not avoid grappling
with this problem.   Appealing to the civilised
world, Christianity was forced to take account of
the past of the non-Hebrew peoples ; making extraordinary and paradoxical claims for the super-
lative importance of Jewish history, it had to
assign to the histories of the Greeks and Romans
their proper place in the universal scheme.   The
Hebrew Scripture determined the six great ages
of human history distinguished by Augustine, of
which the last began with the birth of Christ, and
would endure—such was the confidence of these
interpreters of history—to the end of the world.[2]
The Christian interpretation found the central idea
of world-history in a religious and not in a political

---

[1] The Christian world-chronicle was constructed by Sextus Julius
Africanus, and then, on the basis of his work, by Eusebius.

[2] The succession of the four great monarchies (Assyrian, Persian,
Macedonian, and Roman), in which Greek writers had already seen a
principle of chronological division, was brought into connexion with the
prophecies of Daniel by Jerome ; and Jerome had no doubt that the
Roman was the last.

phenomenon, and it introduced into historiography
a new and pernicious principle. Hitherto history
had been perfectly free. Homer had indeed enjoyed an excessive authority among the Greeks,
but belief in Homer was not a religious doctrine,
and men like Thucydides and Eratosthenes used
the Homeric poems, just as we do, like any other
ancient source. It was with imperfect methods
and inadequate conceptions of the conditions of
the problem that the Greeks had attempted to
order the traditions of their own and other races
into a consistent whole; but they had worked
quite freely, guided by reason alone and unfettered
by dogma. Christian historiography installed the
superior guidance of an indefeasible authority, the
divinely inspired tradition of the Jewish records,
whereby they determined the general frame and
perspective of the history of the world. This was
the first appearance of the principle which Cardinal Manning expressed in his famous saying
that dogma must overcome history, and which
guides all the historiography of the Ultramontane
school.

The Christian reconstruction of history held
men's minds throughout the Middle Ages, imposed as it was by the highest ecclesiastical
authority. But though it marked no advance-
ment of knowledge, though the synthesis was
simply grotesque, it served to emphasize and in-
tensify the idea of the unity of mankind which
had already been preached by the Stoics. With

the Stoics this idea had such a vague application that it came to little more than an abstract theory ; with the Christians it acquired a real and intense meaning, inasmuch as they believed all the inhabitants of the earth to have a common and vital interest, though they might not know it, in the Christian dispensation. In so far as it accustomed men to realise the conception of a solidarity among all the races of humanity, the Christian interpretation assisted in the transition from the ancient to the modern conception of universal history. For this office a price was paid. History submitted to authority, and free inquiry was suspended for centuries.

We may also note that the conception of universal history which prevailed in the Middle Ages was connected with a general theory sometimes described as the first attempt at a philosophy of history, in so far as it professed to supply a guiding clue and a meaning to the whole development. This theory was worked out by Augustine in his *De civitate Dei*, wherein the event to which the whole world moves is defined as the victory of the *civitas Dei* (the Church) over the *civitas Diaboli* (represented by the secular kingdoms). This transcendent principle could give little help to a student desiring to comprehend the causes of the actual course of history ; and the speculation of Augustine no more claims to be called a philosophy of history than the cyclical theories of the Greeks. But though

Geschichtsphilosophie is a modern invention and Herder was its founder, the Christian construction marks an important stage : for the historical process was for the first time definitely conceived as including past and future in a totality which must have a meaning.

In these lectures I hope that I have in some measure explained how the Greeks did not suddenly create, but rather by a gradual process of criticism evolved history, disengaging it from the mythic envelope in which fact and fiction were originally blended ; how this process corresponded to the development of critical thought and scientific inquiry, first in Ionia and then at Athens ; how the early historians were stimulated by those political events which brought Ionia into close contact with the East and by the simultaneous beginnings of geographical exploration ; and how history completed the first stage of its growth and definitely extricated itself from the mythological mists which hung about its infancy and childhood, through the brilliant inspiration which occurred to the genius of Thucydides, the idea of studying critically and recording political events as they occurred. We saw that the chief events in Greek history reacted upon Greek historiography. The Persian conquests led to the investigation of "modern" history ; the defeats of Persia by Greece inspired Herodotus; the Athenian Empire stimulated Thucydides ; the rise of the Macedonian power, suggesting a new possibility of Hellenic unity, suggested also the conception of a comprehensive or universal history of Hellas; the Macedonian conquest of the East enlarged the range of historical interest; and, finally, the Roman conquests created in the mind of Polybius the largest conception of history that had yet emerged. We saw too that history was intimately affected by the general intellectual movements of each successive age—by the scepticism and science of Ionia, by the great illumination of the Sophists, by the literary ideals of Isocrates, by the literary reaction of Asia against Attic convention, by the Peripatetic philosophy which created antiquarian history, and afterwards by Stoicism; we saw that it was governed in its general development by the transcendent influence of rhetoric in Greek life; and we noticed that it was affected by the fact that in some measure it supplied the demand which is now supplied by fiction. Finally, we have seen how Roman historiography followed the lines of Greek historiography from which it sprang.

It still remains to consider the ideas which the ancients entertained as to the use and purpose of studying history and recording it, in the light of modern ideas on the same subject.

LECTURE VIII

VIEWS OF THE ANCIENTS CONCERNING THE
USE OF HISTORY

IT was not reserved for modern historians to ask themselves why history should be studied and why it should be written. The question was considered by ancient writers; and it was first posed by Thucydides. Herodotus indeed announced that the general purpose of his work was to preserve the memory of past events and record great actions which deserve the meed of fame. This statement shows that Herodotus had not asked himself the question; he assumed, and rightly assumed, the human interest of history; but he did not examine what it meant. He was prompted to write his prose epic by the same instinct which prompted the Homeric minstrels to compose their epic poems.

μοῦσ᾽ ἄρ᾽ ἀοιδὸν ἀνῆκεν ἀειδεμέναι κλέα ἀνδρῶν.

The muse inspired the bard to sing of glorious deeds of men.

He esteemed the aim of the historian to be exactly the same as the aim of the epic poet—to entertain an audience. So long as it was written from this

motive, it is clear that history was not likely to
make truth and accuracy its first consideration.

Thucydides definitely asked himself the question
why a record of human events should be kept, and
his answer placed history on a new footing. He
repudiated the view that its only or chief object
was to provide entertainment, and he laid down a
reason for its study, which, so far as we know, was
discovered by himself. "The accurate knowledge
of what has happened," he says, "will be useful,
because, according to human probability, similar
things will happen again." This is the first statement of the opinion that history has another
function than the satisfaction of curiosity or of
patriotic pride, that it has a definite practical
utility, that it contains lessons to instruct the statesman or the military commander. No historian was
more profoundly convinced of the truth of this view
than Polybius. He believed implicitly, as we saw,
that history is a school of statesmanship as well as
of the art of war ; he is never weary of insisting on
the practical utility of his subject ; and the earnestness with which he held and preached this "pragmatical" doctrine is one of the distinctions of his
work. As we have seen, the larger number of the
ancient historiographers at all times laid themselves
out exclusively to please the reading public. But
any ancient writer, subsequent to Thucydides, if
you had asked him what was the use of studying
history beyond the passing entertainment which it
might yield, would have replied that the study

served a practical purpose, supplying examples and warnings, and enabling men to judge the present and future by the past. Moralists (and with many historians the moral interest was predominant) would have insisted further that history supplied object lessons in ethics.

Now the point I would draw your attention to is that the ancients, generally, regarded history as possessing a practical use, and found the chief justification of its study therein. Before going on to consider the assumptions on which their particular view of its utility depends, I must say a word about the general proposition that history is a subject of practical value. It seems to be opposed to a view, promulgated in the last century, which repudiates all practical ends and asserts that history must be studied purely for its own sake, as an end in itself, without any ulterior object, and that any bearings on practical life which may be assigned to it are incidental. This view, if interpreted in an absolute and literal sense, seems to me to be no more than simple nonsense. History cannot be isolated (except provisionally for methodical purposes) from the total complex of human knowledge; and human knowledge has no value out of relation to human life. But if we explain "history for its own sake" as a regulative maxim, it is important and useful. In this sense, it means that history must be studied *as if* it had no bearing on anything beyond itself; the historian, in investigating the facts of the past, must not, at least in the first instance, consider anything beyond the facts themselves. In other words, it assumes that history is a science. The study of *natural* phenomena intimately affects society in its ethics, religion, and politics; the study of *historical* phenomena must affect them too. But like physical sciences and all other branches of knowledge, history requires for its scientific development complete freedom and independence; its value is annulled and its powers are paralysed if it consents to be ancillary to politics, ethics, or theology; in order to fulfil its function, it must (like all sciences) be treated as if it were an end itself. This is the true value and, so far as I can see, the only value of the cry, "History for its own sake!" inscribed on the banner under which history has made such a striking advance in the nineteenth century. But this value, I repeat, is only that of a regulative principle; it concerns only the methods and immediate aims of historians; it does not express the final purpose of their labours.

The Greeks were the founders of antiquarianism, and in a previous lecture I spoke of this as one of their precious contributions to human progress. Once it was started, it was pursued instinctively, unreflectingly, without asking the question, why? But a general answer was given in the circumstances of its origin. It was founded, as I said, by the Aristotelian school of philosophy, and was the result of the importance which Aristotle attached to all phenomena, as things worth study and possessing significance for man's synthesis of the universe.

And without being Aristotelians, or belonging to any school of philosophy, we must admit, that, as all things are interrelated, there must be a point at which every fact has a possible significance for man's view of his world, and therefore a practical value. Take historical phenomena. In the final synthesis of history, which may at least conceivably be achieved in the indefinitely distant future, all facts must have a place. And when we consider the inevitable lacunae in our records, it is clear that every fact is precious; for instance, one trivial detail may be the means of leading us to the right reconstruction, just as in a detective's investigation an apparently insignificant circumstance (such as the spelling of a word) may put the clue in his hands. You never can tell. Thus the antiquarian historian is playing the long game. He collects, sifts, and interprets facts which, if you take the short view, may seem merely curious, without relation to human life, not the business of a man whose interests are human; but at any time one of these facts may enable us to solve a problem, or prove a theory, the human interest of which is evident. We may say then that the cry of "history for its own sake," means that history has begun systematically to play the long game. Let us remember that however long be the game and however technical the rules, human interest is its ultimate justification. Let us not take the phrase "history for its own sake" to mean that it is not the proper function of history to serve any ulterior interest, and that any practical use it may have is thrown in, but not guaranteed. This idea is characteristically academic, one of those cloistral inanities which flourish, preposterous and unashamed, in the congenial air of universities.

But, further, we must not be misled into ignoring or underrating the immediate practical value which the study of history possesses; and this is the point which I would invite you especially to consider. The most important and able ancient historians, although some of them had antiquarian interests, held that the purpose of studying history must be sought in its practical value, and in immediate relations to life. But their idea of what that practical value consisted in, necessarily differs from our view of the matter at the present stage of man's development. The experience of the race and the advance of scientific thought have transformed our ideas of our own position in the universe; and now the human or practical interest in history turns out to be far more vital and deeply founded than the ancients, with their outlook on life, could have suspected.

Let us examine more closely the ancient doctrine. Both Thucydides and Polybius based their view that history possesses direct utility for men of affairs, on the assumption that similar situations recur, and that the problems of the past will come up again for solution in the future. Thucydides, according to his habit, states this doctrine in the briefest form ; Polybius explains the principle with his usual elaboration, and rests it on a philosophical theory. We saw how he presented the theory of *anacyclosis*, a cyclical movement of history. At the end of each cycle a new circuit begins, and history follows, as it were, along the line of its former tracks. This view was widely current; Cicero expresses it in the phrase *miri orbes et quasi circuitus*, "certain strange orbits and revolutions." The *a priori* synthesis of universal history which was launched on the world by the early Christian fathers, in the interest of their religion, threw the cyclical theory into the background. That theory was plainly incompatible with the central dogma of Christianity. *Alter erit tum Tiphys* would have meant *alter erit tum Christus*, and this would have stultified the Christian faith. But cyclical theories reappeared at the Renaissance. Machiavelli, who agreed with the ancients, and went further than they, in his high estimation of history as an instructress in politics, similarly based his view on the principle of a cyclical movement. Guicciardini likewise believed in the doctrine.

Our longer experience has taught us that the assumptions on which the ancients grounded the claim of history to practical utility are untenable. The theory of cycles has been abandoned for the idea of indefinite "progress," and we have ascertained that history does not repeat itself; that the likenesses between historical phenomena at different times are superficial and far less important than the differences.   It follows that the particular kind of use which the ancients ascribed to history cannot be upheld, and that, if it does possess value for the education of men of affairs, that value is either of a more general nature, or entirely different from what they supposed.

And, as a matter of fact, we have ceased to look on history as a storehouse of examples and warnings for the politician, though we recognise that it has an educative value by familiarising him with the variety of political phenomena and by enlarging his horizon.   But the conceptions of causality and development which govern our view, but did not govern the Greek view, of the world, have shown us that any given situation, or any social or political phenomenon, cannot be understood unless we know its antecedents; or in other words, that to comprehend the significance of the present we must be acquainted with the history of the past. This, I think you would agree, is the main reason (according to our present ideas) why a study of history is desirable, if not indispensable, for the man who undertakes to share in the conduct of public affairs, and is desirable also for the private citizen who votes, and criticizes, and contributes to the shaping of public opinion.

We may therefore still make the same claim for the study of history which Polybius made for it, that it is a school for statesmen and citizens, though we base the claim on a different ground. But beyond this direct utility, it has a larger and

deeper practical importance.   For the last two
generations historical investigation has been exercising, steadily and irresistibly, an influence on our
mental attitude; it has been affecting our sense of
our own position in the world and our estimate of
the values of things.   History, in the ordinary and
narrower sense of recorded human transactions, has
been advancing concurrently with that wider history, which is the business of physical science, and
which embraces the evolution of life on our planet,
the evolution of the planet itself, and the evolution
of the cosmos.   But certain results of *historical*
science, though less sensational, have been in some
respects not less effective, than the results of
physical science, because they are closer to us
and, at present at least, concern us more directly.
These results may perhaps be summed up most
concisely in the phrase used by German writers,
"historical relativity."   We have come to see that
all events in the past, however differing in importance, were relative to their historical conditions;
that they cannot be wrenched out of their chronological context and endowed with an absolute
significance.   They are parts of a whole, and have
no meaning except in relation to that whole, just
as a man's arm has no meaning apart from his
body.   The recognition of this truth at once affects
our view of the present; for it follows that the
ideas and events of to-day have no absolute value,
but merely represent a particular stage of human
development.   Ideas and facts are thus put in

their place. Some are abased, others are exalted. If they are dependent on their historical context, they may also be justified by it. For instance, from the point of view of modern conditions, we shudder at the relation which the Church held to the State in the Middle Ages; but when we study the conditions of that period, we may acknowledge that the relation was justified. It is hard to say at which of our present-day Western institutions future generations will shudder most; but we may hope that they will also discover justifications. This principle of historical relativity induces what may be called the historical attitude of mind; it changes our outlook also on the present and the future; and therefore it has a direct practical value. Perhaps it is fair to say that it is one of the most important results of the mental development of the nineteenth century.[1]

I have suggested that this change is not less effective than our new conceptions of the evolution of nature. I may illustrate this by comparing the ways in which the advance of historical science and

[1] Although the principle of historical relativity, with its implication that there are no absolute values in history, that values vary according to time and place, is a modern idea; nevertheless the Greeks made virtual application of it, occasionally and in very simple cases. Thucydides furnishes an instance. He suggests that, if the Greeks of his day regard piracy as an offence against morals, they must not apply their standard to a different stage of civilisation, when piracy was esteemed an honourable profession. This is one of the few examples to be found in ancient writers of what we call an historical sense. Another example is furnished by Eratosthenes, who pointed out that in studying Homer the historical conditions of his age must be taken into account, and that his geographical ideas corresponded to the ignorance which then prevailed; his authority therefore has no value transcending the conditions of his own time.

the advance of physical science have respectively operated on theology. The discoveries of geology, the doctrine of evolution, and the Darwinian theory created loud alarm in the Churches, but they really only touched outworks; and their acceptance by ecclesiastical authorities could not have had a much greater effect on the received body of essential doctrine than the acceptance of the heliocentric system which seemed a diabolical idea to the persecutors of Galilei. Contrast the effects of the *historical* criticism which began with Strauss and Bauer. It has been operating as a steady and powerful solvent of traditional beliefs; and to-day we see that within the Churches the men who have brains and are not afraid to use them are transforming the essential doctrines, under the aegis of historical criticism, so radically that when those doctrines emerge it will be difficult to recognise them.

I may observe here, and by the way, that it is highly important for the historian to be aware that the doctrine of historical relativity applies no less to his own historical judgments than to other facts. His view is conditioned by the mentality of his own age; the focus of his vision is determined within narrow limits by the conditions of contemporary civilisation. There can therefore be nothing final about his judgments, and their permanent interest lies in the fact that they are judgments pronounced at a given epoch and are characteristic of the tendencies and ideas of that epoch. The Greeks had no notion of this. They would have said that the judgment of a wise man at any time might be final or absolutely valid. Older Christian historians thought that they were in possession of absolute criteria; and the illusion that a historical judgment may be the last word is still prevalent. It must ultimately yield to the principle of historical relativity which, as the experience of the race grows, will be more and more fully recognised.

Before I pass from this principle I may note another point. One might think *a priori* that the study of history is eminently adapted to form an antidote to chauvinism, self-satisfaction, and intolerance. It cannot, however, be said that hitherto it has actually done much to counteract these habits of mind; it has been more inclined to subserve them. But it seems probable that it may be more effective in the future. The new historical conception, which we have been considering, is evidently calculated to promote the spirit of tolerance, and cool the spirit of self-satisfaction, more efficaciously than any previous idea. The tolerance of the ordinary man who naïvely urges in excuse of the heathen that they "know no better" must be applied, on the principle of historical relativity, to ourselves; that principle bids us remember that *we* "know no better," that we stand within the strict barriers of our historical conditions, and that we shall be judged hundreds or thousands of years hence by critics who look forth from a higher specular platform of civilisation.

The thought of the judgment of a distant

posterity leads us to another, though closely related, conception which has only in recent times become alive and real for us. It is remarkable how little the Greeks and Romans thought or speculated about the future of the race. The shortness of the period over which their historical records extended, their doctrine of cyclical recurrence, and the widely spread belief in a decline from a golden age, may have hindered them from taking a practical interest in the subject; though they contemplated long periods of time, for instance the *magnus annus*, equivalent in duration to 12,954 ordinary years. Tacitus, in a very interesting passage, asks: What do we mean by using the terms ancient and modern? "The four hundred years, which separate us from Demosthenes, seem long in comparison with the brevity of human life; but they are almost a vanishing quantity if you compare them with the duration of the ages (*ad naturam saeculorum*); why, if you consider even the *magnus annus*, Demosthenes, whom we call an ancient, seems to belong to the same year, nay the same month, as ourselves." This passage stands almost alone, I think, in its appreciation of historical perspective. But such flashes of consciousness of our position in time did not awaken any serious or persistent curiosity about the future fortunes of the race. The Greeks were imbued with what may justly be called a progressive spirit; but they did not asso- ciate their labours for the improvement of civilisa- tion with any notion of an indefinite advance of the human race in knowledge, in mastery of nature, and in the structure of society. I think we may safely say that the general conditions of their own life and thought seemed to the Greeks final, capable only of modification and improvement in details; they never dreamed that more complex forms of civilisation, and entirely different from theirs, might be reached by a gradual development in the course of time. They dreamed of a golden age, but they generally placed it behind them. They sought it in simpler, not in more complex, conditions. And their eagerness to improve the lot of man did not take the form of a conscientious or passionate sense of obligation to posterity. The idea of duty towards posterity which often appears in Greek patriotic orations has mainly a rhetorical value, and does not imply any serious concern about future generations. Afterwards, the fancy of the Christians that the life of the human race on earth would be very brief, and that men would then pass into monotonous states in which there would be no history, excluded any thoughts of future terrestrial progress; and the psychological effects of this error, promulgated by the Church, are a distinct factor in human development. It is only since this fiction has been exploded that the vista of progress in an indefinitely long future has become part of our mental outlook, and has introduced, as all ideas of such a range must introduce, a new ethical principle, namely, duty towards the future heirs of the ages. Progress was a feature in the philosophy of Leibniz. In 1750 Turgot stated a theory of historical progress very clearly. But though the doctrine was not new at the time of the French Revolution, the full significance of the idea was first impressed on the world in the famous book of Turgot's friend, Condorcet, *Esquisse d'un tableau historique des progrès de l'esprit humain* (1795). Here the meaning of the historical process was declared to be social and political progress. It is easy to see that this view, which was diffused by the writings of Comte and Buckle, as well as by the speculations of Saint-Simon and Fourier, was calculated to stimulate interest in the past more powerfully than any previous conception. It imparts to history an intenser meaning. We are led to conceive the short development which is behind us and the long development which is before us as coherent parts of a whole ; our "pragmatic" interest in the destinies of our race necessarily communicates a "pragmatic" interest to its past fortunes.

"Progress" of course implies a judgment of value, and is not scientific. It assumes a standard,— some end or ends, by relation to which we judge historical movements and declare that they mean progress. We have no proof that absolute progress has been made, for we have no knowledge of an absolute end ; and, therefore, scientifically we are not justified in speaking of the history of civilised man as progress ; we can only be sure that it is a causal sequence of transformations.

It may, then, be objected that the indefinite progress of the race is only an assumption, which time may disprove. It may be asked too, what guarantee have we that our Western civilisation, granting that it is on an upward gradient, and that no bounds or bars to its ascent are yet in sight, may not some day reach a definite limit, through the operation of some cause which is now obscure to our vision? Fully admitting that such theoretical scepticism is justifiable, and that persistent progress is an assumption, I submit that it does not affect my point. The idea of progress is, in the present age, an actual, living force; and what I have said as to its bearing on the study of history remains valid. May we not even say that the uncertainty which hangs about the question, with the possibility of man's progress on the one hand, and of his decadence on the other, communicates an appealing interest to the study of the past, as a field in which we may discover, if we can penetrate deep enough, some clue to the destinies of civilisation?

The absence of the idea of an indefinite progress in Greek and Roman speculation is one of the gulfs which separate us from the ancients. Its emergence has had the consequence of making history far more alive. With the Greeks, who applied the inadequate conception of Tyche or Fortune, the reconstruction of the past was an instinct which they justified by reasons which were superficial. For us, because we have a deeper insight into the causal connexion of past and future, because we have grasped the idea of development and dreamed the dream of progress, the reconstruction of history has become a necessity.

It has also become a science. The promotion of history to the rank of a science or *Wissenschaft* is due to the conception of development. We conceive every historical event or phenomenon as a moment in a continuous process of change, and the historian's problem is to determine as completely as possible its connexions with what went before and with what came after, to define its causal relations and its significance in the development to which it belongs. The unattainable ideal of historical research is to explain fully the whole development of human civilisation. This is as much a scientific problem as to trace the history of the solar system or of animal life on the earth, though natural and historical science deal with very different kinds of data, and employ different methods. If the Greeks had possessed records extending over the history of two or three thousand years, the conception of causal development would probably have emerged, and they might have founded scientific history. The limitation of their knowledge of the past to a few centuries disabled them from evolving this idea ; and history therefore always remained subordinate to immediate practical ends. But we must not underrate the importance of the new view which Thucydides announced to the world, that history is

not merely a story book, but an education for
statesmen. That view marked a great advance.
It meant a new conception of the historian's
responsibility and the inauguration of a higher
standard of accuracy. Its proclamation by Thucydides may be placed beside the announcement of
scientific history in 1824 [1] by Ranke, who suggested
that the historian's task is not to teach lessons or
pass judgments, but simply to investigate how
things happened. And as the view of Thucydides
was combined with the requirement of accuracy,
so the appearance of the modern doctrine was
contemporaneous with the introduction of scientific
methods.

As a science, history is disinterested. Yet the
very idea of development, which led to the conception of history as a science, has enhanced its
interest for mankind. So far, indeed, is the Greek
view that history has a value for life from being
exploded, that the bearing of the past on our
mental outlook, on our ideas and judgments, on the
actualities of the present and the eventualities of
the future, is increasing more and more, and is
becoming charged with deeper significance. The
Hellenic conception of history as humanistic is
truer than ever.

[1] Preface to *Geschichten der romanischen und germanischen Völker von
1494 bis 1535.*

APPENDIX

THE RE-HANDLING OF HIS HISTORY BY THUCYDIDES

THE natural probability that Thucydides occupied the years of his exile after the Fifty Years' Peace in finishing and revising the history of the war which was apparently over, is borne out by a number of passages which evidently contemplate only the Ten Years' War, and must have been differently phrased if they had been composed after 404 B.C. But, on the other hand, there are also a number of passages which refer to later events, and imply the Sicilian expedition and the fall of Athens. The obvious explanation is that the author read over the first portion of his work, and made a number of additions and alterations, but allowed some inconsistent phrases to escape his eye.[1]

The most unmistakable of these additions is the passage[2] in which the author escorts Pericles from the scene and characterizes his statesmanship in the light of the subsequent events which approved its wisdom, showing that if his policy had been pursued, and if he had had a successor like himself, the issue would have been different. Here Thucydides comments on the Sicilian expedition and refers to the later events of the war.[3]

But there is a far longer and more important section in

---

[1] As iv. 48. 5 ; ii. 94. 1 (which was not revised in the light of viii. 96. 1).

[2] ii. 65. 5 to end.

[3] The last sentences of ii. 81 were posterior to the Sicilian expedition. The notice of Archelaus (413-399 B.C.), ii. 100. 2, is a late insertion ; likewise iv. 74. 4. E. Meyer has noted that κρῆναι γὰρ οὔπω ἦσαν αὐτόθι, ii. 48. 2, points to a date after 414 B.C. (schol. Arist. *Av.* 997).

the first Book which must be judged a subsequent insertion :
the historical sketch of the growth of Athens from the year
478 to 435 B.C.   The purpose of this sketch is to exhibit the
growth of the Athenian hegemony, and its justification is
that the true cause of the war, so far as the Spartans were
concerned, was to prevent Athens from increasing that
hegemony still more.   Now if Thucydides had grasped this
idea from the first, the appropriate place for his historical
sketch, both logically and chronologically, was at the
beginning of his work, in the Introduction.   It would have
formed a natural continuation of the still earlier history
which he had sketched there.   Instead, it comes in after
the account of the First Assembly of allies at Sparta,
strangely interrupting the narrative.   It serves perhaps an
artistic purpose; for it affords a not unwelcome pause after
the strain of the four speeches in the First Assembly, before
we pass to the immediately following speech of the Corinthians in the Second Assembly.   But while this consideration
may have determined the place chosen for its insertion, it
was, I believe, an afterthought.   There is internal evidence
that it was not originally part of the work.[1]   For the Introduction, where, as I said, we might have expected to find
such a sketch, actually contains a brief summary of the
relevant features of the period.[2]   Further, Thucydides had
before him, as he tells us, the Attic chronicle of Hellanicus ;
the defects of that work supplied him with a special motive
for writing a more adequate and accurate narrative ; and
this work of Hellanicus was not published in its earlier form
till 411 B.C., in its later till 404 B.C.   And may we not fairly
say that these prolegomena had a fuller justification in a
history of a war ending in the catastrophe of the Athenian
empire than in the narrative of a war ending with the

---

[1] The allusion to the destruction of the long walls (c. 93. 5) cannot be
pressed, as it might have been introduced alone. But it is to be noted
that the Pentekontaëteris is ignored in i. 146 ; while i. 23. 6 seems to be a
later insertion.

[2] Cc. 18, 19. The Introduction (i. 1-23) was evidently written before
414 B.C. as a Preface to the history of the Ten Years' War. A few phrases
may have been changed or added, but not so much as an allusion to the
fall of Athens was introduced.

indecisive Peace of 421 B.C., which left things pretty much
as they were?

Again, we may reasonably suspect that the speech of
Hermocrates at Gela in 424 B.C. was composed and inserted
after the Sicilian expedition. While it contains remarks
which seem to imply that the later events were before the
author's mind,[1] the decisive consideration is that the significance of the transactions of 424 B.C. was not apparent till the
events beginning in 415 B.C., and it seems most improbable
that but for those events Thucydides would have emphasized
the Congress of Gela by introducing the speech of Hermocrates.

It is a delicate question whether some of the other
speeches in the early section have been retouched, and reflect
light impinging from what at the time lay in the obscurity
of the future. For instance, in the appeal for peace which
Spartan envoys addressed to the Athenian assembly,[2] at the
time of the Sphacterian episode, they hold up an ideal of
conduct which sounds like an ironical reflexion on Sparta's
own treatment of Athens twenty years later. To Eduard
Meyer, the funeral oration pronounced by Pericles on those
who had fallen in the first year of the war seems designed
by the author to be in truth a funeral oration on Athens
herself. This is a pretty idea, but I cannot find anything
in the speech necessarily implying that it was written after
the catastrophe. On the other hand, in the later speech
of Pericles, delivered to encourage the Athenians in their
despondency, there is a passage which seems to accuse him
of second sight. There is a vein of pessimism or melancholy,
a note which Pericles would not have struck on such an
occasion, and which the author would hardly have introduced
before the worst had befallen. The speaker observes that
decline and fall (ἐλασσοῦσθαι) is a law of nature, and that if
Athens should fall, she will leave a great memory of her
empire, her military successes, and her wealth. This is the
consolation one might proffer after 404 B.C.; it is not what
would have been said to comfort the citizens in 429 B.C.; it
is hardly what would have been written in the interval.

[1] iv. 60 : allusions to the Athenian expedition and to Melos.
[2] iv. 17-20.

The narrative of the last years of the first war may have demanded revision for another reason. The author was absent from Athens ever since he assumed the command of a fleet in Thrace, and there were documents and information which *perhaps* he had no opportunity to procure until he returned to his country after his exile. It has been suggested by Kirchhoff that the text of the armistice between Athens and Sparta in 423 B.C.[1] was a subsequent insertion. It might, of course, have been procured at Sparta. The text too of the Peace of 421 B.C.[2] is inserted in a narrative which reads rather as if it had been composed without accurate knowledge of the precise stipulations; but this can hardly be pressed. In general it seems probable that all the verbal copies of documents which appear in the text would, in the final revision, have been reproduced in the author's own words.

Although Thucydides re-handled his early work, which was now to be only part of a much greater work, he never prepared it finally for publication or gave it the last touches of revision. Passages remain which exhibit the earlier view that the war was over in 421; and there are difficulties here and there which are probably due to want of final correction.

In the transition from the first to the second part of his history (v. 20-26) there are clear signs of imperfect joining, due to the successive views which Thucydides entertained of the war, namely :

(1) Before 414 B.C.: one war of ten years ($\tau o\hat{v}$ $\pi o\lambda\acute{e}\mu o\nu$ $\tau o\hat{v}\delta\epsilon$, 20. 1);

(2) After 414 B.C.: two wars, of which the second began in this year and was in progress;

(3) After 404 B.C.: one war of twenty-seven years.

In the first place we can see, I think, how Thucydides originally concluded his history of the first war, before he thought of a continuation (414 B.C.). We have two conclusions, c. 20 and c. 24. C. 20 is the natural conclusion; it immediately follows the Fifty Years' Peace which terminated the war. But then cc. 21-24 relate the alliance between the

[1] iv. 118-119.   [2] v. 18-19.

Athenians and Lacedaemonians which followed a little later; and a phrase in c. 24 betrays the fact that this was inserted after 404 B.C.: καὶ τὸ θέρος ἦρχε τοῦ ἐνδεκάτου ἔτους. The eleventh year, of what? Of the war of twenty-seven years. After these words there follows: ταῦτα δὲ τὰ δέκα ἔτη ὁ πρῶτος πόλεμος ξυνεχῶς γενόμενος γέγραπται. Obviously this is (1) out of place here; it ought to come in c. 20 after the Peace; and (2) in point of grammar, ταῦτα is not intelligible, for no ten years have been mentioned in the context. But if it came originally in c. 20 (whether after the last sentence or after the first; in both positions ταῦτα would be equally in place), it was considerably altered, for the point of ξυνεχῶς is the contrast between the Ten Years' War and the Twenty-seven Years' War. But the alteration was made hastily and provisionally; and ταῦτα, which betrays it, shows the lack of a careful final revision.

Cc. 25, 26 form the introduction to the second part of the history. C. 26 declares itself to have been written after 404 B.C. C. 25 *may* have been written while Thucydides still considered the second part to be the history of a second war; but there is no proof of this hypothesis.[1] On the other hand, the introduction of πρώτῳ, πρῶτος at the end of the first part (20 *ad fin.*, 24 *ad fin.*) might naturally have been made when he began his continuation after 414 B.C.

It is an interesting philological problem to penetrate into the secrets of the historian's workshop, but here I have been only concerned to illustrate the important facts that the first part of the work was re-handled and that in some parts it needed further revision.

---

[1] It involves the corollary that the words καὶ τὴν ξυμμαχίαν——'Αθηναίων (25. 1) were subsequently added, concurrently with the insertion of 21-24.

BIBLIOGRAPHY

[This selected list comprises works which have been of direct use, great or slight, to the author for the preparation of these lectures. Editions of the historians are not included except in one or two special cases.]

1. GENERAL

BAUER, A. Die Forschungen zur griechischen Geschichte 1888-1898. Munich, 1899.

BELOCH, J. Griechische Geschichte, vols. i.-iii. Strassburg, 1893-1904.

BRUNS, I. Das litterarische Porträt der Griechen im fünften und vierten Jahrhundert v. Chr. Berlin, 1896.

BRUNS, I. Die Persönlichkeit in der Geschichtschreibung der Alten. Berlin, 1898.

BÜDINGER, M. Die Universalhistorie im Altertum. Vienna, 1895.

BUSOLT, G. Griechische Geschichte, vols. i.-iii. Gotha, 1893-1904.

CAUER, F. Thukydides und seine Vorgänger. Historische Zeitschrift, 83, 385 sqq. 1899.

CREUZER, G. F. Die historische Kunst der Griechen in ihrer Entstehung und Fortbildung. (323 pp.) Leipzig, 1803.

DIONYSIUS OF HALICARNASSUS. Opera rhetorica. (Especially, Περὶ Θουκυδίδου, Περὶ τῶν Θουκυδίδου ἰδιωμάτων, Πρὸς Πομπήϊον Γέμινον ἐπιστολή, and the fragments of Περὶ μιμήσεως.)

DRERUP, E. Die historische Kunst der Griechen. Jahrbücher für klassische Philologie, Supplementband xxvii. 443 sqq. 1902.

GOMPERZ, TH. Griechische Denker, vol. i. Leipzig, 1893, etc.

LEO, F. Die griechisch-römische Biographie. Leipzig, 1901.

MAHAFFY, J. P. History of Classical Greek Literature, vol. ii., Parts I. and II., Ed. 3. London, 1890.

MAHAFFY, J. P. Greek Life and Thought, 323-146 B.C. Ed. 2. London, 1896.

MEYER, E. Geschichte des Altertums, vols. ii.-v. Stuttgart, 1893-1902.

MEYER, E. Forschungen zur alten Geschichte, I. Zur älteren griechischen Geschichte. Halle, 1892.

MÜLLER, C. Fragmenta Historicorum Graecorum, vols. i.-iv. Paris, 1841-51.

MÜLLER, C. Scriptores rerum Alexandri Magni (along with Arrian's works, in the Didot series). Paris, 1846.

MURRAY, GILBERT. History of Ancient Greek Literature. London, 1897.

NORDEN, E. Die antike Kunstprosa. Leipzig, 1898.

PETER, H. Die geschichtliche Litteratur über die römische Kaiserzeit bis Theodosius I. und ihre Quellen, 2 vols. Leipzig, 1897.

SCHIRMEISTER, H. Charakteristische Erscheinungen in der antiken Geschichtschreibung. Pyritz, 1896.

SEECK, O. Die Entwicklung der antiken Geschichtschreibung und andere populäre Schriften. Berlin, 1898.

STAHL, TH. Ueber den Zusammenhang der ältesten griechischen Geschichtschreibung mit der epischen Dichtung. Jahrbücher für klassische Philologie, 153, 369 sqq. 1896.

SUSEMIHL, F. Geschichte der griechischen Litteratur in der Alexandrinerzeit, 2 vols. Leipzig, 1892.

WACHSMUTH, C. Einleitung in das Studium der alten Geschichte. Leipzig, 1895.

WACHSMUTH, C. Ueber Ziele und Methoden der griechischen Geschichtschreibung. (Rectoratsrede.) Leipzig, 1897.

WIPPRECHT, F. Zur Entwicklung der rationalistischen Mythendeutung bei den Griechen, i. Tübingen, 1902.

2. SPECIAL

Acusilaus.

KORDT, A. De Acusilao. Basel, 1903.

Antiochus.

WÖLFFLIN, J. Antiochus von Syrakus und Coelius
Antipater. Leipzig, 1872.

Aristotle.

SEECK, O. Quellenstudien zu des Aristoteles Verfas-
sungsgeschichte Athens. Beiträge zur alten Geschichte (Klio), iv. 164 sqq. and 270 sqq. 1904.

WILAMOWITZ - MÖLLENDORFF, U. VON. Aristoteles und
Athen., 2 vols. Berlin, 1893.

Craterus.

KEIL, B. Der Perieget Heliodorus von Athen. Hermes,
xxx. 199 sqq. 1894.

KRECH, J. De Crateri Ψηφισμάτων συναγωγή et de locis
aliquot Plutarchi ex ea petitis. Greifswald, 1888.

Cratippus.

CRATIPPUS. Oxyrhynchus Papyri, Part V. (ed. Grenfell
and Hunt), No. 842. London, 1908.

DE SANCTIS, GAETANO. L' Attide di Androzione e un
papiro di Oxyrhynchos. Turin, 1908.

Dionysius of Miletus.

LEHMANN, C. F. Dionysios von Milet. Beiträge zur
alten Geschichte (Klio), ii. 334 sqq. and iii. 330 sqq.

Ephorus.

SCHWARTZ, E. Article "Ephoros" in Pauly-Wissowa,
Realencyklopädie.

Hecataeus.

PRAŠEK, J. V. Hekataios als Herodots Quelle zur Geschichte Vorderasiens. Beiträge zur alten Geschichte
(Klio), iv. 193 sqq. 1904.

Hellanicus.

KULLMER, H. Hellanikos. Jahrbücher für klassische
Philologie, Supplementband xxvii, 455 sqq. 1902.
[Includes a new edition and redistribution of the
fragments.]

LEHMANN-HAUPT, C. F. Hellanikos, Herodot, Thukydides. Klio, vi. 127 sqq. 1906.

Herodotus.

BAUER, A.   Die Entstehung des herodotischen Geschichtswerkes.   Berlin, 1878.

HAUVETTE, A.   Hérodote historien des guerres médiques.
Paris, 1894.

KIRCHHOFF, A.   Die Entstehungszeit des herodotischen
Geschichtswerkes, Ed. 2.   Berlin, 1878.

KRAUSSE, R.   De Panyasside.   Hanover, 1891.

LEHMANN, C. F.   Die historische Semiramis und
Herodot.   Beiträge zur alten Geschichte (Klio),
i. 256 sqq.   1901.

MACAN, R. W.   Herodotus, Books iv. to vi.   2 vols.
1895.   Books vii. to ix.   2 vols.   1908.

PLUTARCH, Περὶ τῆς Ἡροδότου κακοηθείας.   In vol. 5 of
the Moralia ed. Bernardakis.

SCHWARTZ, E.   Quaestiones Ionicae.   Rostock, 1891.

WIEDEMANN, A.   Herodots zweites Buch mit sachlichen
Bemerkungen.   Leipzig, 1890.

Isocrates.

SCALA, R. VON.   Isokrates und die Geschichtschreibung.
(Vortrag auf der 41. Versammlung deutscher Philo-
logen.)   Leipzig, 1892.

Pherecydes of Leros.

BERTSCH, H.   Pherekydeische Studien.   Tauberbischofs-
heim, 1898.

Polybius.

CUNTZ, O.   Polybius und sein Werk.   Leipzig, 1902.

DAVIDSON, J. STRACHAN.   Selections from Polybius.
Oxford, 1888.

LA-ROCHE, P.   Charakteristik von Polybius.   Leipzig,
1857.

NISSEN, H.   Die Oekonomie der Geschichte des Polybios.   Rheinisches Museum, xxvi. 241 sqq.   1871.

SCALA, R. VON.   Die Studien des Polybios, i.   Stuttgart, 1890.

THOMMEN, R.   Abfassungszeit der Geschichten des
Polybios.   Hermes, xx. 196 sqq.   1885.

WUNDERER, C.   Die psychologischen Anschauungen des
Historikers Polybios.   Erlangen, 1905.

Theopompus.

DIDYMUS. De Demosthene Commenta. Ed. Diels and
Schubart in Berliner Klassikertexte, i. Berlin,
1904, and in Teubner's Volumina Aegyptiaca.
Leipzig, 1904.

Thucydides.

BUSOLT, G. Thukydides und der themistokleische
Mauerbau. Beiträge zur alten Geschichte (Klio),
v. 255 sqq. 1905.

CORNFORD, F. M. Thucydides Mythistoricus. London,
1907.

CWIKLINSKI, L. Quaestiones de tempore quo Thucydides priorem historiae suae partem composuerit.
Berlin, 1873.

HERBST, L. Zur Urkunde in Thukydides v. 47.
Hermes, xxvii. 374 sqq. 1891.

HOLZAPFEL, L. Doppelte Relationen im viii. Buche des
Thukydides. Hermes, xxix. 435 sqq. 1894.

KIRCHHOFF, A. Thukydides und sein Urkundenma-
terial. Berlin, 1895.

KORNEMANN, E. Thukydides und die römische His-
toriographie. Philologus, lxiii. 148 sqq.

MEVES, W. Untersuchungen über das achte Buch
der thukydideischen Geschichte. Brandenburg
a. H., 1865.

NISSEN, H. Der Ausbruch des peloponnesischen
Krieges. Historische Zeitschrift lxiii. (N. F.
xxvii.) 385 sqq. 1890.

STEIN, H. Zur Quellenkritik des Thukydides. Rheinisches Museum lv. 531 sqq. 1900.

STEUP, J. Thukydides, Antiochos und die angebliche
Biographie des Hermokrates [a refutation of Stein's
paper]. Ib. lvi. 443 sqq. 1901.

WILAMOWITZ-MÖLLENDORFF, U. VON. Memoriae oblite-
ratae. Hermes, xi. 294 sqq. 1876.

WILAMOWITZ-MÖLLENDORFF, U. VON. Die Thukydides-
legende. Hermes, xii. 326 sqq. 1877.

Timaeus.

GEFFCKEN. Timaios' Geographie des Westens. Berlin,
1892.

INDEX

Achaeans, Polybius on, 202, 216, 217

Acton, Lord, 232

Acusilaus of Argos, mythographer, 18, 19-21, 25, 103

Aegina, miracle of statues in, 58

Aeschines, *Dialogues* of, 180

Aeschylus, 66, 68, 109

Africanus, Sextus Julius, 237

Agathocles, books on, 168, 169, 172

Agesilaus, 152, 153

αἰτία in Thucydides, 93, 94, in Polybius, 200

Alcibiades, conjectural relations with Thucydides (Kirchhoff), 84; treatment of, by Thucydides, 88, 120, 127 *sq.*; forcible style, 109

Alcidamas, 170

Alcmaeonids, Herodotus on, 61, 64

Alexander the Great, 159, 162; Hegesias on, 171; influence of his conquests on historiography, 175 *sqq.*, 178

Alexandria, libraries, 187; antiquarianism at, 187 *sqq.*

Ammianus Marcellinus, 234

Anacyclosis. See under Cyclical

Anaxagoras, 129

Anaximander, 11, 15, 205

Anaximenes, historian, 162

Androtion, 156, 179, 183

Annus, magnus, 254

Anticleides, 183

Antiochus of Commagene, 170

Antiochus of Syracuse, 26 *sq.*, 103

Antiphon, 103, 120 *sq.*, 144, 179, 180

Antiquarianism, 188 *sqq.*

Antisthenes, 180

Antisthenes of Rhodes, 216

Apollodorus, his use of Hellanicus, 30

Apollonius of Rhodes, 168

Appian, 221

Aratus, Memoirs of, 176, 233

Archidamus, 91, 113

ἀρετή, 119, 144

Aristeas of Proconnesus, 7, 25

Aristobulus, Memoirs of, 175, 176

Aristophanes, 99, 122

Aristotle, 179; 182 *sqq.*, 246

Arrian, 175

Artaxerxes I., reference to, in Herodotus, 37

Artemisium, battle of; incident not recorded by Herodotus, 25

Asconius, 234

Asianic style, 169 *sqq.*, two kinds of, 170 *sq.*; example, 171 *sq.*

Assur-bani-pal, his history of his own reign, 3

Astyochus, Spartan general, 84

Ἀθηναίων πολιτεία, anonymous, 179

Athens, partiality of Herodotus to, 62 *sqq.*; Herodotus at, 36, 65, 69; Athenian tradition of Persian war, 66; Lectures III. and IV. *passim*, 155; educational and literary centre, 161, 167

Atthidographers, 183

Atticism, 148, 170, 206

Augustine, St., 237, 239

Augustus, Emperor, 227, 230

Bérard, V., 7, 100, 219

Bertsch, H., 19, and Bibliography

Biography, 147, 153 *sq.*, 234

Βίος, pregnant meaning of, 153, cp. 187

273

THE END

Catalog
of
DOVER BOOKS

BOOKS EXPLAINING SCIENCE

(Note: The books listed under this category are general introductions, surveys, reviews, and non-technical expositions of science for the interested layman or scientist who wishes to brush up. Dover also publishes the largest list of inexpensive reprints of books on intermediate and higher mathematics, mathematical physics, engineering, chemistry, astronomy, etc., for the professional mathematician or scientist. For our complete Science Catalog, write Dept. catrr., Dover Publications, Inc., 180 Varick Street, New York 14, N. Y.)

CONCERNING THE NATURE OF THINGS, Sir William- Bragg. Royal Institute Christmas Lectures by Nobel Laureate. Excellent plain-language introduction to gases, molecules, crystal structure, etc. explains "building blocks" of universe, basic properties of matter, with simplest, clearest examples, demonstrations. 32pp. of photos; 57 figures. 244pp. 5⅜ x 8.
T31 Paperbound **$1.35**

MATTER AND LIGHT, THE NEW PHYSICS, Louis de Broglie. Non-technical explanations by a Nobel Laureate of electro-magnetic theory, relativity, wave mechanics, quantum physics, philosophies of science, etc. Simple, yet accurate introduction to work of Planck, Bohr, Einstein, other modern physicists. Only 2 of 12 chapters require mathematics. 300pp. 5⅜ x 8.
T35 Paperbound **$1.60**

THE COMMON SENSE OF THE EXACT SCIENCES, W. K. Clifford. For 70 years, Clifford's work has been acclaimed as one of the clearest, yet most precise introductions to mathematical symbolism, measurement, surface boundaries, position, space, motion, mass and force, etc. Prefaces by Bertrand Russell and Karl Pearson. Introduction by James Newman. 130 figures. 249pp. 5⅜ x 8.
T61 Paperbound **$1.60**

THE NATURE OF LIGHT AND COLOUR IN THE OPEN AIR, M. Minnaert. What causes mirages? haloes? "multiple" suns and moons? Professor Minnaert explains these and hundreds of other fascinating natural optical phenomena in simple terms, tells how to observe them, suggests hundreds of experiments. 200 illus; 42 photos. xvi + 362pp.
T196 Paperbound **$1.95**

SPINNING TOPS AND GYROSCOPIC MOTION, John Perry. Classic elementary text on dynamics of rotation treats gyroscopes, tops, how quasi-rigidity is induced in paper disks, smoke rings, chains, etc, by rapid motion, precession, earth's motion, etc. Contains many easy-to-perform experiments. Appendix on practical uses of gyroscopes. 62 figures. 128pp.
T416 Paperbound **$1.00**

A CONCISE HISTORY OF MATHEMATICS, D. Struik. This lucid, easily followed history of mathematics from the Ancient Near East to modern times requires no mathematical background itself, yet introduces both mathematicians and laymen to basic concepts and discoveries and the men who made them. Contains a collection of 31 portraits of eminent mathematicians. Bibliography. xix + 299pp. 5⅜ x 8.
T255 Paperbound **$1.75**

THE RESTLESS UNIVERSE, Max Born. A remarkably clear, thorough exposition of gases, electrons, ions, waves and particles, electronic structure of the atom, nuclear physics, written for the layman by a Nobel Laureate. "Much more thorough and deep than most attempts . . . easy and delightful," CHEMICAL AND ENGINEERING NEWS. Includes 7 animated sequences showing motion of molecules, alpha particles, etc. 11 full-page plates of photographs. Total of nearly 600 illus. 315pp. 6⅛ x 9¼.
T412 Paperbound **$2.00**

WHAT IS SCIENCE?, N. Campbell. The role of experiment, the function of mathematics, the nature of scientific laws, the limitations of science, and many other provocative topics are explored without technicalities by an eminent scientist. "Still an excellent introduction to scientific philosophy," H. Margenau in PHYSICS TODAY. 192pp. 5⅜ x 8.
S43 Paperbound **$1.25**

FADS AND FALLACIES IN THE NAME OF SCIENCE, Martin Gardner. The standard account of the various cults, quack systems and delusions which have recently masqueraded as science: hollow earth theory, Atlantis, dianetics, Reich's orgone theory, flying saucers, Bridey Murphy, psionics, irridiagnosis, many other fascinating fallacies that deluded tens of thousands. "Should be read by everyone, scientist and non-scientist alike," R. T. Birge, Prof. Emeritus, Univ. of California; Former President, American Physical Society. Formerly titled, "In the Name of Science." Revised and enlarged edition. x + 365pp. 5⅜ x 8.

T394 Paperbound **$1.50**

THE STUDY OF THE HISTORY OF MATHEMATICS, THE STUDY OF THE HISTORY OF SCIENCE, G. Sarton. Two books bound as one. Both volumes are standard introductions to their fields by an eminent science historian. They discuss problems of historical research, teaching, pitfalls, other matters of interest to the historically oriented writer, teacher, or student. Both have extensive bibliographies. 10 illustrations. 188pp. 5⅜ x 8. T240 Paperbound **$1.25**

THE PRINCIPLES OF SCIENCE, W. S. Jevons. Unabridged reprinting of a milestone in the development of symbolic logic and other subjects concerning scientific methodology, probability, inferential validity, etc. Also describes Jevons' "logic machine," an early precursor of modern electronic calculators. Preface by E. Nagel. 839pp. 5⅜ x 8. S446 Paperbound **$2.98**

SCIENCE THEORY AND MAN, Erwin Schroedinger. Complete, unabridged reprinting of "Science and the Human Temperament" plus an additional essay "What is an Elementary Particle?" Nobel Laureate Schroedinger discusses many aspects of modern physics from novel points of view which provide unusual insights for both laymen and physicists. 192 pp. 5⅜ x 8.

T428 Paperbound **$1.35**

BRIDGES AND THEIR BUILDERS, D. B. Steinman & S. R. Watson. Information about ancient, medieval, modern bridges; how they were built; who built them; the structural principles employed; the materials they are built of; etc. Written by one of the world's leading authorities on bridge design and construction. New, revised, expanded edition. 23 photos; 26 line drawings, xvii + 401pp. 5⅜ x 8. T431 Paperbound **$1.95**

HISTORY OF MATHEMATICS, D. E. Smith. Most comprehensive non-technical history of math in English. In two volumes. Vol. I: A chronological examination of the growth of mathematics from primitive concepts up to 1900. Vol. II: The development of ideas in specific fields and areas, up through elementary calculus. The lives and works of over a thousand mathematicians are covered; thousands of specific historical problems and their solutions are clearly explained. Total of 510 illustrations, 1355pp. 5⅜ x 8. Set boxed in attractive container. T429, T430 Paperbound, the set **$5.00**

PHILOSOPHY AND THE PHYSICISTS, L. S. Stebbing. A philosopher examines the philosophical implications of modern science by posing a lively critical attack on the popular science expositions of Sir James Jeans and Arthur Eddington. xvi + 295pp. 5⅜ x 8.

T480 Paperbound **$1.65**

ON MATHEMATICS AND MATHEMATICIANS, R. E. Moritz. The first collection of quotations by and about mathematicians in English. 1140 anecdotes, aphorisms, definitions, speculations, etc. give both mathematicians and layman stimulating new insights into what mathematics is, and into the personalities of the great mathematicians from Archimedes to Euler, Gauss, Klein, Weierstrass. Invaluable to teachers, writers. Extensive cross index. 410pp. 5⅜ x 8.

T489 Paperbound **$1.95**

NATURAL SCIENCE, BIOLOGY, GEOLOGY, TRAVEL

A SHORT HISTORY OF ANATOMY AND PHYSIOLOGY FROM THE GREEKS TO HARVEY, C. Singer. A great medical historian's fascinating intermediate account of the slow advance of anatomical and physiological knowledge from pre-scientific times to Vesalius, Harvey. 139 unusually interesting illustrations. 221pp. 5⅜ x 8. T389 Paperbound **$1.75**

THE BEHAVIOUR AND SOCIAL LIFE OF HONEYBEES, Ronald Ribbands. The most comprehensive, lucid and authoritative book on bee habits, communication, duties, cell life, motivations, etc. "A MUST for every scientist, experimenter, and educator, and a happy and valuable selection for all interested in the honeybee," AMERICAN BEE JOURNAL. 690-item bibliography. 127 illus.; 11 photographic plates. 352pp. 5⅜ x 8⅜. S410 Clothbound **$4.50**

TRAVELS OF WILLIAM BARTRAM, edited by Mark Van Doren. One of the 18th century's most delightful books, and one of the few first-hand sources of information about American geography, natural history, and anthropology of American Indian tribes of the time. "The mind of a scientist with the soul of a poet," John Livingston Lowes. 13 original illustrations, maps. Introduction by Mark Van Doren. 448pp. 5⅜ x 8. T326 Paperbound **$2.00**

STUDIES ON THE STRUCTURE AND DEVELOPMENT OF VERTEBRATES, Edwin Goodrich. The definitive study of the skeleton, fins and limbs, head region, divisions of the body cavity, vascular, respiratory, excretory systems, etc., of vertebrates from fish to higher mammals, by the greatest comparative anatomist of recent times. "The standard textbook," JOURNAL OF ANATOMY. 754 illus. 69-page biographical study. 1186-item bibliography. 2 vols. Total of 906pp. 5⅜ x 8.

Vol. I: S449 Paperbound **$2.50**
Vol. II: S450 Paperbound **$2.50**

DOVER BOOKS

THE BIRTH AND DEVELOPMENT OF THE GEOLOGICAL SCIENCES, F. D. Adams. The most complete and thorough history of the earth sciences in print. Covers over 300 geological thinkers and systems; treats fossils, theories of stone growth, paleontology, earthquakes, vulcanists vs. neptunists, odd theories, etc. 91 illustrations, including medieval, Renaissance wood cuts, etc. 632 footnotes and bibliographic notes. 511pp. 308pp. 5⅜ x 8.   T5 Paperbound **$2.00**

FROM MAGIC TO SCIENCE, Charles Singer. A close study of aspects of medical science from the Roman Empire through the Renaissance. The sections on early herbals, and "The Visions of Hildegarde of Bingen," are probably the best studies of these subjects available. 158 unusual classic and medieval illustrations. xxvii + 365pp. 5⅜ x 8.   T390 Paperbound **$2.00**

SAILING ALONE AROUND THE WORLD, Captain Joshua Slocum. Captain Slocum's personal account of his single-handed voyage around the world in a 34-foot boat he rebuilt himself. A classic of both seamanship and descriptive writing. "A nautical equivalent of Thoreau's account," Van Wyck Brooks. 67 illus. 308pp. 5⅜ x 8.   T326 Paperbound **$1.00**

TREES OF THE EASTERN AND CENTRAL UNITED STATES AND CANADA, W. M. Harlow. Standard middle-level guide designed to help you know the characteristics of Eastern trees and identify them at sight by means of an 8-page synoptic key. More than 600 drawings and photographs of twigs, leaves, fruit, other features. xiii + 288pp. 4⅝ x 6½.
T395 Paperbound **$1.35**

FRUIT KEY AND TWIG KEY ("Fruit Key to Northeastern Trees," "Twig Key to Deciduous Woody Plants of Eastern North America"), **W. M. Harlow.** Identify trees in fall, winter, spring. Easy-to-use, synoptic keys, with photographs of every twig and fruit identified. Covers 120 different fruits, 160 different twigs. Over 350 photos. Bibliographies. Glossaries. Total of 143pp. 5⅝ x 8⅜.   T511 Paperbound **$1.25**

INTRODUCTION TO THE STUDY OF EXPERIMENTAL MEDICINE, Claude Bernard. This classic records Bernard's far-reaching efforts to transform physiology into an exact science. It covers problems of vivisection, the limits of physiological experiment, hypotheses in medical experimentation, hundreds of others. Many of his own famous experiments on the liver, the pancreas, etc., are used as examples. Foreword by I. B. Cohen. xxv + 266pp. 5⅜ x 8.
T400 Paperbound **$1.50**

THE ORIGIN OF LIFE, A. I. Oparin. The first modern statement that life evolved from complex nitro-carbon compounds, carefully presented according to modern biochemical knowledge of primary colloids, organic molecules, etc. Begins with historical introduction to the problem of the origin of life. Bibliography. xxv + 270pp. 5⅜ x 8.   S213 Paperbound **$1.75**

A HISTORY OF ASTRONOMY FROM THALES TO KEPLER, J. L. E. Dreyer. The only work in English which provides a detailed picture of man's cosmological views from Egypt, Babylonia, Greece, and Alexandria to Copernicus, Tycho Brahe and Kepler. "Standard reference on Greek astronomy and the Copernican revolution," SKY AND TELESCOPE. Formerly called "A History of Planetary Systems From Thales to Kepler." Bibliography. 21 diagrams. xvii + 430pp. 5⅜ x 8.
S79 Paperbound **$1.98**

URANIUM PROSPECTING, H. L. Barnes. A professional geologist tells you what you need to know. Hundreds of facts about minerals, tests, detectors, sampling, assays, claiming, developing, government regulations, etc. Glossary of technical terms. Annotated bibliography. x + 117pp. 5⅜ x 8.   T309 Paperbound **$1.00**

DE RE METALLICA, Georgius Agricola. All 12 books of this 400 year old classic on metals and metal production, fully annotated, and containing all 289 of the 16th century woodcuts which made the original an artistic masterpiece. A superb gift for geologists, engineers, libraries, artists, historians. Translated by Herbert Hoover & L. H. Hoover. Bibliography, survey of ancient authors. 289 illustrations of the excavating, assaying, smelting, refining, and countless other metal production operations described in the text. 672pp. 6¾ x 10¾. Deluxe library edition.   S6 Clothbound **$10.00**

DE MAGNETE, William Gilbert. A landmark of science by the man who first used the word "electricity," distinguished between static electricity and magnetism, and founded a new science. P. F. Mottelay translation. 90 figures. lix + 368pp. 5⅜ x 8.   S470 Paperbound **$2.00**

THE AUTOBIOGRAPHY OF CHARLES DARWIN AND SELECTED LETTERS, Francis Darwin, ed. Fascinating documents on Darwin's early life, the voyage of the "Beagle," the discovery of evolution, Darwin's thought on mimicry, plant development, vivisection, evolution, many other subjects Letters to Henslow, Lyell, Hooker, Wallace, Kingsley, etc. Appendix. 365pp. 5⅜ x 8.   T479 Paperbound **$1.65**

A WAY OF LIFE AND OTHER SELECTED WRITINGS OF SIR WILLIAM OSLER. 16 of the great physician, teacher and humanist's most inspiring writings on a practical philosophy of life, science and the humanities, and the history of medicine. 5 photographs. Introduction by G. L. Keynes, M.D., F.R.C.S. xx + 278pp. 5⅜ x 8.   T488 Paperbound **$1.50**

LITERATURE

WORLD DRAMA, B. H. Clark. 46 plays from Ancient Greece, Rome, to India, China, Japan. Plays by Aeschylus, Sophocles, Euripides, Aristophanes, Plautus, Marlowe, Jonson, Farquhar, Goldsmith, Cervantes, Molière, Dumas, Goethe, Schiller, Ibsen, many others. One of the most comprehensive collections of important plays from all literature available in English. Over ⅓ of this material is unavailable in any other current edition. Reading lists. 2 volumes. Total of 1364pp. 5⅜ x 8.   Vol. I, T57 Paperbound **$2.00**
Vol. II, T59 Paperbound **$2.00**

MASTERS OF THE DRAMA, John Gassner. The most comprehensive history of the drama in print. Covers more than 800 dramatists and over 2000 plays from the Greeks to modern Western, Near Eastern, Oriental drama. Plot summaries, theatre history, etc. "Best of its kind in English," NEW REPUBLIC. 35 pages of bibliography. 77 photos and drawings. Deluxe edition. xxii + 890pp. 5⅜ x 8.   T100 Clothbound **$5.95**

THE DRAMA OF LUIGI PIRANDELLO, D. Vittorini. All 38 of Pirandello's plays (to 1935) summarized and analyzed in terms of symbolic techniques, plot structure, etc. The only authorized work. Foreword by Pirandello. Biography. Bibliography. xiii + 350pp. 5⅜ x 8.
T435 Paperbound **$1.98**

ARISTOTLE'S THEORY OF POETRY AND THE FINE ARTS, S. H. Butcher, ed. The celebrated "Butcher translation" faced page by page with the Greek text; Butcher's 300-page introduction to Greek poetic, dramatic thought. Modern Aristotelian criticism discussed by John Gassner. lxxvi + 421pp. 5⅜ x 8.

T42 Paperbound **$2.00**

EUGENE O'NEILL: THE MAN AND HIS PLAYS, B. H. Clark. The first published source-book on O'Neill's life and work. Analyzes each play from the early THE WEB up to THE ICEMAN COMETH. Supplies much information about environmental and dramatic influences. ix + 182pp. 5⅜ x 8.   T379 Paperbound **$1.25**

INTRODUCTION TO ENGLISH LITERATURE, B. Dobrée, ed. Most compendious literary aid in its price range. Extensive, categorized bibliography (with entries up to 1949) of more than 5,000 poets, dramatists, novelists, as well as historians, philosophers, economists, religious writers, travellers, and scientists of literary stature. Information about manuscripts, important biographical data. Critical, historical, background works not simply listed, but evaluated. Each volume also contains a long introduction to the period it covers.

Vol. I: **THE BEGINNINGS OF ENGLISH LITERATURE TO SKELTON, 1509, W. L. Renwick. H. Orton.** 450pp. 5⅛ x 7⅛.   T75 Clothbound **$3.50**

Vol. II: **THE ENGLISH RENAISSANCE, 1510-1688, V. de Sola Pinto.** 381pp. 5⅛ x 7⅛.
T76 Clothbound **$3.50**

Vol. III: **THE AUGUSTANS AND ROMANTICS, 1689-1830, H. Dyson, J. Butt.** 320pp. 5⅛ x·7⅛.
T77 Clothbound **$3.50**

Vol. IV: **THE VICTORIANS AND AFTER, 1830-1914, E. Batho, B. Dobrée.** 360pp. 5⅛ x 7⅛.
T78 Clothbound **$3.50**

EPIC AND ROMANCE, W. P. Ker. The standard survey of Medieval epic and romance by a foremost authority on Medieval literature. Covers historical background, plot, literary analysis, significance of Teutonic epics, Icelandic sagas, Beowulf, French chansons de geste, the Niebelungenlied, Arthurian romances, much more. 422pp. 5⅜ x 8.   T355 Paperbound **$1.95**

THE HEART OF EMERSON'S JOURNALS, Bliss Perry, ed. Emerson's most intimate thoughts, impressions, records of conversations with Channing, Hawthorne, Thoreau, etc., carefully chosen from the 10 volumes of The Journals. "The essays do not reveal the power of Emerson's mind . . .as do these hasty and informal writings," N. Y. TIMES. Preface by B. Perry. 370pp. 5⅜ x 8.   T447 Paperbound **$1.85**

A SOURCE BOOK IN THEATRICAL HISTORY, A. M. Nagler. (Formerly, "Sources of Theatrical History.") Over 300 selected passages by contemporary observers tell about styles of acting, direction, make-up, scene designing, etc., in the theatre's great periods from ancient Greece to the Théâtre Libre. "Indispensable complement to the study of drama," EDUCATIONAL THEATRE JOURNAL. Prof. Nagler, Yale Univ. School of Drama, also supplies notes, references. 85 illustrations. 611pp. 5⅜ x 8.   T515 Paperbound **$2.75**

THE ART OF THE STORY-TELLER, M. L. Shedlock. Regarded as the finest, most helpful book on telling stories to children, by a great story-teller. How to catch, hold, recapture attention; how to choose material; many other aspects. Also includes: a 99-page selection of Miss Shedlock's most successful stories; extensive bibliography of other stories. xxi + 320pp. 5⅜ x 8.   T245 Clothbound **$3.50**

THE DEVIL'S DICTIONARY, Ambrose Bierce. Over 1000 short, ironic definitions in alphabetical order, by America's greatest satirist in the classical tradition. "Some of the most gorgeous witticisms in the English language," H. L. Mencken. 144pp. 5⅜ x 8.   T487 Paperbound **$1.00**

MUSIC

A DICTIONARY OF HYMNOLOGY, John Julian. More than 30,000 entries on individual hymns, their authorship, textual variations, location of texts, dates and circumstances of composition, denominational and ritual usages, the biographies of more than 9,000 hymn writers, essays on important topics such as children's hymns and Christmas carols, and hundreds of thousands of other important facts about hymns which are virtually impossible to find anywhere else. Convenient alphabetical listing, and a 200-page double-columned index of first lines enable you to track down virtually any hymn ever written. Total of 1786pp. 6¼ x 9¼. 2 volumes. T133. The Set, Clothbound **$15.00**

STRUCTURAL HEARING, TONAL COHERENCE IN MUSIC, Felix Salzer. Extends the well-known Schenker approach to include modern music, music of the middle ages, and Renaissance music. Explores the phenomenon of tonal organization by discussing more than 500 compositions, and offers unusual new insights into the theory of composition and musical relationships. "The foundation on which all teaching in music theory has been based at this college," Leopold Mannes, President, The Mannes College of Music. Total of 658pp. 6½ x 9¼. 2 volumes. S418 The set, Clothbound **$8.00**

A GENERAL HISTORY OF MUSIC, Charles Burney. The complete history of music from the Greeks up to 1789 by the 18th century musical historian who personally knew the great Baroque composers. Covers sacred and secular, vocal and instrumental, operatic and symphonic music; treats theory, notation, forms, instruments; discusses composers, performers, important works. Invaluable as a source of information on the period for students, historians, musicians. "Surprisingly few of Burney's statements have been invalidated by modern research . . . still of great value," NEW YORK TIMES. Edited and corrected by Frank Mercer. 35 figures. 1915pp. 5½ x 8½. 2 volumes. T36 The set, Clothbound **$12.50**

JOHANN SEBASTIAN BACH, Phillp Spitta. Recognized as one of the greatest accomplishments of musical scholarship and far and away the definitive coverage of Bach's works. Hundreds of individual pieces are analyzed. Major works, such as the B Minor Mass and the St. Matthew Passion are examined in minute detail. Spitta also deals with the works of Buxtehude, Pachelbel, and others of the period. Can be read with profit even by those without a knowledge of the technicalities of musical composition. "Unchallenged as the last word on one of the supreme geniuses of music," John Barkham, SATURDAY REVIEW SYNDICATE. Total of 1819pp. 5⅜ x 8. 2 volumes. T252 The set, Clothbound **$10.00**

HISTORY

THE IDEA OF PROGRESS, J. B. Bury. Prof. Bury traces the evolution of a central concept of Western civilization in Greek, Roman, Medieval, and Renaissance thought to its flowering in the 17th and 18th centuries. Introduction by Charles Beard. xl + 357pp. 5⅜ x 8.
T39 Clothbound **$3.95**
T40 Paperbound **$1.95**

THE ANCIENT GREEK HISTORIANS, J. B. Bury. Greek historians such as Herodotus, Thucydides, Xenophon; Roman historians such as Tacitus, Caesar, Livy; scores of others fully analyzed in terms of sources, concepts, influences, etc., by a great scholar and historian. 291pp. 5⅜ x 8. T397 Paperbound **$1.50**

HISTORY OF THE LATER ROMAN EMPIRE, J. B. Bury. The standard work on the Byzantine Empire from 395 A.D. to the death of Justinian in 565 A.D., by the leading Byzantine scholar of our time. Covers political, social, cultural, theological, military history. Quotes contemporary documents extensively. "Most unlikely that it will ever be superseded," Glanville Downey, Dumbarton Oaks Research Library. Genealogical tables. 5 maps. Bibliography. 2 vols. Total of 965pp. 5⅜ x 8. T398, T399 Paperbound, the set **$4.00**

GARDNER'S PHOTOGRAPHIC SKETCH BOOK OF THE CIVIL WAR, Alexander Gardner. One of the rarest and most valuable Civil War photographic collections exactly reproduced for the first time since 1866. Scenes of Manassas, Bull Run, Harper's Ferry, Appomattox, Mechanicsville, Fredericksburg, Gettysburg, etc.; battle ruins, prisons, arsenals, a slave pen, fortifications; Lincoln on the field, officers, men, corpses. By one of the most famous pioneers in documentary photography. Original copies of the "Sketch Book" sold for $425 in 1952. Introduction by E. Bleiler. 100 full-page 7 x 10 photographs (original size). 244pp. 10¾ x 8½
T476 Clothbound **$6.00**

THE WORLD'S GREAT SPEECHES, L. Copeland and L. Lamm, eds. 255 speeches from Pericles to Churchill, Dylan Thomas. Invaluable as a guide to speakers; fascinating as history past and present; a source of much difficult-to-find material. Includes an extensive section of informal and humorous speeches. 3 indices: Topic, Author, Nation. xx + 745pp. 5⅜ x 8.
T468 Paperbound **$2.49**

FOUNDERS OF THE MIDDLE AGES, E. K. Rand. The best non-technical discussion of the transformation of Latin paganism into medieval civilization. Tertullian, Gregory, Jerome, Boethius, Augustine, the Neoplatonists, other crucial figures, philosophies examined. Excellent for the intelligent non-specialist. "Extraordinarily accurate," Richard McKeon, THE NATION. ix + 365pp. 5⅜ x 8. T369 Paperbound **$1.85**

THE POLITICAL THOUGHT OF PLATO AND ARISTOTLE, Ernest Barker. The standard, comprehensive exposition of Greek political thought. Covers every aspect of the "Republic" and the "Politics" as well as minor writings, other philosophers, theorists of the period, and the later history of Greek political thought. Unabridged edition. 584pp. 5⅜ x 8.
T521 Paperbound **$1.85**

PHILOSOPHY

THE GIFT OF LANGUAGE, M. Schlauch. (Formerly, "The Gift of Tongues.") A sound, middle-level treatment of linguistic families, word histories, grammatical processes, semantics, language taboos, word-coining of Joyce, Cummings, Stein, etc. 232 bibliographical notes. 350pp. 5⅜ x 8.
T243 Paperbound **$1.85**

THE PHILOSOPHY OF HEGEL, W. T. Stace. The first work in English to give a complete and connected view of Hegel's entire system. Especially valuable to those who do not have time to study the highly complicated original texts, yet want an accurate presentation by a most reputable scholar of one of the most influential 19th century thinkers. Includes a 14 x 20 fold-out chart of Hegelian system. 536pp. 5⅜ x 8.
T254 Paperbound **$2.00**

ARISTOTLE, A. E. Taylor. A lucid, non-technical account of Aristotle written by a foremost Platonist. Covers life and works; thought on matter, form, causes, logic, God, physics, metaphysics, etc. Bibliography. New index compiled for this edition. 128pp. 5⅜ x 8.
T280 Paperbound **$1.00**

GUIDE TO PHILOSOPHY, C. E. M. Joad. This basic work describes the major philosophic problems and evaluates the answers propounded by great philosophers from the Greeks to Whitehead, Russell. "The finest introduction," BOSTON TRANSCRIPT. Bibliography, 592pp. 5⅜ x 8.
T297 Paperbound **$2.00**

LANGUAGE AND MYTH, E. Cassirer. Cassirer's brilliant demonstration that beneath both language and myth lies an unconscious "grammar" of experience whose categories and canons are not those of logical thought. Introduction and translation by Susanne Langer. Index. x + 103pp. 5⅜ x 8.
T51 Paperbound **$1.25**

SUBSTANCE AND FUNCTION, EINSTEIN'S THEORY OF RELATIVITY, E. Cassirer. This double volume contains the German philosopher's profound philosophical formulation of the differences between traditional logic and the new logic of science. Number, space, energy, relativity, many other topics are treated in detail. Authorized translation by W. C. and M. C. Swabey. xii + 465pp. 5⅜ x 8.
T50 Paperbound **$2.00**

THE PHILOSOPHICAL WORKS OF DESCARTES. The definitive English edition, in two volumes, of all major philosophical works and letters of René Descartes, father of modern philosophy of knowledge and science. Translated by E. S. Haldane and G. Ross. Introductory notes. Total of 842pp. 5⅜ x 8.
T71 Vol. 1, Paperbound **$2.00**
T72 Vol. 2, Paperbound **$2.00**

ESSAYS IN EXPERIMENTAL LOGIC, J. Dewey. Based upon Dewey's theory that knowledge implies a judgment which in turn implies an inquiry, these papers consider such topics as the thought of Bertrand Russell, pragmatism, the logic of values, antecedents of thought, data and meanings. 452pp. 5⅜ x 8.
T73 Paperbound **$1.95**

THE PHILOSOPHY OF HISTORY, G. W. F. Hegel. This classic of Western thought is Hegel's detailed formulation of the thesis that history is not chance but a rational process, the realization of the Spirit of Freedom. Translated and introduced by J. Sibree. Introduction by C. Hegel. Special introduction for this edition by Prof. Carl Friedrich, Harvard University. xxxix + 447pp. 5⅜ x 8.
T112 Paperbound **$1.85**

THE WILL TO BELIEVE and **HUMAN IMMORTALITY, W. James.** Two of James's most profound investigations of human belief in God and immortality, bound as one volume. Both are powerful expressions of James's views on chance vs. determinism, pluralism vs. monism, will and intellect, arguments for survival after death, etc. Two prefaces. 429pp. 5⅜ x 8.
T294 Clothbound **$3.75**
T291 Paperbound **$1.65**

INTRODUCTION TO SYMBOLIC LOGIC, S. Langer. A lucid, general introduction to modern logic, covering forms, classes, the use of symbols, the calculus of propositions, the Boole-Schroeder and the Russell-Whitehead systems, etc. "One of the clearest and simplest introductions," MATHEMATICS GAZETTE. Second, enlarged, revised edition. 368pp. 5⅜ x 8.
S164 Paperbound **$1.75**

MIND AND THE WORLD-ORDER, C. I. Lewis. Building upon the work of Peirce, James, and Dewey, Professor Lewis outlines a theory of knowledge in terms of "conceptual pragmatism," and demonstrates why the traditional understanding of the a priori must be abandoned. Appendices. xiv + 446pp. 5⅜ x 8.
T359 Paperbound **$1.95**

THE GUIDE FOR THE PERPLEXED, M. Maimonides One of the great philosophical works of all time, Maimonides' formulation of the meeting-ground between Old Testament and Aristotelian thought is essential to anyone interested in Jewish, Christian, and Moslem thought in the Middle Ages. 2nd revised edition of the Friedlander translation. Extensive introduction. lix + 414pp. 5⅜ x 8.
T351 Paperbound **$1.85**

DOVER BOOKS

THE PHILOSOPHICAL WRITINGS OF PEIRCE, J. Buchler, ed. (Formerly, "The Philosophy of Peirce.") This carefully integrated selection of Peirce's papers is considered the best coverage of the complete thought of one of the greatest philosophers of modern times. Covers Peirce's work on the theory of signs, pragmatism, epistemology, symbolic logic, the scientific method, chance, etc. xvi + 386pp. 5 ⅜ x 8.
T216 Clothbound **$5.00**
T217 Paperbound **$1.95**

HISTORY OF ANCIENT PHILOSOPHY, W. Windelband. Considered the clearest survey of Greek and Roman philosophy. Examines Thales, Anaximander, Anaximenes, Heraclitus, the Eleatics, Empedocles, the Pythagoreans, the Sophists, Socrates, Democritus, Stoics, Epicureans, Sceptics, Neo-platonists, etc. 50 pages on Plato; 70 on Aristotle. 2nd German edition tr. by H. E. Cushman. xv + 393pp. 5⅜ x 8.
T357 Paperbound **$1.75**

INTRODUCTION TO SYMBOLIC LOGIC AND ITS APPLICATIONS, R. Carnap. A comprehensive, rigorous introduction to modern logic by perhaps its greatest living master. Includes demonstrations of applications in mathematics, physics, biology. "Of the rank of a masterpiece," Z. für Mathematik und ihre Grenzgebiete. Over 300 exercises. xvi + 241pp. 5⅜ x 8.
Clothbound **$4.00**
S453 Paperbound **$1.85**

SCEPTICISM AND ANIMAL FAITH, G. Santayana. Santayana's unusually lucid exposition of the difference between the independent existence of objects and the essence our mind attributes to them, and of the necessity of scepticism as a form of belief and animal faith as a necessary condition of knowledge. Discusses belief, memory, intuition, symbols, etc. xii + 314pp. 5⅜ x 8.
T235 Clothbound **$3.50**
T236 Paperbound **$1.50**

THE ANALYSIS OF MATTER, B. Russell. With his usual brilliance, Russell analyzes physics, causality, scientific inference, Weyl's theory, tensors, invariants, periodicity, etc. in order to discover the basic concepts of scientific thought about matter. "Most thorough treatment of the subject," THE NATION. Introduction. 8 figures. viii + 408pp. 5⅜ x 8.
T231 Paperbound **$1.95**

THE SENSE OF BEAUTY, G. Santayana. This important philosophical study of why, when, and how beauty appears, and what conditions must be fulfilled, is in itself a revelation of the beauty of language. "It is doubtful if a better treatment of the subject has since appeared," PEABODY JOURNAL. ix + 275pp. 5⅜ x 8.
T238 Paperbound **$1.00**

THE CHIEF WORKS OF SPINOZA. In two volumes. Vol. I: The Theologico-Political Treatise and the Political Treatise. Vol. II: On the Improvement of Understanding, The Ethics, and Selected Letters. The permanent and enduring ideas in these works on God, the universe, religion, society, etc., have had tremendous impact on later philosophical works. Introduction. Total of 862pp. 5⅜ x 8.
T249 Vol. I, Paperbound **$1.50**
T250 Vol. II, Paperbound **$1.50**

TRAGIC SENSE OF LIFE, M. de Unamuno. The acknowledged masterpiece of one of Spain's most influential thinkers. Between the despair at the inevitable death of man and all his works, and the desire for immortality, Unamuno finds a "saving incertitude." Called "a masterpiece," by the ENCYCLOPAEDIA BRITANNICA. xxx + 332pp. 5⅜ x 8.
T257 Paperbound **$1.95**

EXPERIENCE AND NATURE, John Dewey. The enlarged, revised edition of the Paul Carus lectures (1925). One of Dewey's clearest presentations of the philosophy of empirical naturalism which reestablishes the continuity between "inner" experience and "outer" nature. These lectures are among the most significant ever delivered by an American philosopher. 457pp. 5⅜ x 8.
T471 Paperbound **$1.85**

PHILOSOPHY AND CIVILIZATION IN THE MIDDLE AGES, M. de Wulf. A semi-popular survey of medieval intellectual life, religion, philosophy, science, the arts, etc. that covers feudalism vs. Catholicism, rise of the universities, mendicant orders, and similar topics. Bibliography. viii + 320pp. 5⅜ x 8.
T284 Paperbound **$1.75**

AN INTRODUCTION TO SCHOLASTIC PHILOSOPHY, M. de Wulf. (Formerly, "Scholasticism Old and New.") Prof. de Wulf covers the central scholastic tradition from St. Anselm, Albertus Magnus, Thomas Aquinas, up to Suarez in the 17th century; and then treats the modern revival of. scholasticism, the Louvain position, relations with Kantianism and positivism, etc. xvi + 271pp. 5⅜ x 8.
T296 Clothbound **$3.50**
T283 Paperbound **$1.75**

A HISTORY OF MODERN PHILOSOPHY, H. Höffding. An exceptionally clear and detailed coverage of Western philosophy from the Renaissance to the end of the 19th century. Both major and minor figures are examined in terms of theory of knowledge, logic, cosmology, psychology. Covers Pomponazzi, Bodin, Boehme, Telesius, Bruno, Copernicus, Descartes, Spinoza, Hobbes, Locke, Hume, Kant, Fichte, Schopenhauer, Mill, Spencer, Langer, scores of others. A standard reference work. 2 volumes. Total of 1159pp. 5⅜ x 8.
T117 Vol. 1, Paperbound **$2.00**
T118 Vol. 2, Paperbound **$2.00**

LANGUAGE, TRUTH AND LOGIC, A. J. Ayer. The first full-length development of Logical Positivism in English. Building on the work of Schlick, Russell, Carnap, and the Vienna school, Ayer presents the tenets of one of the most important systems of modern philosophical thought. 160pp. 5⅜ x 8.
T10 Paperbound **$1.25**

ORIENTALIA AND RELIGION

THE MYSTERIES OF MITHRA, F. Cumont. The great Belgian scholar's definitive study of the Persian mystery religion that almost vanquished Christianity in the ideological struggle for the Roman Empire. A masterpiece of scholarly detection that reconstructs secret doctrines, organization, rites. Mithraic art is discussed and analyzed. 70 illus. 239pp. 5⅜ x 8.
T323 Paperbound **$1.85**

CHRISTIAN AND ORIENTAL PHILOSOPHY OF ART. A. K. Coomaraswamy. The late art historian and orientalist discusses artistic symbolism, the role of traditional culture in enriching art, medieval art, folklore, philosophy of art, other similar topics. Bibliography. 148pp. 5⅜ x 8.
T378 Paperbound **$1.25**

TRANSFORMATION OF NATURE IN ART, A. K. Coomaraswamy. A basic work on Asiatic religious art. Includes discussions of religious art in Asia and Medieval Europe (exemplified by Meister Eckhart), the origin and use of images in Indian art, Indian Medieval aesthetic manuals, and other fascinating, little known topics. Glossaries of Sanskrit and Chinese terms. Bibliography. 41pp. of notes. 245pp. 5⅜ x 8.
T368 Paperbound **$1.75**

ORIENTAL RELIGIONS IN ROMAN PAGANISM, F. Cumont. This well-known study treats the ecstatic cults of Syria and Phrygia (Cybele, Attis, Adonis, their orgies and mutilatory rites); the mysteries of Egypt (Serapis, Isis, Osiris); Persian dualism; Mithraic cults; Hermes Trismegistus, Ishtar, Astarte, etc. and their influence on the religious thought of the Roman Empire. Introduction. 55pp. of notes; extensive bibliography. xxiv + 298pp. 5⅜ x 8.
T321 Paperbound **$1.75**

ANTHROPOLOGY, SOCIOLOGY, AND PSYCHOLOGY

PRIMITIVE MAN AS PHILOSOPHER, P. Radin. A standard anthropological work based on Radin's investigations of the Winnebago, Maori, Batak, Zuni, other primitive tribes. Describes primitive thought on the purpose of life, marital relations, death, personality, gods, etc. Extensive selections of õriginal primitive documents. Bibliography. xviii + 420pp. 5⅜ x 8.
T392 Paperbound **$2.00**

PRIMITIVE RELIGION, P. Radin. Radin's thoroughgoing treatment of supernatural beliefs, shamanism, initiations, religious expression, etc. in primitive societies. Arunta, Ashanti, Aztec, Bushman, Crow, Fijian, many other tribes examined. "Excellent," NATURE. New preface by the author. Bibliographic notes. x + 322pp. 5⅜ x 8. T393 Paperbound **$1.85**

SEX IN PSYCHO-ANALYSIS, S. Ferenczi. (Formerly, "Contributions to Psycho-analysis.") 14 selected papers on impotence, transference, analysis and children, dreams, obscene words, homosexuality, paranoia, etc. by an associate of Freud. Also included: THE DEVELOPMENT OF PSYCHO-ANALYSIS, by Ferenczi and Otto Rank. Two books bound as one. Total of 406pp. 5⅜ x 8.
T324 Paperbound **$1.85**

THE PRINCIPLES OF PSYCHOLOGY, William James. The complete text of the famous "long course," one of the great books of Western thought. An almost incredible amount of information about psychological processes, the stream of consciousness, habit, time perception, memory, emotions, reason, consciousness of self, abnormal phenomena, and similar topics. Based on James's own discoveries integrated with the work of Descartes, Locke, Hume, Royce, Wundt, Berkeley, Lotse, Herbart, scores of others. "A classic of interpretation," PSYCHIATRIC QUARTERLY. 94 illus. 1408pp. 2 volumes. 5⅜ x 8.
T381 Vol. 1, Paperbound **$2.50**
T382 Vol. 2, Paperbound **$2.50**

THE POLISH PEASANT IN EUROPE AND AMERICA, W. I. Thomas, F. Znaniecki. Monumental sociological study of peasant primary groups (family and community) and the disruptions produced by·a new industrial system and emigration to America, by two of the foremost sociologists of recent times. One of the most important works in sociological thought. Includes hundreds of pages of primary documentation; point by point analysis of causes of social decay, breakdown of morality, crime, drunkenness, prostitution, etc. 2nd revised edition. 2 volumes. Total of 2250pp. 6 x 9. T478 2 volume set, Clothbound **$12.50**

FOLKWAYS, W. G. Sumner. The great Yale sociologist's detailed exposition of thousands of social, sexual, and religious customs in hundreds of cultures from ancient Greece to Modern Western societies. Preface by A. G. Keller. Introduction by William Lyon Phelps. 705pp. 5⅜ x 8.
S508 Paperbound **$2.49**

BEYOND PSYCHOLOGY, Otto Rank. The author, an early associate of Freud, uses psychoanalytic techniques of myth-analysis to explore ultimates of human existence. Treats love, immortality, the soul, sexual identity, kingship, sources of state power, many other topics which illuminate the irrational basis of human existence. 291pp. 5⅜ x 8. T485 Paperbound **$1.75**

ILLUSIONS AND DELUSIONS OF THE SUPERNATURAL AND THE OCCULT, D. H. Rawcliffe. A rational, scientific examination of crystal gazing, automatic writing, table turning, stigmata, the Indian rope trick, dowsing, telepathy, clairvoyance, ghosts, ESP, PK, thousands of other supposedly occult phenomena. Originally titled "The Psychology of the Occult." 14 illustrations. 551pp. 5⅜ x 8.
T503 Paperbound **$2.00**

YOGA: A SCIENTIFIC EVALUATION, Kovoor T. Behanan. A scientific study of the physiological and psychological effects of Yoga discipline, written under the auspices of the Yale University Institute of Human Relations. Foreword by W. A. Miles, Yale Univ. 17 photographs. 290pp. 5⅜ x 8.   T505 Paperbound **$1.65**

HOAXES, C. D. MacDougall. Delightful, entertaining, yet scholarly exposition of how hoaxes start, why they succeed, documented with stories of hundreds of the most famous hoaxes. "A stupendous collection . . . and shrewd analysis, "NEW YORKER. New, revised edition. 54 photographs. 320pp. 5⅜ x 8.   T465 Paperbound **$1.75**

CREATIVE POWER: THE EDUCATION OF YOUTH IN THE CREATIVE ARTS, Hughes Mearns. Named by the National Education Association as one of the 20 foremost books on education in recent times. Tells how to help children express themselves in drama, poetry, music, art, develop latent creative power. Should be read by every parent, teacher. New, enlarged, revised edition. Introduction. 272pp. 5⅜ x 8.   T490 Paperbound **$1.50**

LANGUAGES

NEW RUSSIAN-ENGLISH, ENGLISH-RUSSIAN DICTIONARY, M. A. O'Brien. Over 70,000 entries in new orthography! Idiomatic usages, colloquialisms. One of the few dictionaries that indicate accent changes in conjugation and declension. "One of the best," Prof. E. J. Simmons, Cornell. First names, geographical terms, bibliography, many other features. 738pp. 4½ x 6¼.   T208 Paperbound **$2.00**

MONEY CONVERTER AND TIPPING GUIDE FOR EUROPEAN TRAVEL, C. Vomacka. Invaluable, handy source of currency regulations, conversion tables, tipping rules, postal rates, much other travel information for every European country plus Israel, Egypt and Turkey. 128pp. 3½ x 5¼.   T260 Paperbound **60¢**

MONEY CONVERTER AND TIPPING GUIDE FOR TRAVEL IN THE AMERICAS (including the United States and Canada), **C. Vomacka.** The information you need for informed and confident travel in the Americas: money conversion tables, tipping guide, postal, telephone rates, etc. 128pp. 3½ x 5¼.   T261 Paperbound **65¢**

DUTCH-ENGLISH, ENGLISH-DUTCH DICTIONARY, F. G. Renier. The most convenient, practical Dutch-English dictionary on the market. New orthography. More than 60,000 entries: idioms, compounds, technical terms, etc. Gender of nouns indicated. xviii + 571pp. 5½ x 6¼.   T224 Clothbound **$2.50**

LEARN DUTCH!, F. G. Renier. The most satisfactory and easily-used grammar of modern Dutch. Used and recommended by the Fulbright Committee in the Netherlands. Over 1200 simple exercises lead to mastery of spoken and written Dutch. Dutch-English, English-Dutch vocabularies. 181pp. 4¼ x 7¼.   T441 Clothbound **$1.75**

PHRASE AND SENTENCE DICTIONARY OF SPOKEN RUSSIAN, English-Russian, Russian-English. Based on phrases and complete sentences, rather than isolated words; recognized as one of the best methods of learning the idiomatic speech of a country. Over 11,500 entries, indexed by single words, with more than 32,000 English and Russian sentences and phrases, in immediately usable form. Probably the largest list ever published. Shows accent changes in conjugation and declension; irregular forms listed in both alphabetical place and under main form of word. 15,000 word introduction covering Russian sounds, writing, grammar, syntax. 15-page appendix of geographical names, money, important signs, given names, foods, special Soviet terms, etc. Travellers, businessmen, students, government employees have found this their best source for Russian expressions. Originally published as U.S. Government Technical Manual TM 30-944. iv + 573pp. 5⅝ x 8⅜.   T496 Paperbound **$2.75**

PHRASE AND SENTENCE DICTIONARY OF SPOKEN SPANISH, Spanish-English, English-Spanish. Compiled from spoken Spanish, emphasizing idiom and colloquial usage in both Castilian and Latin-American. More than 16,000 entries containing over 25,000 idioms—the largest list of idiomatic constructions ever published. Complete sentences given, indexed under single words —language in immediately usable form, for travellers, businessmen, students, etc. 25-page introduction provides rapid survey of sounds, grammar, syntax, with full consideration of irregular verbs. Especially apt in modern treatment of phrases and structure. 17-page glossary gives translations of geographical names, money values, numbers, national holidays, important street signs, useful expressions of high frequency, plus unique 7-page glossary of Spanish and Spanish-American foods and dishes. Originally published as U.S. Government Technical Manual TM 30-900. iv + 513pp. 5⅝ x 8⅜.   T495 Paperbound **$1.75**

SAY IT language phrase books

"SAY IT" in the foreign language of your choice! We have sold over ½ million copies of these popular, useful language books. They will not make you an expert linguist overnight, but they do cover most practical matters of everyday life abroad.

Over 1000 useful phrases, expressions, with additional variants, substitutions.

Modern! Useful! Hundreds of phrases not available in other texts: "Nylon," "air-conditioned," etc.

The ONLY inexpensive phrase book **completely indexed.** Everything is available at a flip of your finger, ready for use.

Prepared by native linguists, travel experts.

Based on years of travel experience abroad.

This handy phrase book may be used by itself, or it may supplement any other text or course; it provides a living element. Used by many colleges and institutions: Hunter College; Barnard College; Army Ordnance School, Aberdeen; and many others.

Available, 1 book per language:

Danish (T818) 75¢
Dutch T(817) 75¢
English (for German-speaking people) (T801) 60¢
English (for Italian-speaking people) (T816) 60¢
English (for Spanish-speaking people) (T802) 60¢
Esperanto (T820) 75¢
French (T803) 60¢
German (T804) 60¢
Modern Greek (T813) 75¢
Hebrew (T805) 60¢

Italian (T806) 60¢
Japanese (T807) 60¢
Norwegian (T814) 75¢
Russian (T810) 75¢
Spanish (T811) 60¢
Turkish (T821) 75¢
Yiddish (T815) 75¢
Swedish (T812) 75¢
Polish (T808) 75¢
Portuguese (T809) 75¢

LISTEN & LEARN language record sets

LISTEN & LEARN is the only language record course designed especially to meet your travel needs, or help you learn essential foreign language quickly by yourself, or in conjunction with any school course, by means of the automatic association method. Each set contains three 33⅓ rpm long- playing records — 1½ hours of recorded speech by eminent native speakers who are professors at Columbia, N.Y.U., Queens College and other leading universities. The sets are priced far below other sets of similar quality, yet they contain many special features not found in other record sets.

* Over 800 selected phrases and sentences, a basic vocabulary of over 3200 words.
* Both English and foreign language recorded; with a pause for your repetition.
* Designed for persons with limited time; no time wasted on material you cannot use immediately.
* Living, modern expressions that answer modern needs: drugstore items, "air-conditioned," etc.
* 128-196 page manuals contain everything on the records, plus simple pronunciation guides.
* Manual is fully indexed; find the phrase you want instantly.
* High fidelity recording—equal to any records costing up to $6 each.

The phrases on these records cover 41 different categories useful to the traveller or student interested in learning the living, spoken language: greetings, introductions, making yourself understood, passing customs, planes, trains, boats, buses, taxis, nightclubs, restaurants, menu items, sports, concerts, cameras, automobile travel, repairs, drugstores, doctors, dentists, medicines, barber shops, beauty parlors, laundries, many, many more.

"Excellent . . . among the very best on the market," Prof. Mario Pei, Dept. of Romance Languages, Columbia University. "Inexpensive and well-done . . . an ideal present," CHICAGO SUNDAY TRIBUNE. "More genuinely helpful than anything of its kind which I have previously encountered," Sidney Clark, well-known author of "ALL THE BEST" travel books. Each set contains 3 33⅓ rpm pure vinyl records, 128- 196 page with full record text, and album. One language per set. LISTEN & LEARN record sets are now available in—

FRENCH — the set $4.95
ITALIAN — the set $4.95
RUSSIAN — the set $5.95
* Available Sept. 1, 1959

GERMAN — the set $4.95
SPANISH — the set $4.95
JAPANESE * — the set $5.95

UNCONDITIONAL GUARANTEE: Dover Publications stands behind every Listen and Learn record set. If you are dissatisfied with these sets for any reason whatever, return them within 10 days and your money will be refunded in full.

ART HISTORY

STICKS AND STONES, Lewis Mumford. An examination of forces influencing American architecture: the medieval tradition in early New England, the classical influence in Jefferson's time, the Brown Decades, the imperial facade, the machine age, etc. "A truly remarkable book," SAT. REV. OF LITERATURE. 2nd revised edition. 21 illus. xvii + 228pp. 5⅜ x 8.
T202 Paperbound **$1.60**

THE AUTOBIOGRAPHY OF AN IDEA, Louis Sullivan. The architect whom Frank Lloyd Wright called "the master," records the development of the theories that revolutionized America's skyline. 34 full-page plates of Sullivan's finest work. New introduction by R. M. Line. xiv + 335pp. 5⅜ x 8.
T281 Paperbound **$1.85**

THE MATERIALS AND TECHNIQUES OF MEDIEVAL PAINTING, D. V. Thompson. An invaluable study of carriers and grounds, binding media, pigments, metals used in painting, al fresco and al secco techniques, burnishing, etc. used by the medieval masters. Preface by Bernard Berenson. 239pp. 5⅜ x 8.
T327 Paperbound **$1.85**

PRINCIPLES OF ART HISTORY, H. Wölfflin. This remarkably instructive work demonstrates the tremendous change in artistic conception from the 14th to the 18th centuries, by analyzing 164 works by Botticelli, Dürer, Hobbema, Holbein, Hals, Titian, Rembrandt, Vermeer, etc., and pointing out exactly what is meant by "baroque," "classic," "primitive," "picturesque," and other basic terms of art history and criticism. "A remarkable lesson in the art of seeing," SAT. REV. OF LITERATURE. Translated from the 7th German edition. 150 illus. 254pp. 6⅛ x 9¼.
T276 Paperbound **$2.00**

FOUNDATIONS OF MODERN ART, A. Ozenfant. Stimulating discussion of human creativity from paleolithic cave painting to modern painting, architecture, decorative arts. Fully illustrated with works of Gris, Lipchitz, Léger, Picasso, primitive, modern artifacts, architecture, industrial art, much more. 226 illustrations. 368pp. 6⅛ x 9¼.
T215 Paperbound **$1.95**

HANDICRAFTS, APPLIED ART, ART SOURCES, ETC.

WILD FOWL DECOYS, J. Barber. The standard work on this fascinating branch of folk art, ranging from Indian mud and grass devices to realistic wooden decoys. Discusses styles, types, periods; gives full information on how to make decoys. 140 illustrations (including 14 new plates) show decoys and provide full sets of plans for handicrafters, artists, hunters, and students of folk art. 281pp. 7⅞ x 10¾. Deluxe edition.
T11 Clothbound **$8.50**

METALWORK AND ENAMELLING, H. Maryon. Probably the best book ever written on the subject. Tells everything necessary for the home manufacture of jewelry, rings, ear pendants, bowls, etc. Covers materials, tools, soldering, filigree, setting stones, raising patterns, repoussé work, damascening, niello, cloisonné, polishing, assaying, casting, and dozens of other techniques. The best substitute for apprenticeship to a master metalworker. 363 photos and figures. 374pp. 5½ x 8½.
T183 Clothbound **$7.50**

SHAKER FURNITURE, E. D. and F. Andrews. The most illuminating study of Shaker furniture ever written. Covers chronology, craftsmanship, houses, shops, etc. Includes over 200 photographs of chairs, tables, clocks, beds, benches, etc. "Mr. & Mrs. Andrews know all there is to know about Shaker furniture," Mark Van Doren, NATION. 48 full-page plates. 192pp. Deluxe cloth binding. 7⅞ x 10¾.
T7 Clothbound **$6.00**

PRIMITIVE ART, Franz Boas. A great American anthropologist covers theory, technical virtuosity, styles, symbolism, patterns, etc. of primitive art. The more than 900 illustrations will interest artists, designers, craftworkers. Over 900 illustrations. 376pp. 5⅜ x 8.
T25 Paperbound **$1.95**

ON THE LAWS OF JAPANESE PAINTING, H. Bowie. The best possible substitute for lessons from an oriental master. Treats both spirit and technique; exercises for control of the brush; inks, brushes, colors; use of dots, lines to express whole moods, etc. 220 illus. 132pp. 6⅛ x 9¼.
T30 Paperbound **$1.95**

HANDBOOK OF ORNAMENT, F. S. Meyer. One of the largest collections of copyright-free traditional art: over 3300 line cuts of Greek, Roman, Medieval, Renaissance, Baroque, 18th and 19th century art motifs (tracery, geometric elements, flower and animal motifs, etc.) and decorated objects (chairs, thrones, weapons, vases, jewelry, armor, etc.). Full text. 3300 illustrations. 562pp. 5⅜ x 8.
T302 Paperbound **$2.00**

THREE CLASSICS OF ITALIAN CALLIGRAPHY. Oscar Ogg, ed. Exact reproductions of three famous Renaissance calligraphic works: Arrighi's OPERINA and IL MODO, Tagliente's LO PRESENTE LIBRO, and Palatino's LIBRO NUOVO. More than 200 complete alphabets, thousands of lettered specimens, in Papal Chancery and other beautiful, ornate handwriting. Introduction. 245 plates. 282pp. 6⅛ x 9¼.
T212 Paperbound **$1.95**

THE HISTORY AND TECHNIQUES OF LETTERING, A. Nesbitt. A thorough history of lettering from the ancient Egyptians to the present, and a 65-page course in lettering for artists. Every major development in lettering history is illustrated by a complete alphabet. Fully analyzes such masters as Caslon, Koch, Garamont, Jenson, and many more. 89 alphabets, 165 other specimens. 317pp. 5⅜ x 8.
T427 Paperbound **$2.00**

LETTERING AND ALPHABETS, J. A. Cavanagh. An unabridged reissue of "Lettering," containing the full discussion, analysis, illustration of 89 basic hand lettering tyles based on Caslon, Bodoni, Gothic, many other types. Hundreds of technical hints on construction, strokes, pens, brushes, etc. 89 alphabets, 72 lettered specimens, which may be reproduced permission-free. 121pp. 9¾ x 8.   **T53 Paperbound $1.25**

THE HUMAN FIGURÉ IN MOTION, Eadweard Muybridge. The largest collection in print of Muybridge's famous high-speed action photos. 4789 photographs in more than 500 action-strip-sequences (at shutter speeds up to 1/6000th of a second) illustrate men, women, children—mostly undraped—performing such actions as walking, running, getting up, lying down, carrying objects, throwing, etc. "An unparalleled dictionary of action for all artists," AMERICAN ARTIST. 390 full-page plates, with 4789 photographs. Heavy glossy stock, reinforced binding with headbands. 7⅞ x 10¾.   **T204 Clothbound $10.00**

ANIMALS IN MOTION, Eadweard Muybridge. The largest collection of animal action photos in print. 34 different animals (horses, mules, oxen, goats, camels, pigs, cats, lions, gnus, deer, monkeys, eagles—and 22 others) in 132 characteristic actions. All 3919 photographs are taken in series at speeds up to 1/1600th of a second, offering artists, biologists, car-toonists a remarkable opportunity to see exactly how an ostrich's head bobs when running, how a lion puts his foot down, how an elephant's knee bends, how a bird flaps his wings, thousands of other hard-to-catch details. "A really marvelous series of plates," NATURE. 380 full-pages of plates. Heavy glossy stock, reinforced binding with headbands. 7⅞ x 10¾.   **T203 Clothbound $10.00**

THE BOOK OF SIGNS, R. Koch. 493 symbols—crosses, monograms, astrological, biological symbols, runes, etc.—from ancient manuscripts, cathedrals, coins, catacombs, pottery. May be reproduced permission-free. 493 illustrations by Fritz Kredel. 104pp. 6⅛ x 9¼.
T162 Paperbound $1.00

A HANDBOOK OF EARLY ADVERTISING ART, C. P. Hornung. The largest collection of copyright-free early advertising art ever compiled. Vol. I: 2,000 illustrations of animals, old automo-biles, buildings, allegorical figures, fire engines, Indians, ships, trains, more than 33 other categories! Vol II: Over 4,000 typographical specimens; 600 Roman, Gothic, Barnum, Old English faces; 630 ornamental type faces; hundreds of scrolls, initials, flourishes, etc. "A remarkable collection," PRINTERS' INK.

Vol. I: Pictorial Volume. Over 2000 illustrations. 256pp. 9 x 12.   **T122 Clothbound $10.00**
Vol. II: Typographical Volume. Over 4000 speciments. 319pp. 9 x 12.   **T123 Clothbound $10.00**
Two volume set, Clothbound, only **$18.50**

DESIGN FOR ARTISTS AND CRAFTSMEN, L. Wolchonok. The most thorough course on the creation of art motifs and designs. Shows you step-by-step, with hundreds of examples and 113 detailed exercises, how to create original designs from geometric patterns, plants, birds, animals, humans, and man-made objects. "A great contribution to the field of design and crafts," N. Y. SOCIETY OF CRAFTSMEN. More than 1300 entirely new illustrations. xv + 207pp. 7⅞ x 10¾.   **T274 Clothbound $4.95**

HANDBOOK OF DESIGNS AND DEVICES, C. P. Hornung. A remarkable working collection of 1836 basic designs and variations, all copyright-free. Variations of circle, line, cross, diamond, swastika, star, scroll, shield, many more. Notes on symbolism. "A necessity to every designer who would be original without having to labor heavily," ARTIST and ADVERTISER. 204 plates. 240pp. 5⅜ x 8.

T125 Paperbound $1.90

THE UNIVERSAL PENMAN, George Bickham. Exact reproduction of beautiful 18th century book of handwriting. 22 complete alphabets in finest English roundhand, other scripts, over 2000 elaborate flourishes, 122 calligraphic illustrations, etc. Material is copyright-free. "An essential part of any art library, and a book of permanent value," AMERICAN ARTIST. 212 plates. 224pp. 9 x 13¾.   **T20 Clothbound $10.00**

AN ATLAS OF ANATOMY FOR ARTISTS, F. Schider. This standard work contains 189 full-page plates, more than 647 illustrations of all aspects of the human skeleton, musculature, cutaway portions of the body, each part of the anatomy, hand forms, eyelids, breasts, location of muscles under the flesh, etc. 59 plates illustrate how Michelangelo, da Vinci, Goya, 15 others, drew human anatomy. New 3rd edition enlarged by 52 new illustrations by Cloquet, Barcsay. "The standard reference tool," AMERICAN LIBRARY ASSOCIATION. "Excellent," AMERICAN ARTIST. 189 plates, 647 illustrations. xxvi + 192pp. 7⅞ x 10⅝.   **T241 Clothbound $6.00**

AN ATLAS OF ANIMAL ANATOMY FOR ARTISTS, W. Ellenberger, H. Baum, H. Dittrich. The largest, richest animal anatomy for artists in English. Form, musculature, tendons, bone structure, expression, detailed cross sections of head, other features, of the horse, lion, dog, cat, deer, seal, kangaroo, cow, bull, goat, monkey, hare, many other animals. "Highly recommended," DESIGN. Second, revised, enlarged edition with new plates from Cuvier, Stubbs, etc. 288 illustrations. 153pp. 11⅜ x 9.   **T82 Clothbound $6.00**

ANIMAL DRAWING: ANATOMY AND ACTION FOR ARTISTS, C. R. Knight. 158 studies, with full accompanying text, of such animals as the gorilla, bear, bison, dromedary, camel, vulture, pelican, iguana, shark, etc., by one of the greatest modern masters of animal drawing. Innumerable tips on how to get life expression into your work. "An excellent reference work,' SAN FRANCISCO CHRONICLE. 158 illustrations. 156pp. 10½ x 8½.
T426 Paperbound $2.00

DOVER BOOKS

THE CRAFTSMAN'S HANDBOOK, Cennino Cennini. The finest English translation of IL LIBRO DELL' ARTE, the 15th century introduction to art technique that is both a mirror of Quatrocento life and a source of many useful but nearly forgotten facets of the painter's art. 4 illustrations. xxvii + 142pp. D. V. Thompson, translator. 6⅛ x 9¼. T54 Paperbound **$1.50**

THE BROWN DECADES, Lewis Mumford. A picture of the "buried renaissance" of the post-Civil War period, and the founding of modern architecture (Sullivan, Richardson, Root, Roebling), landscape development (Marsh, Olmstead, Eliot), and the graphic arts (Homer, Eakins, Ryder). 2nd revised, enlarged edition. Bibliography. 12 illustrations. xiv + 266 pp. 5⅜ x 8. T200 Paperbound **$1.65**

STIEGEL GLASS, F. W. Hunter. The story of the most highly esteemed early American glassware, fully illustrated. How a German adventurer, "Baron" Stiegel, founded a glass empire; detailed accounts of individual glasswork. "This pioneer work is reprinted in an edition even more beautiful than the original," ANTIQUES DEALER. New introduction by Helen McKearin. 171 illustrations, 12 in full color. xxii + 338pp. 7⅞ x 10¾. T128 Clothbound **$10.00**

THE HUMAN FIGURE, J. H. Vanderpoel. Not just a picture book, but a complete course by a famous figure artist. Extensive text, illustrated by 430 pencil and charcoal drawings of both male and female anatomy. 2nd enlarged edition. Foreword. 430 illus. 143pp. 6⅛ x 9¼. T432 Paperbound **$1.45**

PINE FURNITURE OF EARLY NEW ENGLAND, R. H. Kettell. Over 400 illustrations, over 50 working drawings of early New England chairs, benches, beds cupboards, mirrors, shelves, tables, other furniture esteemed for simple beauty and character. "Rich store of illustrations . . . emphasizes the individuality and varied design," ANTIQUES. 413 illustrations, 55 working drawings. 475pp. 8 x 10¾. T145 Clothbound **$10.00**

BASIC BOOKBINDING, A. W. Lewis. Enables both beginners and experts to rebind old books or bind paperbacks in hard covers. Treats materials, tools; gives step-by-step instruction in how to collate a book, sew it, back it, make boards, etc. 261 illus. Appendices. 155pp. 5⅜ x 8. T169 Paperbound **$1.35**

DESIGN MOTIFS OF ANCIENT MEXICO, J. Enciso. Nearly 90% of these 766 superb designs from Aztec, Olmec, Totonac, Maya, and Toltec origins are unobtainable elsewhere! Contains plumed serpents, wind gods, animals, demons, dancers, monsters, etc. Excellent applied design source. Originally $17.50. 766 illustrations, thousands of motifs. 192pp. 6⅛ x 9¼. T84 Paperbound **$1.85**

AFRICAN SCULPTURE, Ladislas Segy. 163 full-page plates illustrating masks, fertility figures, ceremonial objects, etc., of 50 West and Central African tribes—95% never before illustrated. 34-page introduction to African sculpture. "Mr. Segy is one of its top authorities," NEW YORKER. 164 full-page photographic plates. Introduction. Bibliography. 244pp. 6⅛ x 9¼. T396 Paperbound **$2.00**

THE PROCESSES OF GRAPHIC REPRODUCTION IN PRINTING, H. Curwen. A thorough and practical survey of wood, linoleum, and rubber engraving; copper engraving; drypoint, mezzotint, etching, aquatint, steel engraving, die sinking, stencilling, lithography (extensively); photographic reproduction utilizing line, continuous tone, photoengravure, collotype; every other process in general use. Note on color reproduction. Section on bookbinding. Over 200 illustrations, 25 in color. 143pp. 5½ x 8½. T512 Clothbound **$4.00**

CALLIGRAPHY, J. G. Schwandner. First reprinting in 200 years of this legendary book of beautiful handwriting. Over 300 ornamental initials, 12 complete calligraphic alphabets, over 150 ornate frames and panels, 75 calligraphic pictures of cherubs, stags, lions, etc., thousands of flourishes, scrolls, etc., by the greatest 18th century masters. All material can be copied or adapted without permission. Historical introduction. 158 full-page plates. 368pp. 9 x 13. T475 Clothbound **$10.00**

* * *

A DIDEROT PICTORIAL ENCYCLOPEDIA OF TRADES AND INDUSTRY, Manufacturing and the Technical Arts in Plates Selected from "L'Encyclopédie ou Dictionnaire Raisonné des Sciences, des Arts, et des Métiers," of Denis Diderot, edited with text by C. Gillispie. Over 2000 illustrations on 485 full-page plates. Magnificent 18th century engravings of men, women, and children working at such trades as milling flour, cheesemaking, charcoal burning, mining, silverplating, shoeing horses, making fine glass, printing, hundreds more, showing details of machinery, different steps in sequence, etc. A remarkable art work, but also the largest collection of working figures in print, copyright-free, for art directors, designers, etc. Two vols. 920pp. 9 x 12. Heavy library cloth. T421 Two volume set **$18.50**

* * *

SILK SCREEN TECHNIQUES, J. Biegeleisen, M. Cohn. A practical step-by-step home course in one of the most versatile, least expensive graphic arts processes. How to build an inexpensive silk screen, prepare stencils, print, achieve special textures, use color, etc. Every step explained, diagrammed. 149 illustrations, 8 in color. 201pp. 6⅛ x 9¼. T433 Paperbound **$1.45**

PUZZLES, GAMES, AND ENTERTAINMENTS

MATHEMATICS, MAGIC AND MYSTERY, Martin Gardner. Astonishing feats of mind reading, mystifying "magic" tricks, are often based on mathematical principles anyone can learn. This book shows you how to perform scores of tricks with cards, dice, coins, knots, numbers, etc., by using simple principles from set theory, theory of numbers, topology, other areas of mathematics, fascinating in themselves. No special knowledge required. 135 illus. 186pp. 5⅜ x 8.
T335 Paperbound **$1.00**

MATHEMATICAL PUZZLES FOR BEGINNERS AND ENTHUSIASTS, G. Mott-Smoth. Test your problem-solving techniques and powers of inference on 188 challenging, amusing puzzles based on algebra, dissection of plane figures, permutations, probabilities, etc. Appendix of primes, square roots, etc. 135 illus. 2nd revised edition. 248pp. 5⅜ x 8.
T198 Paperbound **$1.00**

LEARN CHESS FROM THE MASTERS, F. Reinfeld. Play 10 games against Marshall, Bronstein, Najdorf, other masters, and grade yourself on each move. Detailed annotations reveal principles of play, strategy, etc. as you proceed. An excellent way to get a real insight into the game. Formerly titled, "Chess by Yourself." 91 diagrams. vii + 144pp. 5⅜ x 8.
T362 Paperbound **$1.00**

REINFELD ON THE END GAME IN CHESS, F. Reinfeld. 62 end games of Alekhine, Tarrasch, Morphy, other masters, are carefully analyzed with emphasis on transition from middle game to end play. Tempo moves, queen endings, weak squares, other basic principles clearly illustrated. Excellent for understanding why some moves are weak or incorrect, how to avoid errors. Formerly titled, "Practical End-game Play." 62 diagrams. vi + 177pp. 5⅜ x 8.
T417 Paperbound **$1.25**

101 PUZZLES IN THOUGHT AND LOGIC, C. R. Wylie, Jr. Brand new puzzles you need no special knowledge to solve! Each one is a gem of ingenuity that will really challenge your problem-solving technique. Introduction with simplified explanation of scientic puzzle solving. 128pp. 5⅜ x 8.
T167 Paperbound **$1.00**

THE COMPLETE NONSENSE OF EDWARD LEAR. The only complete edition of this master of gentle madness at a popular price. The Dong with the Luminous Nose, The Jumblies, The Owl and the Pussycat, hundreds of other bits of wonderful nonsense. 214 limericks, 3 sets of Nonsense Botany, 5 Nonsense Alphabets, 546 fantastic drawings, much more. 320pp. 5⅜ x 8.
T167 Paperbound **$1.00**

28 SCIENCE FICTION STORIES OF H. G. WELLS. Two complete novels, "Men Like Gods" and "Star Begotten," plus 26 short stories by the master science-fiction writer of all time. Stories of space, time, future adventure that are among the all-time classics of science fiction. 928pp. 5⅜ x 8.
T265 Clothbound **$3.95**

SEVEN SCIENCE FICTION NOVELS, H. G. Wells. Unabridged texts of "The Time Machine," "The Island of Dr. Moreau," "First Men in the Moon," "The Invisible Man," "The War of the Worlds," "The Food of the Gods," "In the Days of the Comet." "One will have to go far to match this for entertainment, excitement, and sheer pleasure," N. Y. TIMES. 1015pp. 5⅜ x 8.
T264 Clothbound **$3.95**

MATHEMAGIC, MAGIC PUZZLES, AND GAMES WITH NUMBERS, R. V. Heath. More than 60 new puzzles and stunts based on number properties: multiplying large numbers mentally, finding the date of any day in the year, etc. Edited by J. S. Meyer. 76 illus. 129pp. 5⅜ x 8.
T110 Paperbound **$1.00**

FIVE ADVENTURE NOVELS OF H. RIDER HAGGARD. The master story-teller's five best tales of mystery and adventure set against authentic African backgrounds: "She," "King Solomon's Mines," "Allan Quatermain," "Allan's Wife," "Maiwa's Revenge." 821pp. 5⅜ x 8.
T108 Clothbound **$3.95**

WIN AT CHECKERS, M. Hopper. (Formerly "Checkers.") The former World's Unrestricted Checker Champion gives you valuable lessons in openings, traps, end games, ways to draw when you are behind, etc. More than 100 questions and answers anticipate your problems. Appendix. 75 problems diagrammed, solved. 79 figures. xi + 107pp. 5⅜ x 8.
T363 Paperbound **$1.00**

CRYPTOGRAPHY, L. D. Smith. Excellent introductory work on ciphers and their solution, history of secret writing, techniques, etc. Appendices on Japanese methods, the Baconian cipher, frequency tables. Bibliography. Over 150 problems, solutions. 160pp. 5⅜ x 8.
T247 Paperbound **$1.00**

CRYPTANALYSIS, H. F. Gaines. (Formerly, "Elementary Cryptanalysis.") The best book available on cryptograms and how to solve them. Contains all major techniques: substitution, transposition, mixed alphabets, multafid, Kasiski and Vignere methods, etc. Word frequency appendix. 167 problems, solutions. 173 figures. 236pp. 5⅜ x 8.
T97 Paperbound **$1.95**

FLATLAND, E. A. Abbot. The science-fiction classic of life in a 2-dimensional world that is considered a first-rate introduction to relativity and hyperspace, as well as a scathing satire on society, politics and religion. 7th edition. 16 illus. 128pp. 5⅜ x 8.
T1 Paperbound **$1.00**

DOVER BOOKS

HOW TO FORCE CHECKMATE, F. Reinfeld. (Formerly "Challenge to Chessplayers.") No board needed to sharpen your checkmate skill on 300 checkmate situations. Learn to plan up to 3 moves ahead and play a superior end game. 300 situations diagrammed; notes and full solutions. 111pp. 5⅜ x 8. T439 Paperbound **$1.25**

MORPHY'S GAMES OF CHESS, P. W. Sergeant, ed. Play forcefully by following the techniques used by one of the greatest chess champions. 300 of Morphy's games carefully annotated to reveal principles. Bibliography. New introduction by F. Reinfeld. 235 diagrams. x + 352pp. 5⅜ x 8. T386 Paperbound **$1.75**

MATHEMATICAL RECREATIONS, M. Kraitchik. Hundreds of unusual mathematical puzzlers and odd bypaths of math, elementary and advanced. Greek, Medieval, Arabic, Hindu problems; figurate numbers, Fermat numbers, primes; magic, Euler, Latin squares; fairy chess, latruncles, reversi, jinx, ruma, tetrachrome other positional and permutational games. Rigorous solutions. Revised second edition. 181 illus. 330pp. 5⅜ x 8. T163 Paperbound **$1.75**

MATHEMATICAL EXCURSIONS, H. A. Merrill. Revealing stimulating insights into elementary math, not usually taught in school. 90 problems demonstrate Russian peasant multiplication, memory systems for pi, magic squares, dyadic systems, division by inspection, many more. Solutions to difficult problems. 50 illus. 5⅜ x 8. T350 Paperbound **$1.00**

MAGIC TRICKS & CARD TRICKS, W. Jonson. Best introduction to tricks with coins, bills, eggs, ribbons, slates, cards, easily performed without elaborate equipment. Professional routines, tips on presentation, misdirection, etc. Two books bound as one: 52 tricks with cards, 37 tricks with common objects. 106 figures. 224pp. 5⅜ x 8. T909 Paperbound **$1.00**

MATHEMATICAL PUZZLES OF SAM LOYD, selected and edited by **M. Gardner.** 177 most ingenious mathematical puzzles of America's greatest puzzle originator, based on arithmetic, algebra, game theory, dissection, route tracing, operations research, probability, etc. 120 drawings, diagrams. Solutions. 187pp. 5⅜ x 8. T498 Paperbound **$1.00**

THE ART OF CHESS, J. Mason. The most famous general study of chess ever written. More than 90 openings, middle game, end game, how to attack, sacrifice, defend, exchange, form general strategy. Supplement on "How Do You Play Chess?" by F. Reinfeld. 448 diagrams. 356pp. 5⅜ x 8. T463 Paperbound **$1.85**

HYPERMODERN CHESS as Developed in the Games of its Greatest Exponent, ARON NIMZOVICH, F. Reinfeld, ed. Learn how the game's greatest innovator defeated Alekhine, Lasker, and many others; and use these methods in your own game. 180 diagrams. 228pp. 5⅜ x 8. T448 Paperbound **$1.35**

A TREASURY OF CHESS LORE, F. Reinfeld, ed. Hundreds of fascinating stories by and about the masters, accounts of tournaments and famous games, aphorisms, word portraits, little known incidents, photographs, etc., that will delight the chess enthusiast captivate the beginner. 49 photographs (14 full-page plates), 12 diagrams. 315pp. 5⅜ x 8. T458 Paperbound **$1.75**

A NONSENSE ANTHOLOGY, collected by Carolyn Wells. 245 of the best nonsense verses ever written: nonsense puns, absurd arguments, mock epics, nonsense ballads, "sick" verses, dog-Latin verses, French nonsense verses, limericks. Lear, Carroll, Belloc, Burgess, nearly 100 other writers. Introduction by Carolyn Wells. 3 indices: Title, Author, First Lines. xxxiii + 279pp. 5⅜ x 8. T499 Paperbound **$1.25**

SYMBOLIC LOGIC and THE GAME OF LOGIC, Lewis Carroll. Two delightful puzzle books by the author of "Alice," bound as one. Both works concern the symbolic representation of traditional logic and together contain more than 500 ingenious, amusing and instructive syllogistic puzzlers. Total of 326pp. 5⅜ x 8. T492 Paperbound **$1.50**

PILLOW PROBLEMS and A TANGLED TALE, Lewis Carroll. Two of Carroll's rare puzzle works bound as one. "Pillow Problems" contain 72 original math puzzles. The puzzles in "A Tangled Tale" are given in delightful story form. Total of 291pp. 5⅜ x 8. T493 Paperbound **$1.50**

PECK'S BAD BOY AND HIS PA, G. W. Peck. Both volumes of one of the most widely read of all American humor books. A classic of American folk humor, also invaluable as a portrait of an age. 100 original illustrations. Introduction by E. Bleiler. 347pp. 5⅜ x 8. T497 Paperbound **$1.35**

Dover publishes books on art, music, philosophy, literature, languages, history, social sciences, psychology, handcrafts, orientalia, puzzles and entertainments, chess, pets and gardens, books explaining science, intermediate and higher mathematics mathematical physics, engineering, biological sciences, earth sciences, classics of science, etc. Write to:

Dept. catrr.
Dover Publications, Inc.
180 Varick Street, N. Y. 14, N. Y.